THE ENDURING VILLAGE

JOYCE PRINCE

The Enduring Village

Tragedy and Triumph in the Life of Chettle

PRINCE PUBLISHING · *London*

First published in Great Britain in 2008 by
Prince Publishing
177 Battersea Bridge Road
London
SW11 3AS

2 4 6 8 9 7 5 3 1

A catalogue record for this book is
available from the British Library

ISBN 978-0-9559698-0-5

Typeset in Minion

Printed by Blackmore Ltd
Longmead
Shafestbury
Dorset
SP7 8PX

Contents

List of illustrations

The Castleman farmhouse.
William Beale's box tomb, Chettle churchyard.
William Beale's box tomb.
St Mary's farmhouse, Chettle.
Edward Castleman (2).
Mary Dean, Mrs William Castleman.
Mrs Fuidge.
Mrs Esther Bourke.
Edward Castleman (3).
Edward Castleman (1).
Cranborne chase keeper's hat and truncheon.
Mrs Anne Castleman.
William Castleman.
William Castleman with two of his grand-daughters Emily and
    Elizabeth.
Alice Roe, Esther Bourke's mother.
Isaac Gulliver and his wife Elizabeth.
Chettle House.
Chettle Church.
The Keeper's cottage residents 1892.
The Keeper's cottage.

CHAFIN FAMILY TREE

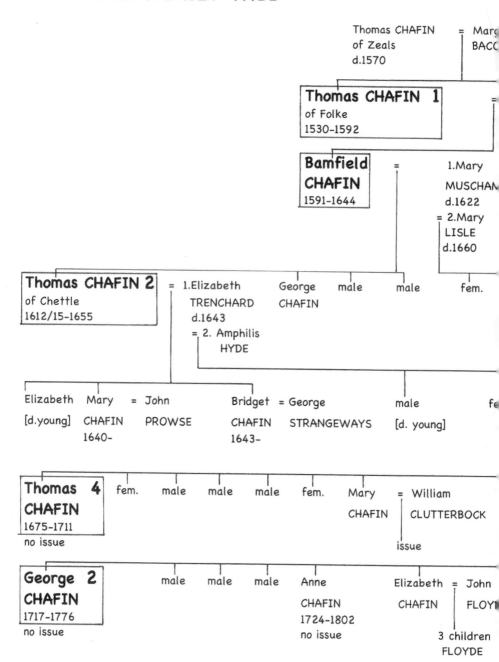

Thomas CHAFIN
of Zeals
d.1570
= Marg
BACO

Thomas CHAFIN 1
of Folke
1530-1592
=

Bamfield CHAFIN
1591-1644
=
1.Mary
MUSCHAM
d.1622
= 2.Mary
LISLE
d.1660

Thomas CHAFIN 2
of Chettle
1612/15-1655
= 1.Elizabeth
TRENCHARD
d.1643
= 2. Amphilis
HYDE

George   male   male   fem.
CHAFIN

Elizabeth   Mary   = John   Bridget = George   male   fe
[d.young]   CHAFIN   PROWSE   CHAFIN   STRANGEWAYS   [d. young]
             1640-   1643-

Thomas 4 CHAFIN
1675-1711
no issue

fem.   male   male   male   fem.   Mary   = William
                                        CHAFIN   CLUTTERBOCK

                                                        issue

George 2 CHAFIN
1717-1776
no issue

male   male   male   Anne   Elizabeth = John
                        CHAFIN   CHAFIN   FLOYI
                        1724-1802
                        no issue   3 children
                                                  FLOYDE

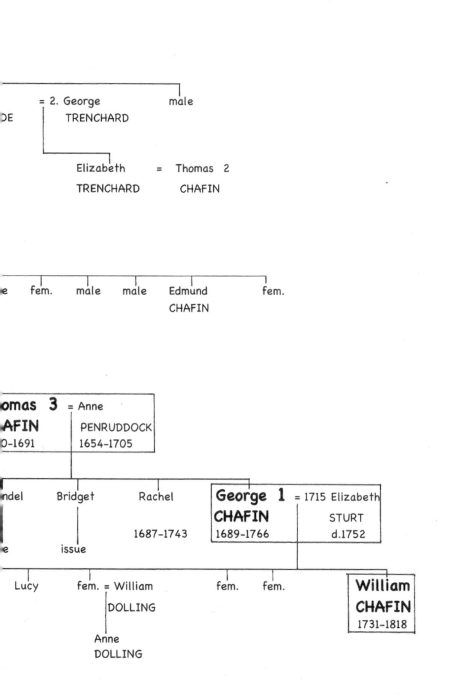

= 2. George   male
TRENCHARD

Elizabeth   = Thomas 2
TRENCHARD   CHAFIN

fem.   male   male   Edmund   fem.
CHAFIN

omas 3 = Anne
AFIN   PENRUDDOCK
0-1691   1654-1705

ndel   Bridget   Rachel   **George 1** = 1715 Elizabeth
                            CHAFIN   STURT
              1687-1743   1689-1766   d.1752
e   issue

Lucy   fem. = William   fem.   fem.   **William**
           DOLLING   **CHAFIN**
                                               1731-1818
      Anne
      DOLLING

GULLIVER FAMILY TREE

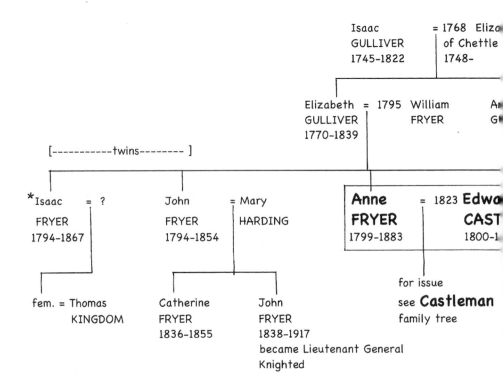

```
                                        Isaac       = 1768  Eliza
                                        GULLIVER    |  of Chettle
                                        1745-1822   |  1748-
                                            |
                                            |
                                    Elizabeth  = 1795  William    An
                                    GULLIVER   |       FRYER      G
                                    1770-1839  |
  [-----------twins-------- ]                  |
                                               |
        |                    |                 |
  *Isaac     = ?         John     = Mary      Anne      = 1823 Edwa
  FRYER                  FRYER      HARDING   FRYER             CAST
  1794-1867             1794-1854            1799-1883          1800-1
        |                    |                      |
        |                    |                      |
  fem. = Thomas        Catherine      John       for issue
        KINGDOM        FRYER          FRYER      see Castleman
                       1836-1855      1838-1917  family tree
                                      became Lieutenant General
                                      Knighted
```

*appointed Master Extraordinary
  in the High Court of Chancery

E

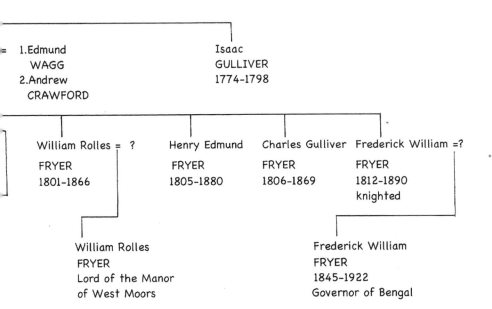

=   1.Edmund   Isaac
      WAGG   GULLIVER
   2.Andrew   1774-1798
      CRAWFORD

William Rolles = ?   Henry Edmund   Charles Gulliver Frederick William =?

FRYER   FRYER   FRYER   FRYER

1801-1866   1805-1880   1806-1869   1812-1890
                                              knighted

    William Rolles   Frederick William
    FRYER   FRYER
    Lord of the Manor   1845-1922
    of West Moors   Governor of Bengal

CASTLEMAN / BOURKE FAMILY TREE

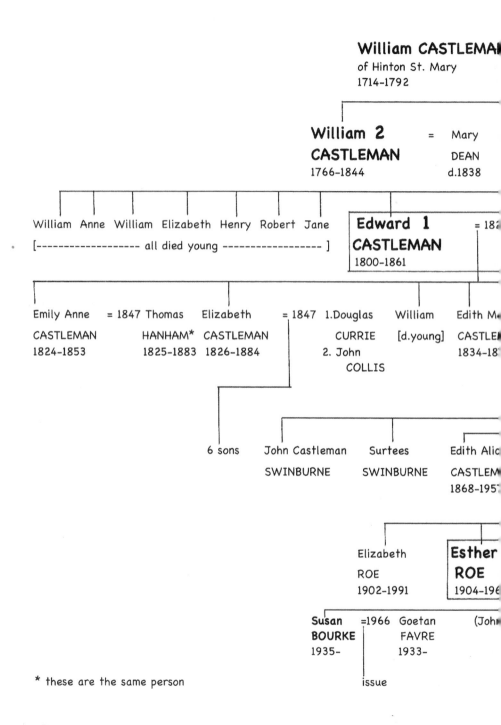

William CASTLEMAN
of Hinton St. Mary
1714-1792

William 2 CASTLEMAN
1766-1844
= Mary DEAN d.1838

William Anne William Elizabeth Henry Robert Jane
[------------------ all died young ------------------]

Edward 1 CASTLEMAN
1800-1861
= 182

Emily Anne CASTLEMAN 1824-1853 = 1847 Thomas HANHAM* 1825-1883

Elizabeth CASTLEMAN 1826-1884 = 1847 1.Douglas CURRIE 2. John COLLIS

William [d.young]

Edith M. CASTLE 1834-18

6 sons

John Castleman SWINBURNE

Surtees SWINBURNE

Edith Alic CASTLEM 1868-195

Elizabeth ROE 1902-1991

Esther ROE 1904-196

Susan BOURKE 1935- =1966 Goetan FAVRE 1933-

(John

issue

* these are the same person

nne

'INING

.727-1810

le

ed in infancy]

	Henry	= Emma	Charles	= 1.
	CASTLEMAN	STEPHENS	CASTLEMAN	2.
83	1805-1863		1808-1876	3.

5 1. John Jane = 1856 Edwin Augustus

'INBURNE   SMITH

29-1867   1836-1905   821-1898

68 2.Thomas
      HANHAM*
      1825-1883

Edward 2
CASTLEMAN
1841-1874

=1866 Fanny Martha
FUIDGE
1848-1907

Bernhard Oswald

ROE

1870-1937

Edward William 3 = Jessie Ann
CASTLEMAN   MORRIS
1870-1946   1860-1936

no issue

fem.   male   fem.

et = **Leslie Ernest**
     BOURKE
      1903-1987

Corrie
ROE
1907-1992

Dora
ROE
1909-1990

= Burton
  ABBOTT

= Janet Elizabeth
  GRIFFITHS
  1943-

Edward
BOURKE
1941-

= Barbara
  GARNSWORTHY

Stella Mary
ABBOTT
1952-

ue

Preface

Several years ago my journalist son Dominic was urging me to do some research on the village of Chettle: *'I think there's a good story somewhere,'* he said, journalistic antennae aquiver and arm sweeping round the full extent of the village in one easy gesture.

Forty generations have succeeded one another here since William the Conqueror granted the small estate of Coetel [1] to Airard toward the end of the eleventh century. There have been fat years and lean years but the size of the population has varied little. Individual men and women have tilled the soil, built their houses, reared their children, buried their dead and passed on their skills, traditions and values down through the long vista of history. The community of Chettle has survived through centuries of gradual and evolutionary change. The vestiges that emerge to evoke this long past and hint at a tale worth telling are not misleading. There is a story with several strands.

The survival of a small estate from the time of the Norman Conquest is one. On three separate occasions it has come very near to breaking up. In the seventeenth century during the English Civil War it was sequestrated by the Parliamentarians. During the eighteenth and early nineteenth centuries its wealth was recklessly squandered by its custodians and in 1946 it was bequeathed to four siblings in the expectation that they would all realize their assets in it. On each

---

[1] Coetel was the Anglo-Saxon for Chettle.

occasion it was saved by the determination and independent-mindedness of a few individuals who loved these thousand quiet acres of Dorset.

It is also the story of two families who have either held or owned the estate of Chettle. The Chafin family held it as feudal property from 1572 till 1818. The Castleman/Bourkes owned it as freehold property from 1847 to the present day. In the interregnum the Bank of England held it as security for a debt.

It is also a story in miniature of the agricultural enterprise of England, once the primary occupation of the country. Chettle testifies to the changes wrought by the need for more and cheaper food, driven by population growth and industrialization. In Chettle we can witness at close quarters the transfer from the medieval strip and furrow system to consolidated fields; from rights of common to enclosure; from hand flailing and reaping, to threshing and mowing machine; from feudal to allodial landholding. Agricultural improvements of the eighteenth and nineteenth centuries meant that landowners required money for investment and lending banks grew up to fulfil the need. One of the local bankers was William Castleman whose family finally acquired Chettle. The Corn Laws that prevailed from 1815 till 1846 prohibited imports of corn until homegrown reached eighty shillings a quarter. Protected landholders and farmers benefitted but the price of bread periodically rose beyond the reach of the pockets of labourers. Hunger riots disturbed the countryside. The repeal of the Corn Laws marked the watershed when England irrevocably became an industrial nation and agriculture as a major source of its wealth was a thing of the past. Chettle never made the step into modern industrial Britain. Its continued dependence upon the land is one of the features contributing to its rarity. In and around Chettle the aristocratic privilege of deer owning and hunting on Cranborne Chase had its pervasive influence from the eleventh till the nineteenth century. By imposing a superordinate authority above local landowners it created an ambiguity of responsibility that was at first an irritant and eventually became a source of serious conflict.

It is a story told through a small number of people; a few of them quite outstanding, one or two of them rogues and simpletons, in influential positions. There is smuggling, gambling and money making (and losing) in some of its many chameleon disguises.

Above all it is the story of a place – Coetel – a wooded hollow, that has held not a few in an enchanted embrace, and continues to affect many who come to Chettle today.

ONE

Introduction

Take a turning north from the A 354 between Salisbury and Blandford – the old Great Western Turnpike Road – for about half a mile
and you will find the village of Chettle. The great rolling chalk landscape with its ancient hill forts and burial mounds through which
you have been travelling will be obscured by the tousled hedgerows
on either side of the lane to the village. One or two wild creatures
may scurry out in mild protest at this incursion into their territory.
Approaching the village, hedgerow gives place to fence and a more
open view. To the left across the meadow can be seen the fine eighteenth-century red brick mansion that dominates the village to an
inappropriate degree. It was built in the 1720's as the centrepiece of
a very large estate that was dispersed within a few years of the completion of the mansion.

On the right is Lower Farm House with the farmyard bordering
the lane, and a row of pretty brick cottages. A great spreading horse
chestnut tree marks the parting of the ways. A lane to the left wends
its way, subdividing into footpaths and tracks, to the church, the
mansion, timber yard, several dwellings and the village hall. In dry
weather the way is dusty and uneven; after a rainstorm Wellington
boots are advisable. The road that continues through the village to
Farnham leads to the shop, post office, the hotel and several more
houses. There have been repairs, renovations and re-thatching but no
new house has been built here in the last half century. There is no
street lighting, no pavement, the side roads are unmetalled and the

only street sign is an old wooden finger post, green with lichen.

In 1991 approximately half of the population of sixty-nine was engaged in agriculture (as compared with 1.85% nationally). Forty percent of the population of the village had a higher educational qualification (as compared with 13.4% nationally) and there were fourteen children under the age of sixteen, which is 20% of the village population.[2] At the beginning of the twenty-first century this is an exceptional community, predominantly soil dependent, cultivated and forward looking. Yet it has deep roots. Some family histories are recorded in the church registries going back hundreds of years. This is a village from which people move rarely and reluctantly, and when they do there is no shortage of folk anxious to move in. In the middle of the nineteenth century the lord of the manor had a hill lowered to improve the view. At that time too, a few of the very elderly and infirm residents were uprooted and transferred to the workhouse in Wimborne, under the New Poor Law system. These are rare examples of intentional and radical disturbance. Change in Chettle is seasonal, adaptive and evolutionary.

It is a place of quiet pursuits, where animals are rather more in evidence than human beings. Lower Farm has a prize winning dairy herd whose demanding routine is readily observable. The surrounding woods are alive with squabbling squirrels and the dark nights eerie with the cries of owl and fox. Deer and pheasant – both viewed unsentimentally by their human co-residents as potential food supply – are likely to be encountered on any walk through the woods or meadows. Horse riding is popular. Pervading all are country smells: hay, wet grass, musty leaves, farm yard manure, the occasional waft of wood smoke and the myriad unidentifiable scents that constitute the communication systems of animal, insect and flower. A dog, with a nose more sensitive than a human's, becomes ecstatic.

The village road goes only to the next village. There is little traffic. The seasons, length of day, sun and rain, growth and decay, will strike any town-bred visitor with stimulating effect, as there are few of the

[2] Census 1991.

screens and buffers commonly provided in urban living. Occasionally a tractor or timber lorry creates a commotion and a burst of petrol fume, both sound and smell the more remarkable against the foil of stillness.

But this is no quiet backwater or genteel retirement village. It has the appearance of a small tight-lipped community living close to the land, observant and respectful of nature and attuned to the seasons.

Chettle is one of the dwindling number of 'closed' villages owned by one family. The term 'estate' village was used when all the residents were also employees on the estate. This is no longer the case in Chettle, but the entire property is under the control of the Bourke family, a sister and two brothers – Susan, Patrick and Edward. Once a common landholding pattern in England, there are now no more than a dozen villages owned by one family. That makes it rare. It is the owners themselves who make Chettle entirely unique. They came to the village as very young children (Edward was born in the mansion in 1941). It was a harbour of safety from a very different world. Chettle moulded them in their formative years. Their friends were other children in the village where they made their own adventures, discovered for themselves the ways of the wild wood, the chalk down and the lush meadow. Supervision varied from light to non-existent. The adult world was occupied with 'the war effort' and left the young to cultivate their independent interests and resources. The childhood friends they made then have remained their friends. When the responsibility of the estate eventually fell to them their perspective was not that of superordinate landlord, but of first among equals. Rents are arranged, not according to what the market will bear, but with a view to the well being of a small rural community. Family ties and potential for contribution to the general weal take priority. The wholesale displacement of local people by urban wealth, which is damaging village life in much of England, does not happen in Chettle. Long roots are respected and tended with consideration.

The general plan of the village and conformity of the land around would be recognized by a returning Tudor resident, even a Roman soldier from 350 AD could probably find his bearings. It has found its way into literary history since it was nearby at Marnhull that Tess of the d'Urbervilles grew up in this *'engirdled and secluded region, for the most part untrodden as yet by tourist or landscape-painter, though within a four hours' journey from London'.*[3]

Aerial photography enables us to look through the long lens of history to the Iron Age, the Roman occupation of Britain and to the Anglo-Saxons. Long barrows mark prehistoric burial sites, and there is a more recent one to the south of the village where the victims of the Black Death of the fourteenth century were buried.

By the time of the Domesday Book in 1087 the area of northeast Dorset was held of the King, by Aiulf the Chamberlain. Aiulf himself retained control of all his considerable domain[4] with the exception of one hide, which was held of him, by Airard, his subordinate: that individual property was Coetel,[5] now known as Chettle. It had *'land for one plough. There are 12 acres of pasture. It is worth 20s.'* Airard, at the head of an extended household at Coetel would have been responsible for his immediate family and the several villeins, serfs and slaves that constituted the small community or household. A hide was the land that could support one household, and varied in extent from about 40 to 120 acres depending upon its fertility and productivity. The welfare of Airard and all his dependents rested entirely on his hide of land and self-sufficiency was essential. A glance at other properties held by Aiulf indicates how device and chance over a millennium have affected relative values. Blandford is recorded in the Domesday Book as one and a half hides: *'it was worth 20s. now 30s.'* Farnham was two hides, worth 30s. and Long Crichel four hides, worth 65s.8d. Blandford (present population 8,800) and Chettle were of similar size; Farnham twice and Long Crichel four times the size of both.

This hide of Airard's at Coetel became the centrepiece around

---

[3] Thomas Hardy *Tess of the d'Urbervilles* Folio Society Edition 1988 p6.
[4] The area held by Aiulf in the eleventh century was very similar to the great Dorset and Somerset estate of Lord Uxbridge, which plays a part in the story of Chettle in the nineteenth century.
[5] Anglo-Saxon for a wooded hollow.

which the Dorset estate of Chettle accreted; assessed in 1918 as a total of 850 acres, 2 roods and 26 poles,[6] today it is assessed as 1126 acres with a seven mile circumference. It is in the years following the Norman invasion that the economic structure of the village was laid down and its legacy is there today. Its biography is a microcosm of the history of the agricultural enterprise of England.

In Chettle the agricultural community has never been swept aside by factory or bulldozer. Its survival as a single entity has been in serious jeopardy on three separate occasions, each threat of a different nature. In the seventeenth century the fines imposed by Parliamentarians on the Royalist lord of the manor were crippling. In the eighteenth and nineteenth centuries it was bankrupted by family recklessness, and in the twentieth century it was a victim of agricultural depression. The management and warding off of these hazards forms a considerable part of the story of Chettle through which we can read a wider story about the trials and successes of agricultural England. The survival of this village is nevertheless something of a miracle. Elements of rational calculation, devoted hard work in both legal and illegal enterprises, chance events and good fortune have all made their contribution.

The population has varied between about sixty and one hundred and seventy: today it is eighty.[7] Christenings, weddings and funerals ensure a full church, as do the great celebrations of the church calendar. The gusto with which singing and organ playing are performed more than compensates for any shortcomings in musical refinement. The advowson[8] is still retained by the lord of the manor, though the rector can no longer claim a tithe of the farm produce. Changes evolve slowly and many of the practices that have been abandoned elsewhere in England prevail to this day. Transactions between residents are often on a barter system. Eggs, tomatoes, flowers, pheasant,

---

[6] 4 roods = 1 acre, 40 poles = 1 rood, therefore this is 850.625 acres or just over 340 hectares. Recent Census data gives the size as 1126 acres. Land measurement here has often been approximate.

[7] Census 2001.

[8] An advowson is the right to appoint a vicar in English Ecclesiastical Law.

pea sticks, firewood, strawberries, rhubarb, green beans all enter the system in their season. Personal eccentricities are generally contained and irritations absorbed. Vestigial remnants of feudal organization can be detected, although attitudes and behaviour that arose from a strictly enforced hierarchical system are nowhere to be found. Inevitably today's residents are dependent for all the services required for modern living – educational, medical, public transport, financial, etc – on organizations from further afield, but the heart of the village functions as it has for hundreds of years and no resident has a main occupation in either manufacturing or the service industries.[9]

Chettle has an enigmatic place in the England of the twenty-first century. Successive generations who have lived here have experienced at close quarters and often in painful detail the great tectonic movements that in many parts of England divided large landholdings into a collection of smaller freeholds and that swept away field and farmstead, replacing them with mill and factory. In Chettle the landholding arranged under Norman rule is still apparent; agriculture predominates. While much of England became feverishly busy with factories and finance, competition and colonization, Chettle kept to a pace dictated by seasons and the soil. On the rare occasions when urban outsiders have come to impose their will, their failure to appreciate these subliminal rhythms has contributed to their confusion.

This fertile protected valley has been attractive as a place of settlement from prehistoric times. The Romans have left their indelible mark. Coins, vessels and other domestic paraphernalia have frequently been unearthed; farming was carried on though there is no evidence of a villa having been built at Chettle. With their departure a veil descends upon Chettle for six and a half centuries, until the Norman invasion. From the eleventh till the sixteenth century a succession of medieval landholders farmed at Chettle and it became part of the property of the Church of Rome. Following Henry VIII's dissolution of the monasteries Chettle was granted to the Chafin family in 1572 though little of the fabric of the village changed. They

[9] Census 2001.

were then the Chafins of Folke as that village, about twenty miles from Chettle, was their family home and centre of their already extensive holdings.

From 1572 our story of the village becomes firmer and records more reliable. Two interdependent narratives become interwoven. There is Chettle, a settlement of dwellings housing an agricultural community of shepherd, ploughman, dairyman, labourer, woodman, carpenter, groom, parson, cook, domestic servant, seamstress, laundress, farrier and their families. Then there are the Chafin and the Castleman/Bourke families who have held or owned the property upon which all rests. The story of the village cannot be told without the Chafins and the Castleman/Bourkes. Likewise the human story does not exist without its geographical setting.

The two families who have held Chettle for nearly four and a half centuries have played a dominant role in its history. The rector, yeoman farmer, gamekeeper, shopkeeper, and generations of children have played their part, though the records they have left are fragmentary. The biography of two families forms the core of the story. Landowning men wielded the power and their decisions had disproportionate influence. Their opinions and actions are the ones that have been recorded and hence constitute the most obvious stuff of history. The jigsaw pieces for the whole picture have been scattered, and some may never be found. Prior to the arrival of the Chafins Chettle must be read from the general history of the area. No personality emerges with his life's chronicle. We have to interpret from the living history of the Roman road, the ploughed up coin, the sytem of feudal land tenure and the monarch's grant of privilege to his favourites.

The records that have been tracked down and pieced together provide, in the chapters that follow, an outline of affairs until the sixteenth century. Then with the arrival of the Chafin family the image becomes clearer. The name of Chafin had been prominent in Wiltshire from the fifteenth century. The Folke and Chettle branch of the family with which our story is concerned had found favour with Queen Elizabeth in the sixteenth century and she granted Chettle to

Thomas Chafin (1). It became incorporated into the very large estate the family owned that extended into parts of what are now Somerset, Dorset, Hampshire, Gloucestershire and Surrey. In 1635 the Chafin heir moved to Chettle and it then became the centre of the estate. The family adopted the title the Chafins of Chettle. During the Civil War of the seventeenth century both the Chafin family and Chettle suffered many losses and privations. The family was Royalist. For the eleven years of the Protectorate from 1649 till 1660 they, like many Royalists, faced great hardship. There was an energetic recovery at the Restoration, though at the time the nominal lord of the manor was a minor. He was much influenced by Sir Ralph Bankes and his family who lived in Chettle while Sir Ralph planned his new home at Kingston Lacey. They were all recovering from their experiences as Royalists during the eleven years that the Parliamentarians had been in the ascendent. Thomas Chafin (3) was able to take his place amongst the West Country elite when he became of age in 1671. The next twenty years constituted the peak of achievement for both the Chafin family and for Chettle. All this changed during the eighteenth century when the Chafins were ruined irrevocably. The great turning point for both came in the 1730's when the wealth upon which both depended was lost. Gambling was the great scourge of the period and such evidence as there is points to this as the most likely explanation. A family catastrophe that affected not only the Chafins and Chettle, but also many workers in the area, was hushed up. The cause of the disaster has been obfuscated and it was kept out of the public eye. How this was achieved is one of the biggest of several puzzling events in the Chafin story. The last two Chafin lords of the manor of Chettle were financially, morally and biologically bankrupt. The last of them died in 1818 and not long afterwards Chettle became the hapless victim of a prolonged legal dispute. For almost thirty years it was not at all clear who owned the estate. While the case was argued between numerous lawyers, a very elderly man who thought he had purchased it spent thirteen years in prison, Chettle was neglected and parts were sold off as freehold property.

The recovery of Chettle and its re-instatement as an integrated whole was effected in the nineteenth century by the Castleman family. There are essential digressions in the story, to pursue the question of how the wealth for its rescue was accumulated. William Castleman, lawyer, banker, land agent, and son of a local yeoman farmer is one source. An appreciable amount came from smuggling, a pursuit that kept several residents of Chettle and the local excise men busy. Smugglers and deer poachers combined their local knowledge and their transgressing minds together and made the area, with Chettle at its centre, lawless and unbiddable. The ringleader of the smugglers of the Dorset coast, Isaac Gulliver, became conspicuously wealthy. His granddaughter Anne Fryer married William Castleman's son Edward. Together they took over Chettle in 1847. Anne's grandmother had been a Chettle girl. The daughter of the village farrier, she had married Isaac Gulliver in 1768. It was a fabric tightly woven around Chettle. Their descendents live there today.

The men and women of this small community are not always clearly visible, and their families cannot be accurately traced. Democracy, now lauded as a political ideal, was, for most of the period under consideration, dismissed as a term of disparagement. It is to the Chafins and the Castlemans that we must look to give the story coherence. They were its leaders, who built houses, appointed the rector, and exerted control. The people of Chettle who made the living village, appear as well, and without them there would be neither Chafin nor Castleman.

Chettle, in the twenty-first century, secluded and quiet in its wooded hollow, a compact community held in a loose nexus by unspecified affiliations and with a one-family landlord, may not have changed very much in appearance for several centuries. It has known some fearful and lawless times. Some of the turbulent secrets shrouded in its mature heart we may glimpse, but Delphic-like it retains some of its ancient ambiguities.

TWO

Chettle under the Romans

Julius Caesar came to Britain in 55 BC and again in 54 BC. He came, he saw, but he went away again and did not conquer. *'All the Britons dye themselves with woad,'* he wrote, *'which makes them a sky-blue colour and thereby more terrible to their enemies.'* Woad is a dye derived from the leaves of a cruciferous plant, Isatis Tinctoria. It thrives where there is chalk soil and sunshine. It was entirely suited to the area that is now known as Cranborne Chase, of which Chettle is a part. Woad continued to be used for dying fabrics until the middle of the seventeenth century, though Queen Elizabeth forbade its production within five miles of her palaces because of its foul smell.[10]

What is now Dorset was then inhabited by the Celtic tribe of the Durotriges. They used woad, minted their own coins and marked their territory with a series of hill forts. Maiden Castle, the grandest of them all, still stands as a memorial to the Durotriges near Dorchester. Hambledon and Hod Hill and Knowlton Circles are within a few miles of Chettle. Within the present boundary of the Chettle estate to the north west of the village is a Neolithic long barrow; a burial chamber from pre-history, indicating perhaps the earliest human settlement in the valley.

Almost a hundred years after the blue Britons had startled the great Caesar, Emperor Claudius ((10 BC–54 AD) appointed Aulius

---

[10] Deni Brown *Encyclopaedia of Herbs* RHS 1995.

Plautius to go north to subdue the barbarians who were constantly making mischief by crossing the channel to Gaul. He landed at Richborough in Kent in 43 AD and dispatched the Second Legion under their commander Flavius Vespasianus (9–79 AD) to the west. They landed at Hamworthy, a sheltered inlet, fourteen miles due south of Chettle. Despite their fierce resistance the Durotriges were subdued, and in time, the area became romanized. The hill forts were evacuated and their inhabitants accommodated in small low-lying planned townships.

Aulius Plautius became the first Roman Governor of Britain, and Flavius Vespasianus became the Emperor Vespasian. He marked his reign by starting the rebuilding of the Colosseum in Rome for the entertainment of fifty thousand people who went to see animal and gladiator fights and the martyring of the troublesome Christians.

By the mid 70's Maiden Castle, about twenty-two miles from Chettle, had given place to Durnovaria (Dorchester) on the river Frome occupying eighty acres. The Romans made it the cantonal capital, and it is now the county town of Dorset. A part of the Roman wall built to enclose Durnovaria can still be seen at the upper end of West Walks near Princes Street in Dorchester. To the south of the town just off the Weymouth Road are the remains of the great Roman amphitheatre for thirteen thousand spectators, Maumbury Rings. Built at about the same time as the Colosseum in Rome it provided similar facilities for Roman soldiers and the local people. Cirque of the Gladiators was Thomas Hardy's name for Maumbury Rings. When his house, Max Gate, was being built nearby in 1884, many Roman artefacts were found. He kept many of them in his study and they were deposited in Dorchester County Museum after his death. They were also woven into the fabric of the novel he was writing, *The Mayor of Casterbridge* (Hardy's name for Dorchester).

'Casterbridge announced old Rome in every street, alley, and precinct. It looked Roman, bespoke the art of Rome, concealed dead men of Rome. It was impossible to dig more than a foot or two deep about the town fields and gardens without coming upon some tall soldier or other of the Empire, who had lain there in his silent unobtrusive rest for a space of fifteen hundred years.'[11]

Other towns in England, Chester, York and Cirencester, for example, have more spectacular and obvious evidence of their Roman history but in the area of the Durotriges testimony of Roman residence is never far below the surface. Garden spade, plough and metal detector are ever finding mementos of the four hundred years that Britain was the northern outpost of the great Roman Empire.

Territory conquered by the Romans was secured by forts and roads. Whoever lived at Chettle in this first century AD continued to make a living with their customary primitive mode of agriculture. But they knew things were changing, for very close by one of the fine straight roads was being built from Badbury Rings to the northeast. Another ran to the south of Chettle between Badbury and Sorbiodunum (Old Sarum). This is still visible and is now known as Ackling Dyke. Roman structures in the vicinity, at Rockbourne Cashmore and Woodyates, still exist.

By the beginning of the fourth century AD the Roman Empire was under threat from perpetual waves of barbarian invasion along its immense periphery. Defensive contraction meant the recall of the Roman army from its northern territory. After the last Roman legionary left, the roads and townships, the system of government, the communications and economy gradually fell into disrepair; the recording of events and history was no longer maintained

The ancient glory of a nation-wide road system could be seen by shepherd and ox drover for generations. They are still there, some now surfaced for use by modern cars and lorries, and some in more remote areas used by walkers and horseriders. The ploughshares of Chettle periodically turned over Roman coins. But it was not until the 1880's that General Augustus Pitt Rivers (designated the father of British archaeology) painstakingly excavated several of the Romano-British villages situated on the chalk of the Cranborne Chase. The

[11] Thomas Hardy *The Mayor of Casterbridge* 1886.

first Pitt Rivers Museum was established in a house that was built in the 1830's as a school for gypsy children in Farnham, the adjacent parish a mile to the west of Chettle, to accommodate the treasures that he unearthed. This museum no longer exists. Salisbury Museum and the Pitt Rivers Museum in Oxford now house many of the items.

That Chettle had been part of a Roman colonized area there was no doubt. In August 2003, however, a group of fine Roman vessels was discovered in Middle Field in the Parish of Chettle. Margaret Hamilton, a local amateur archaeologist was alerted to them by her metal detector and Wessex Archaeology excavated and supervised the care and analysis of the well preserved items.

There was one Iron Age decorated bronze mirror plate, four complete bronze Roman vessels, one broken bronze bowl and two broken Roman glass vessels. This is the most recent and most valuable of the many marks of Roman influence – coins, brooches and other ornamentation – that have been found in the area over many years.

The Wessex Archaeology Report states that

'the most likely reason for the burial of these finds was as gifts to accompany a dead person in their journey to the next world. Such a burial, which is likely to have been a cremation, would be very rare in Dorset. However, the only alternative for a hoard of objects buried as an offering to the gods would be rarer still.'

A burial of this kind implies some settled habitation with established religious practices. Edward Bourke, who has lived in Chettle all his life and has made a study of the Roman period, thinks this is unlikely.

'At the time the hoard was buried in Middle Field in 60–70 AD there was', he writes, no settlement and 'certainly it was much too early for there to have been any settlement influenced by Roman architecture or building methods which could be described as a Roman villa'; but 'there is considerable evidence that Middle Field … was often crossed by local inhabitants.'

Bourke's hypothesis is that these items were deposited in Middle Field either by members of the Second Legion or by a local inhabitant who had perhaps stolen them. The position and style of their burial points to its having been done in a great hurry, and it lacks the care that would have prevailed for a religious ceremony. There was no food or other item such as was so often included to assist the dead person on his journey, and no evidence of burning for cremation.

The Roman acculturation of this area came well after the time of this burial. Who buried these spectacular vessels and for what purpose we can only speculate. Their beauty and preservation we may marvel over. Some unknown craftsman of the first century AD is now commemorated with a photograph of his beautifully wrought amphora on the wine list of the Castleman Hotel Chettle, owned and run by Edward and Barbara Bourke.

THREE

Feudal Chettle

The outlines of life at Chettle during the Roman period are discernible. Nearby townships, ports, and roads were established and were commercially and socially active and well administered; their foundations remain. After the Romans departed in 410 AD traces of their legacy began to disappear. Not until Britain was again subdued by an invader, William of Normandy in 1066, does the area re-emerge into the historical landscape.

The administrative genius of the Romans departed with them. From about 410 AD the business of life – farming, trading, travelling, building, living and dying – continued in Britain, but almost nothing was recorded in writing. The materials used for domestic purposes were less durable. Housing of wood and straw does not stand the test of archaeological time, which leaves little in material recording of our forebears during this period. During the six and a half centuries between 410 AD and 1066 very little recorded data has been found to illuminate our understanding of the conditions of life. Waves of invaders took advantage of the absence of an efficient defence system and by the fifth century the Angles and Saxons had settled in Britain.

William the Conqueror arrived in 1066. Nineteen years later he commissioned a survey of the country. The land, held previously by the English, had by then been redistributed to the men and women who had come from France with the Conqueror in accordance with the strictly hierarchical feudal system. Under this system the land was held by the king, who granted it to his lords, in exchange for specified services – mainly military. They in turn could grant parts of the land to their subordinates in exchange for other agreed services, and so on down to the landless serf who worked in exchange for protection and food. An essential element of the feudal system is that land could not be owned and was therefore not purchasable. It was held *of the king* (who in theory held it of God). When the holder no longer required it, or could no longer meet his agreed obligations, it returned to the lord, or to the king, and was re-granted. This system of land tenure had dramatic consequences for Chettle, particularly in the eighteenth and nineteenth centuries.

Inadequacies in record keeping in the centuries preceding the Conquest meant that William had little to guide him as to the value of the prize he had won. Commissioners appointed *'by the King's will'* went to every part of the country and recorded how much land (woodland, pasture, meadow, arable) and how many animals, buildings, mills, and fisheries existed. All of this data was brought together in the Domesday Book. Chettle is one of the thirteen and a half thousand towns and villages chronicled in this eleventh century tome. The very large area of Blandford, Morden, Hampreston, Selavestune,[12] Tarrant, Stubhampton, Chettle, Farnham, Bradle, Tatton, Durweston, Wooton Fitzpaine, Bridge, Hethfelton, Lulworth and Long Crichel was held by Aiulf the Chamberlain and was worth a total of £60 0s.8d. Most of these names can be recognized today. All were held *'by Aiulf himself'* with one exception. *'The same Aiulf holds CHETTLE, and Airard [holds] it of him,'*[13] so Chettle, of one hide and worth 20s. had Airard as an intermediate lord. Aiulf could manage the rest of his very large property but Chettle qualified for closer control.

William of Normandy's system of land tenure influenced Chettle for almost eight hundred years. Of equal importance was his designation of Cranborne Chase as a royal hunting ground. This too lasted for nearly eight hundred years. Cranborne Chase is the three

---

[12] Probably Winterbourne Zelston, the old form of which was Selyston.
[13] Dr Ann Williams & Professor G H Martin Eds. *Domesday Book A Complete Translation* Penguin Books 1992.

hundred and eighty square miles of chalk down that lies within a rec-
tangle formed by lines joining Shaftesbury, Salisbury, Ringwood and
Blandford. Chettle lies in the southwest quadrant. The royal hunting
grounds were subject to Forest, or Chase, law. The monarch, or his
appointed representative, claimed the monopolistic right to maintain and hunt deer over the area, regardless of who farmed the land.
The protected deer damaged boundaries and crops and competed
with domestic animals for pasturage. In the main it was the new
men, the invaders, who had hunting rights and the dispossessed
Anglo-Saxons who were incommoded in their farming. Forest Law
was heartily disliked throughout England. The legends of Robin Hood
and his Merry Men standing up for the dispossessed against the imposition of Forest Law by the monarch (then King John, 1199–1216)
or his representative, the Sheriff of Nottingham, resonate down the
centuries.

Enjoyable sport hunting may have been, but the deer were a natural, invaluable source of protein. Famine was an ever-present threat,
which for centuries concentrated the minds of the populace as every
winter approached. In essence and origin deer hunting was part of
the essential food economy but it became, as food production methods and transport changed, symbolic of landholding rights, as vigorously defended as the Norman and Plantagenet kings had defended
their access to good meat. No Robin Hood has been found at Chettle, but King John's Hunting Lodge still stands at Tollard Royal three
miles north of the village.[14] No doubt Aiulf, and Airard his appointee,
and their successors, like the Sheriff of Nottingham, dealt with some
rebellious Anglo-Saxons constrained within their hide of land at
Chettle. The overarching monarchical authority wielded by the Lord
of the Chase stretched its long and haughty arm down to the nineteenth century, even then imposing a sentence of seven years' transportation for deer poaching.

The local Anglo-Saxon community of Coetel did not settle easily
under their Norman overlords. *Their* land was now controlled by

---

[14] A. Pitt-Rivers *King John's House Tollard Royal* 1890.

Airard and all were bound into a system of grant and obligation. Service was demanded for tilling land previously their own. The capture of deer was forbidden. Airard was responsible to Aiulf for getting this small part of his great domain into Norman order. The resistance of the wooded hollow to modernizing change made his job difficult.

Airard would have been followed by a sequence of landholders farming the hide at Chettle. By the seventh century Britain had been Christianized and at some time Chettle came into ownership of the Church. It is recorded that in 1389 *'Thomas Chesterton, Abbott of Tewkesbury held, at his death, the Manor of Tarrant Monkton, Cranborne Priory, Chettle, Upwimborne and Boveridge.'*[15] Chettle was then supporting a nunnery. The combination of two or more parcels of land in church ownership to form the nunnery would have been economically beneficial to the Church. Of the Benedictine nuns at Chettle there is no record, but the principal buildings would in all likelihood have been grouped around the cloister, and charitable work of feeding the poor and caring for the sick undertaken. Unmarriageable daughters and widows of wealthy families, together with their endowments and jewellery, were welcomed into convents and they became repositories of considerable riches. The Abbot of Tewkesbury still received the tithe (a tenth of all farm produce in kind) of Chettle when Henry VIII embarked upon the Dissolution of the Monasteries in 1536. Vast acres of church property were confiscated and redistributed, much of it to secular interests. Many of the monastic establishments had been centres of learning, education and places where the sick and indigent might be cared for. Within a few years these treasure houses, their contents and their welfare functions had been ruthlessly destroyed.

As the monasteries were closed their residents were turned out. Some of the clerics, being well educated, found jobs as tutors in wealthy families. Many became mendicants[16] and added to the disorderly

---

[15] *Chronicle of Cranborne* 1841 p21.
[16] Mendicant Friars had been dependent on alms as part of their discipline. With the demolition of their religious base they became simple beggars.

rabble of the Tudor homeless. The nursery song *'Hark hark, the dogs do bark, the beggars are coming to town'* alludes to this roaming band which struck fear in town and country. The authorities, reluctant to have the women of religious orders compounding the vagabond problem, delayed in closing their establishments so it was not until the year after Elizabeth became Queen, 1559, that the *'manor* [of Chettle] *and advowson, parcel of Tewkesbury Abbey and manor of Pimperne were granted to William Tooke and Edward Balsh esquires and their heirs.'*[17] Many of the Tudor beneficiaries of the Dissolution had found favour with the monarch and were able to acquire, or had granted to them, assets that had belonged to the church. Remnants of the nunnery probably survived until the present Chettle House was built on the site in the early eighteenth century.

Thirteen years later in 1572 the property was transferred to the ownership of Thomas Chafin (1) under a grant from the Queen. It is from that date, 1572 that the ownership of, and events at, Chettle emerge into a clearer light.

The Norman feudal administrative structure was based on land as the only source of wealth and its assessment. With increasing economic diversification the feudal system gradually eroded, first in towns and ports where trade and commerce took precedence, later in rural areas. Chettle, as its story will reveal, has had an idiosyncratic relationship with feudalism. Throughout its history it has been dependent upon land, and is so, to a very large extent, today. Some of its personalities however overrode legalities to break the restrictions imposed by feudal law. Its development, as perhaps Airard could have foretold, has been sporadic, sometimes delinquent, often unruly.

---

[17] John Hutchins *The History and Antiquities of the County of Dorset* 1773.

FOUR

Thomas Chafin (1) of Folke

Thomas Chafin (1) came from a family of good standing in the West Country. He could trace his forebears back through five generations to John Chafin, a card maker who lived in Warminster in the early fifteenth century. Carding was the process of combing the fibres of wool to remove small loose fibres before spinning, and also to raise the nap on the woven cloth. John Chafin was making the carding machines for this purpose. Wool was the principal source of England's wealth at the time and the West Country one of its most productive areas.

The *History of Parliament* records that the Chafin *'family of Wiltshire origin produced a member for Salisbury in 1475'*.[18] This was during the turbulent period of the Wars of the Roses (1455–1485), a civil war between the York and Lancaster branches of the royal family. The decimation of the aristocratic families in this carnage meant that many of the positions of power were left untenanted. The social vacuum thus created enabled men from relatively modest background to come forward, and a new stratum emerged into the political arena. The *'middling sort'*, as they were known, could not claim membership of the old nobility but their skills, achievements and acquisitions made them eligible to fill some of the empty places. Some of them had acquired land, by means fair and foul; some had benefited from a trading niche; a few forwarded their cause through

---

[18] Desmond Hawkins *The Grove Diaries* 1995.

education, particularly in the law. The Chafins were involved in the prosperous wool trade in the fifteenth century, making money, buying land and education and moving into positions of influence.

Henry VII, the first Tudor, needed the ability of these new men to get his divided realm into some order. During the long rule of the Tudors (1475–1603) their ambitions were exploited. They were promoted to posts in government at central and county level where they enjoyed authority and influence, but had no pay. Tudor government was carried on efficiently at very little cost to the exchequer. A member of the Chafin family was one of the first to take his place in this new scheme of things.

From 1537 the Chafin family tree and coat of arms was recorded with the College of Heralds. The date and the family motto suggest that this promotion was connected with Henry VIII's policy of severance from Rome. In 1536 he divorced Queen Katherine (of Aragon) and made a divorce between the English Church and the Church of Rome. Henry appointed himself *'Defender of the Faith'*. The Chafins chose *'Watch Dogs of the Lord'*. The Chafins could be relied upon to support the Crown in those difficult times and were prominent amongst the prosperous merchant-mercers of the West Country, particularly in New Sarum (Salisbury), Bristol and Mere.[19]

In 1548 a Thomas Chafin Junior was Mayor of New Sarum with Thomas Chafin Senior, Clerk of the Statute Merchant.[20] These two posts were crucial to the administration of the Statute Merchant Bonds that had been set up by Henry VIII in 1510 to facilitate credit arrangements and was one of several early Tudor devices for the encouragement of commerce and trade. The Bond (a promise to pay) was *'recorded before the Clerk of the Statute and the Lord Mayor of the City of London … or person appointed… if the obliger pay not the debt at the day, execution may be awarded against his body, lands and goods…till the debt be levied'*. Shakespeare (1564–1616) made fine dramatic capital from this clause in *The Merchant of Venice* that

---

[19] The family in some documents is described as from Zeals. Zeals and Mere are about a mile apart and were the same estate.

[20] Somerset & Dorset Notes & Queries Vol 10 1907.

was first produced in 1596. The bond between Antonio and Shylock was recorded before a notary who would have been the equivalent of the Clerk of the Statute Merchant, the position held by Thomas Chafin Senior of New Sarum.

Shakespeare's acting company The King's Men, based at the Globe Theatre, London, played *The Merchant of Venice 'for the sovereign'* at *'Wilton, the Earl of Pembroke's estate near Salisbury in Wiltshire…on 2 December'* 1603.[21] (King James would have come to Wilton for deer hunting.) The Earl of Pembroke was the king's appointed representative as Lord of the Chase and the Chafins by then had game hunting rights so might have anticipated an invitation to take part in seasonal festivities with the king.

By the mid sixteenth century when Queen Elizabeth came to the throne the Chafins were not only commercially successful, they were influential in civic affairs and trusted by authority. Their reward was the manor of Chettle, purloined a few years before from the Catholic Church. It was added to what was by then extensive Chafin property in different parts of the West Country, the centre and family home of which was at Folke in the Blackmore Vale – known in Tudor times as the Vale of the White Hart – about twenty miles distant.

Chettle came with some responsibilities and not a few compensatory privileges, as a charter dated 1572, *'confirmed by diverse princes'* and issued by *'Mr Uvedaele, Highe Sherieffe of the County of Dorset'*[22] tells us. *'Roialties. The Lord of the manor of Chettle is chiefe lorde of the soile, and kepe the court and leet, and hath weifes* (orphans) *and straies* (homeless) *fellones* (criminals) *goods etc and hath the royalties of fowling fishinge and huntinge; and hath by speciall wordes in Charter graunted…the hunting in certaine groundes, as well within his own several manors, as also within Cranborne Chace and Chetred Chace, without vexation of anie person.'* Time and custom modified the terms of this charter over the next two and a half centuries, during which six successive generations of Chafins were lords of the manor

---

[21] Peter Ackroyd *Shakespeare: The Biography* 2005.
[22] A fine monument to this man, Sir Edmund Uvedale can be seen in Wimborne Minster.

of Chettle. They continued to enjoy most of the privileges and the social position throughout.

Within a few years of becoming Lord of Chettle Thomas (1) was appointed High Sheriff of Dorset, thus following Mr Uvedale who had issued the Charter of Chettle to him. The High Sheriff was one of the monarch's agents in the county. The job came with considerable responsibilities, influence and distinction, but no pay. Nevertheless keen competition marked these appointments. Local peers made nomination to the Lord Chancellor who advised the monarch. It was the duty of the High Sheriff to summon members to Parliament, to arrest those charged with crime, to empanel juries, and to enforce judgements made by Justices of the Peace (another honorary crown office), and to appoint an under sheriff and constables for the county.

Portraits of both men and women of the time display their elaborate dress and ornament. Paintings of Henry VIII and Queen Elizabeth and their courtiers, are rich with lovely fabrics, embroidery, furs, jewels at neck, wrist and ear, and fingers laden with rings. With the increase in geographical and social mobility it was especially important for men of the *'middling sort'* to make display of their newfound position, to assure themselves that all knew of their importance. No painting of Thomas Chafin (1) exists, but he certainly dressed to impress. He had invested in plate and jewels and wore a chain of gold.[23] When he was on *'some duty of the Queen's service'* in 1580 with another High Sheriff, Benjamin Tichborne of Hampshire, they met with Henry Howard *'during one of his insane fits'*. Thomas was attacked by Henry who, Chafin reported, *'tore down my shirt and doublet and brake the chain which I had about my neck into two pieces... called me scab and papistical knave.'*[24] Henry Howard was about twenty when this skirmish took place. A search for a crucifix on the gold chain was the likely motivation for this attack, for Thomas Chafin (1) was, like many of the landowners of the southwest, reluctant to bend the knee to the new Anglican Church. This

[23] Will of Thomas Chafin.
[24] State Papers 12/140 f 11, quoted by Rachel Lloyd in *Dorset Elizabethans at Home and Abroad* 1967.

event took place nine years after Henry's father, the fourth Duke of Norfolk, had been executed in 1572 for his part in the Ridolfi plot, one of the many Catholic attempts to replace the Anglican Queen Elizabeth with the Catholic Mary Queen of Scots. Perhaps we can catch here a glimpse of the traumatic effects, on an impressionable and not very stable young man, of being at such close quarters with the intense religious anxiety that followed the Dissolution. Queen Elizabeth managed to turn a blind eye on recusant practice in the early part of her reign. Her much-valued Lord Chancellor (some thought her paramour as well), Sir Christopher Hatton (1540–1591) was an acquaintance and near neighbour of the Chafins at Corfe Castle. He had always been suspected of Catholicism. Many devout and worthy people, Thomas Chafin amongst them, managed the tricky balancing act of being loyal to the English Crown at the same time as worshipping according to the edicts of Rome.

On 9th February 1589 Thomas married Jane, the daughter of Hugh Bampfylde of North Cadbury in Somerset. Jane was a young woman, but Thomas was then fifty-nine, a late age for a first marriage at any time, but in the sixteenth century quite exceptional. If the marriage had been urged by the need for an heir, success crowned their efforts. Their only child Bamfield was born two years later and named after his mother's family. (Consistency of spelling is not a strong feature of early records and I have kept, as far as is practicable, to the name as recorded.)

The Bampfylde family, which was the longer established, wielded considerable influence in the area. Their family seat was at Poltimore near Exeter where they had lived since 1306. Jane came with an appreciable dowry. Advantageous marriages became as important to the rising gentry class as they had always been to European royalty and nobility, and the association with the Bampfylde family was recurrently celebrated by a male child in every generation being baptized Bamfield.

Thomas fitted the role of the ambitious aspiring gentleman to perfection, though the marriage was short lived as Thomas died in February 1592. His memorial stone in the south aisle of St Michael's

Church, North Cadbury is no longer visible, now being covered with pews.

Thomas (1)'s will is in the approved format of the Anglican Church and gives no sign of recusancy. He was able to leave to his wife Jane all his *'stock and store of cattle'* at his farms in Folke and Sydling, or *'wheresoever'.* To his year-old son he bequeathed the gold chain that had caused a commotion in 1580, and £500 *'to be delivered by his mother … when he shall accomplish twenty and two years.'* Jane was the sole executrix of his will, but she had two overseers to help and advise her. One was the distinguished Lord Thomas Howard (1561–1626) who was then aged thirty-one and Lord Lieutenant of Dorset. He was the brother of Henry who had attacked Chafin the High Sheriff. He had gone some way to redeeming the family name so besmirched by his father, by a spectacularly brave performance at the time of the Spanish Armada in 1588. He later became Lord High Treasurer for King James I. (There are four paintings of him, grandly accoutred, in the National Portrait Gallery).

Twenty years after Chettle had been granted to the Chafin family it passed to a year-old child. Bamfield has a baptismal record at St Michael's Church, North Cadbury, the home of his mother, and another later one, dated September/October 1592, at Chettle. He was baptized at Chettle more than six months after his father's death. It was wise to have the child's existence recorded there. For some years after the Dissolution there were difficulties over establishing title to property. Sheep rearing was so profitable that land was being enclosed often without too much regard as to who actually owned it. A young child with no record of having been in the parish might have had some greedy eyes turned upon his property. Jane Chafin made a second marriage to Sir George Trenchard, another Dorset landowner, whose home was at Wolfeton House, Charminster. The village of Chettle, with its empty nunnery laid waste, had no resident Lord of the Manor and no Chafin in authority there. Thomas Chafin (1) had been grant-ed the land in 1572 but he, and later his son Bamfield chose to stay in Folke. It was not until his grandson, Thomas (2) married Elizabeth Trenchard in the 1630's that a Chafin came to live at Chettle.

Like many families of the time they used a very limited repertoire of Christian names. Four Thomases, two Georges, a Bamfield and a William were holders of the property. The table below shows their dates of birth, death and their years of tenure.

Christian Name	Born	Inherited	Died	Years as Lord of Manor	Age at which Lord of of Manor
Thomas (1)	1530	1572	1592	20	42–62
Bamfield	1591	1592	1644	52	1–53
Thomas (2)	1612/15	1644	1655	11	29/32–40/43
Thomas (3)	1650	1655	1691	36	5–41
Thomas (4) brother to	1675	1691	1711	20	16–36
George (1)	1689	1711	1766	55	22–77
George (2) brother to	1717	1766	1776	10	49–59
William	1731	1776	1818	42	45–87

(see also the Chafin family tree at p.viii & ix)

Unresolved problems of church and state exploded with the Civil War for the next generation of Chafins.

FIVE

The Parish of Chettle

For hundreds of years Chettle had been centred upon a religious establishment governed from Rome. Some time after 1558, the year that Queen Elizabeth came to the throne, this core of the village was ransacked and its inhabitants, the Roman Catholic nuns, were turned out. The officers of the crown appointed to take over the religious establishments were not fastidious; damage to property and to social fabric was often brutal.

During the reign of Queen Elizabeth the parish church of St Mary, then about three hundred years old, became the centrepiece of the village. The Church of England rector was strictly bound by Elizabeth's Act of Uniformity to the Book of Common Prayer in place of the Mass, English in place of Latin, loyalty to the English monarch, and with the ritual detail of each religious service, clerical dress and conduct punctiliously prescribed. Church attendance was compulsory upon pain of a £20 a month fine. A labourer's weekly wage was reckoned in shillings or pence not pounds, so this might have been a year's wages. Precise comparison is misleading. Rural labourers were never far from subsistence, which depended on the exercise of their rights of common, barter, and gifts. They had not completely entered the money economy. Thus the threat of such a fine kept all but wealthy Catholics in obedient attendance. It would have been a brave, or foolhardy, resident of Chettle who tried to resist. The struggle to turn a population embedded for a millennium in the Catholic faith to the Anglican Church, and to fashion a diverse population, bound in allegiance to the different landholding barons, into one nation, was a long one. More than four fifths of Queen Elizabeth's subjects lived in rural England so it fell largely to the parish rectors to carry out this radical central government policy. How vigorously they did so no doubt varied with their own views, their distance from London and their local bishop. While the secular overlord of Chettle, suspected of recusancy, lived at Folke, the rectors of the parish wielded considerable local authority. With their ability to read and write they would have been particularly important as conduits for news. They also had a judicial function as civil order was largely maintained through the ecclesiastical courts.

When the nunnery in Chettle was destroyed the practice of the nuns of looking after the sick, making herbal medicines, taking in orphans, helping folk at the extremity of exhaustion or desperation was destroyed as well. Church assets had been redistributed by the monarch and those of Chettle had been granted to Thomas Chafin (1) though responsibility for the welfare functions was not included. The consequent social and economic distress that was apparent throughout the land was dealt with towards the end of Elizabeth's reign by the enactment of the Poor Law of 1601. This was administered through the parish. Before any Chafin had taken up residence in Chettle a few local dignitaries, the rector, the bailiff, one of the bigger farmers, maybe a tradesman had formed the Parish Vestry to carry out the requirements of this legislation. As we shall see, the parish came to define the individual's existence. For more than three hundred years, with few modifications the parish was second only to the family in regulating one's life.

In 1538 Thomas Cromwell, Henry VIII's Lord Chancellor[25] ordered the recording of baptisms, marriages and burials. He needed the information for population statistics and taxation. Chettle parish registers at St Mary's date from 1538 and are amongst the best in the county. Robert Ratcliff was the rector from 1525 till 1558 and started recording events at his church so promptly that it suggests he

---

[25] Also referred to as the King's Lord Great Chamberlain.

was keen to show his support for, or at least not to offend, Thomas Cromwell. His survival through the four reigns with their four changes of 'official' religion[26] may hint at a man with a fairly flexible attitude to his calling. The record that he started however continues to this day. The present rector, Father William Johnstone appointed in 1998, entered the baptism of my granddaughter Lara Prince in October 1998 in the four hundred and sixtieth year of the parish record.

Some of the entries are illegible. Bad handwriting by clerics over the centuries, mice, damp and mildew all take their toll. There was no standard spelling of surnames until 1870. Births and deaths are not the same as baptisms and burials – the latter deal only with events within the purview of the church. The *'ditch delivered brat'*, common law marriage and clandestine death did not enter Cromwell's calculations. The clergy often resented the unpaid civil service task that had been imposed upon them. It is plain in looking at the parish records of Chettle and Folke that the written record was sometimes made well after the event when the rector's recall was but hazy. On the early baptismal records only the father's name is given. The high death rate meant there were many second marriages. Shoals of children, from two or more marriages, are not easy to sort out when only one parent is named. Families often limited themselves to a narrow range of Christian names, even to the point of having two children identically named. Nevertheless from these records and from the surviving wills of some of the residents a picture emerges of life in sixteenth century Chettle.

Roger Phillips followed Robert Ratcliff and was appointed rector in the year of Queen Elizabeth's coronation. He would have witnessed the expulsion of the nuns from the religious house in the village. The previous twenty years had seen four changes of officially

---

[26] Henry VIII remained a Catholic, but not Roman. Edward VI was very Protestant, Mary a Roman Catholic. Queen Elizabeth, with the Act of Supremacy and the Act of Conformity, established herself as head of the Anglican Church. Between Henry's death in 1547 and Elizabeth's accession to the throne in 1558 there were changes with each new monarch, often brutally enforced.

sanctioned Christianity with cruel and public punishments for non-compliance. Fears and anxieties crept in every shadowy corner and every overturned religious house. If God kept changing, who could be relied upon? It was a time of great uncertainty with recurrent epidemics, and with each onset of winter the threat of famine. Free-floating amorphous anxiety gave rise to the terror of the day, witchcraft. Witches, sorcery, demonology are to be found in many societies and the concept of witchcraft has beguiled human thought for centuries, but it emerged with unusual strength from the middle of the sixteenth century. Witches were attributed with supernatural powers for either good or evil, they were believed to be in league with the Devil and a local witch would be under suspicion if, for example, a crop failed, a woman miscarried, a child fell ill or an animal died. Who were these witches? Suspicion fell on those who were not well integrated into the community. Indigent old women who lived alone were particularly suspect. In 1563 a law aimed at keeping witches at bay was enacted. '*Conjuration, enchantments and witchcraft*' were forbidden as being '*contrary to Almighty God, to the peril of their own soules and to the great infamy and disquietness of this Realm.*' It was not until 1736 that the legislation on witchcraft was repealed.

It was part of Roger Phillips' church duties to maintain social order in the village, and if necessary he had recourse to ecclesiastical law. He would have adjudicated on quarrels between neighbours, accusations of witchcraft, and domestic disputes. There were various shaming rituals employed against men and women who flouted their prescribed roles. The Skimmity ride, which was well known in Dorset,[27] was a ritual for the public shaming of men who could not keep control of their wives and families. The ducking stool in the village pond was punishment for deviant women. It is all too easy to imagine the unruly merriment enjoyed by the inhabitants of Chettle while watching their neighbours being ridiculed. These public humiliations provided a rowdy release of social tension, though

---

[27] Montacute House, built between 1588 and 1601, a little more than twenty-five miles to the east of Chettle, has a fine plaster representation of the Skimmity ride across the north doorway of the Hall.

disaster did sometimes supervene: drowning and death from exposure were not unknown. The quiet pond near the lane leading to the
church could have been the site where the over-bold women of the
parish were taken to task. The Court Book of the Manor of Chettle
periodically records the decision that *'the Water that Runs down the
Street shall not be turned out of its course or prevented from going to
…Hardinge Pond'.*[28] For most of his time at Chettle Roger Phillips
would have been the authority, and probably the only literate person,
in the village. In those changing and fearful times his was no
sinecure.

In 1579 James Feltham became the rector, seven years after the
property was transferred to Thomas Chafin (1). The Anglican min-
istry by this time had become more firmly established. It was almost
entirely graduate and was emerging as distinctly professional. James
Feltham exemplifies the changes taking place in the Anglican
Church. He was a man of some substance who owned property at
Burcombe in Wiltshire (a village about fourteen miles northeast of
Chettle near Wilton) as well as some leasehold property. On his
death he was able to bequeath property to Avis his wife, and to sons
William and Edward. He left money for his son William, but Edward
received only forgiveness for *'twenty shillings of old debt'*. Edward had
anticipated his patrimony, to his father's annoyance. He left thirteen
shillings and fourpence to both the church and to the *'poor people of
Chettle'.*[29] James Feltham's will was proved in the Prerogative Court of
Canterbury in 1609, which dealt only with wills of some substance.
It is indicative of the changing values promoted by the Anglican
Church and the altered circumstances of churchmen who were no
longer bound by vows of poverty, chastity and obedience. His assets
to some extent reflect those of Chettle as he had a tithe of the income
of all parishioners. James Feltham was a man of property with an
established family for whom he had made good material provision.

---

[28] B F P, Chettle Court Book.

[29] The sum of thirteen shillings and fourpence was not as eccentric as it now seems.
A mark was a third of a pound (twenty shillings) so the sum bequeathed was two
marks.

He also wished to be remembered by his church and parishioners.

In 1603 Queen Elizabeth died and was succeeded by James I of England, VI of Scotland. James inherited troublesome unresolved religious discords. The Gunpowder Plot in 1605 revived anxieties about foreign Catholic mischief that had been allayed with the defeat of the Spanish Armada in 1588. At the other extreme Puritans were active in promoting further church reform, wanting amongst other things the removal of all bishops from office. Puritan agitation was quite vigorous in Dorset, though no documents have been found identifying Chettle as a trouble spot for either its religious fervour or its witchcraft. There was always potential for witchcraft in this quiet secluded valley, but radicalism in religion would have been extremely unlikely. This tended to flourish in towns and ports along the Dorset coast where trade and commerce brought the population into contact with the larger world.

When James Feltham died in 1608 Robert Palmer was appointed to the benefice of St Mary's Chettle and he held it for thirty-two years. The Gunpowder Plotters had been motivated in part by their disappointment that King James was not as supportive of Catholicism as they had hoped. A few years later a group of Puritans, equally disappointed with constitutional restrictions on their religious practice, sailed away from Plymouth on the Mayflower and emigrated to America. These were the extremities of the complex range of beliefs, fears and faiths that confronted King James when he came to England. He commissioned a new translation of the Bible *'for what James, the self styled Rex Pacificus, and his councillors hoped… might be an ideal world'.*[30] The new translation would usher in harmony and unification. The King James Version of the Holy Bible was launched upon the nation in 1611. This has recently been described as *'the greatest creation of the seventeenth century England…England's equivalent of the great baroque cathedral it never built…a national shrine built only of words.'*[31] Fifty men from key positions in church and

[30] Adam Nicholson *Power and Glory* 2003.
[31] Adam Nicholson op.cit.

university worked in six teams translating the books of the Bible from their original Greek and Hebrew.

The ordinary folk of Chettle would have known little of the regal aspirations for peace and unity associated with the new Authorized Version of the Bible. Although the population of England was becoming more literate, education was slow to reach rural areas. The parishioners knew however, that their church was being refurbished and equipped with a fine new pulpit from which Robert Palmer was to introduce them to the new translation in 1611, as was required in every church in the land. Reading desks, favoured in the Elizabethan era, gave place to the Jacobean pulpit, which provided the rector with a more commanding position. The *'national shrine, built only of words'* was to be delivered with power and glory. This was state control exerted through the church and the rector knew that he was expected to maintain peace, good order and amity in his parish. Between 1603, when James I became king of England, and the outbreak of the Civil War nearly forty years later *'it seems every village joiner in England must have been engaged in making'* pulpits for this noble enterprise.[32] The nave of St Mary's Church, Chettle was repaired at the same time *'to such an extent as to leave but little of the original style remaining'*, writes Hutchins.[33] Under Robert Palmer the scene was set for the new one-size-fits-all Christianity. Chettle's Jacobean pulpit, remodelled in the nineteenth century to make two chairs, is still part of the church furnishing in the twenty-first century. The skilful hands of a local carpenter made it in about 1610: his proud contribution to the refurbishment of the church for the new reign.

For most of Robert Palmer's ministry (1608–1640) the parish was without a secular overlord. (Thomas Chafin (2) did not move to Chettle till 1635.) Nicholas Dunning, the bailiff, looked after the secular affairs of the parish. The estate had been incorporated into the many Chafin acres for about thirty-five years by then. Nicholas was a

[32] Gerald Randall *The English Parish Church* 1982.
[33] John Hutchins *The History and Antiquities of the County of Dorset* 1773.

generation older than the rector, Robert Palmer but they were friends and the parish ran peaceably enough. The seasonal tasks of the farming year imposed their discipline and provided the food on every cottage table. The bedrock of Chafin prosperity however was the trade in wool and cloth. The year brought its round of lambing, shearing, and slaughtering. Some of the women in the village spun the wool and then it had to be taken to the weavers' shops in the vicinity where men fashioned it into cloth for sale or export from Poole and Melcombe Regis. Nicholas kept accounts for these transactions and had to be constantly aware of price movements. That meant attending markets and meeting other men in the business. He could combine a day at Sturminster Newton market with a visit to Folke and sometimes a social visit to Sir Thomas Freke's bailiff at Shroton.

Nicholas Dunning was bailiff for Chettle from about the time that Queen Elizabeth died in 1603 till 1625. The arrival of King James I from Scotland was particularly remembered in the area because Robert Cecil, his chief minister, was appointed Viscount Cranborne and Lord of Cranborne Chase shortly afterwards. He was known locally as *'the crooked earl'*. He did have a hunch back, and he was so clever and calculating that people suspected that he might have been crooked in other ways. But he died in great debt.

Until Bamfield Chafin was old enough to take responsibility in connection with Chettle Nicholas Dunning had occasionally to go to Charminster to see Lady Trenchard, Bamfield's mother. That was a long journey but it meant a visit to Blandford and Dorchester where he occasionally stayed.

His wages as bailiff were good and he kept some animals of his own on the common land. He and his wife Anne and their family worked hard but lived contentedly. Their six children, Richard, Anne, Honor, Mary, John and Humphrey, were all baptized by Robert Palmer in St Mary's Church, Chettle. Nicholas died in 1625 and was able to leave £20 each to four of his children. Humphrey and John had £5 each. He left small sums of money to several neighbours, Goodwife Cutler, Anny Ash, Walter Parker, George Brice and Stephen Greene, something for the church and all else to his wife Anne. Thus he disposed very precisely of the £90.8s he had saved. It was a sizable sum and would have given his children a chance to start in some small way of business of their own. '*I bequeath my soule*', he wrote, '*into the hands of Christ Jesus my redeemer by whose merritts I hope to be saved. And my body to be buried in the churchyard of Chettle.*'

The ordinary folk of Chettle were a long way from London where autocratic monarchs promulgated changes in the law, civil administration and church practice. Recoverable fragments from the lives of four rectors, Ratcliff, Phillips, Feltham and Palmer, and the Dunning family between 1525 and 1640 show how Tudor and Stuart reforms gradually seeped into this quiet corner of the realm. We can see too, how the feudal economy of grant and obligation was giving way to capitalism and a money economy.

There was a further duty in connection with provision for the poor that was imposed upon the dignitaries of the parish during this period. It lasted, with some modifications, until 1930. The demolition of the religious houses from 1536 onward had destroyed their charitable work at the same time. The indigent who had been beneficiaries of Catholic welfare added to the long-standing Tudor vagabondage problem. The Elizabethan Poor Law implemented in 1601 was an attempt by central government to deal with the resulting social and economic difficulties: to provide the necessities of life for those unable to do so for themselves and to provide work for the 'sturdy beggar'. The parish was the administrative unit. It was required to provide for those parishioners who, through incapacity or sloth, were failing in life's struggle, and to raise the necessary money through a tax on the land of the parish. There was periodic unemployment. Orphans and widows needed food and clothing. The disabled and sick could not be forever ignored. There were the layabouts too. Discriminating between the deserving and the undeserving has ever been a problem in the administration of charity. The Elizabethan Poor Law made legal distinctions between those who could not, and those who would not, stand on their own two feet. With recurrent cycles of unemployment the application of the law was not always equitable.

Nicholas Dunning and Robert Palmer, friends and colleagues were the men on the spot to set in hand the necessary arrangements for the parish of Chettle. An assessment was made each year of the demand to be expected from the poor of the parish and on that basis a rate per acre was calculated. The Poor Rate was payable by anyone holding land. It was for very many years the only national system of welfare in the world, and arguably the three and a half centuries of communal concern did something to pave the way for an acceptance of the proposals for a welfare state at the end of the Second World War. The overseers in the parish carried considerable responsibility. The books had to be balanced and both receivers of welfare and providers of the same had to live in accord with each other and with the administrators of the system. The more modest providers also knew that their turn might come to be receivers. A bad harvest, an accidental fire, an outbreak of disease in cattle or poultry could change the status of a small tenant farmer who lived constantly near the margin. The implementation of the Poor Law brought the conditions of men, women and children, rich and poor, within the purview of their fellow parishioners, the overseers. It helped to bind them into a recognized condition of interdependence and gave the parish a firm identity. It was the parish that defined one's existence.

When Robert Palmer's ministry at Chettle came to an end in 1640 the parish was well and truly established as the determinant of an individual's locus, second only to his family. Here his baptism, marriage and burial were recorded. The parish provided a mutual support system where it was understood that the 'haves' had some obligation, however resentfully it might have been fulfilled, enforced by the overseers of the parish, to the 'have nots'. It was to this parish, shaping itself into self-respect after the sixteenth century religious turmoil and the destruction of its nunnery, that the first resident Chafin came in 1635.

SIX

The Move to Chettle

Bamfield Chafin, only child of the first holder of Chettle, Thomas (1), had been baptized by James Feltham in St Mary's Church Chettle in September 1591. The long reign of the Tudors was nearing its end. They had, to a considerable extent, succeeded in their aim of replacing old loyalties to the nobility with loyalty to the Crown. The Chafins typified the new men; mercantile, bowing the knee to no overlord, taking a leading role in local government and affairs, and enjoying a certain degree of crown patronage. Bamfield was twelve years old when Queen Elizabeth died and the new era of the Stuarts opened with King James I.

Bamfield's father had died when he was one, his mother remarried to Sir George Trenchard who lived at Wolfeton House, Charminster. Bamfield came into the inheritance, together with the family name, Chafin of Folke when he came of age. He was the sole survivor of this branch of the family and its future was therefore looking precarious. An early marriage was urged upon him. At the age of twenty-one he married Mary Muschamp, the daughter of another worthy of Folke, William Muschamp, in 1612. Consolidation of property was a traditional part of marriage arrangements. Their home at Folke was the centre of a very large property extending over parts of what are now Dorset, Hampshire, Surrey, Somerset and Wiltshire. For the next thirty years Bamfield established both his growing family in Folke, and the repute of the name of Chafin.

The first-born child was Thomas Chafin (2) followed by his

37

younger brother George. Two further sons died in infancy and their mother Mary also died in 1622 in her mid twenties, and is buried at Folke, though no memorial is to be found there. Bamfield remarried within two years. His second wife, another Mary, was the daughter of Thomas and Elizabeth Lisle from the Isle of Wight, another fine sheep rearing area. (Sheep on chalk made very fine wool, but poor meat. The wool of sheep grown for mutton did not enjoy such a good market.)

A third of all children at this period had lost one parent before the age of fourteen; a quarter of all marriages were terminated by the woman's death in childbirth. Remarriage was often an economic necessity rather than an emotional comfort; the unhappy circumstances that sometimes followed have given us the fearsome nursery stories that are woven around the character of the wicked stepmother.

Thomas (2) was about eight years old when his mother died. He had already lost two brothers and was to witness the death of a further five half-siblings in the next fifteen years. Seven small children from this family alone were buried in Folke churchyard. Bamfield Junior died when he was one, John at two, Mary eleven, Harry a few days, Frances five, George lived for a week or two and Charles was just over a year old. Infant and child mortality on this scale is difficult now to imagine. Some historians have surmised that, with the prospect of grief to come, parents held aloof from loving their children. Shakespeare, a near contemporary writes movingly affectionate scenes between parents and their children. Ben Jonson's poem on the death of his son is not from the pen of an unfeeling parent.

> 'Farewell, thou child of my right hand, and joy;
> My sin was too much hope of thee, loved boy.
> Rest in soft peace, and, asked, say here doth lie
> Ben Jonson, his best piece of poetry.'

In contemporary diaries, letters and memorial stones these children are often accorded an identity and a place in the annals of the family that suggests they, and the remembrance of them, were cherished, and some solace was afforded by the widely held belief in reunion in the afterlife. Despite the high child mortality the Folke nursery of Bamfield Chafin's family was kept busy with the four surviving children and the home had come to life.

Bamfield took an active part in both local and national politics from his early thirties. His father had been High Sheriff of Dorset and Bamfield followed in his footsteps in 1624. Bamfield Chafin's appointment as sheriff is recorded in the diary of a local farmer, William Whiteway. On 4 October 1624 he tells us that '*Mr Bamfill Chafin of Folke was chosen as Sheriffe for Dorset*' and another entry in the following February records that he was '*elected as Member of Parliament for Bridport.*' William Whiteway, with both time and ability to write a diary, was of the local squirarchy and kept a weather eye on political developments in the locality.

Bamfield could have had no recollection of his father but had grown up in an ambitious and political milieu. The years preceding the Civil War were economically reasonably prosperous. For men like Bamfield who were rising in the world the readily perceived potential was a spur to action. Though his branch of the family was as yet sparsely populated there were many more distant relatives scattered about the West Country making and taking opportunities for advancement. His mother's second marriage had been into the wealthy landowning Trenchard family. Bamfield had grown up on respectful but amicable terms with some of the great men of the period. He held land on part of Viscount Cranborne's Chase; the Earl of Pembroke at Wilton also had an interest in the Chase. Lord Thomas Howard had been overseer of his father's will and had in his young days played his part as his guardian. In addition Bamfield was well acquainted with a number of families like his own who had been beneficiaries of the Dissolution and had been promoted into the county government posts and been elected to become Members of Parliament.

Bamfield did not lack for friends in high places to help him forward. His mother's family the Bampfyldes were influential in Devon, his stepfather, Sir George Trenchard was well known and of good repute in Dorset and Lord Thomas Howard, King James I's Lord Treasurer, was a family friend. Bamfield, with neither father nor siblings, had every motivation to secure a position of honour and respect for himself and his family. Chafin was a prominent name in the West Country though his branch of the Chafins had but a tenuous toehold to the future. Family building and assuring an heir was a precarious and always unpredictable enterprise. By 1624 Bamfield had two thriving little sons, Thomas and George and hopeful prospects that came with his second marriage. It was time to take on some public responsibility befitting the name of Chafin of Folke.

In February 1624[34] Bamfield, as William Whiteway had recorded, was elected as Member of Parliament for Bridport. Bridport, eighteen miles from Folke and thirty miles from Chettle, had a centuries old thriving rope and net making industry, based on locally grown hemp. This trade ensured contact with sea-going vessels, sailors and ideas from a wider world that contributed to the long tradition of independence displayed by several of the coastal towns of Dorset. Bridport had been a borough with a Member of Parliament for centuries. In 1619 King James I had granted it a mayor and corporation, thereby enhancing its status and no doubt the assertiveness of the town's leaders. Boroughs had idiosyncratic ways of selecting who should represent them in Parliament. Some relied upon nominees, others appointed a civic officer, but elections were unusual. Complaints were made in the House of Commons as to the validity of Bamfield Chafin's election as Member for Bridport, and a committee of enquiry appointed to look into the matter declared the election to be void, as not enough notice had been given. Chafin's political antennae did not resonate with those of the radical townsfolk and the burgesses of Bridport who would have considered the Chafins as outsiders, but the origin of the complaint is enigmatic.[35] King James I died in March 1625 so no further Parliaments were called

---

[34] The year ended on 31st March until 1752.

[35] Similar objections had previously been made to the election of Sir Lewis D'Yves as M P for Bridport by the Duke of Buckingham.

and the matter seems therefore to have been dropped.

Ten years later in 1635 Bamfield's son Thomas (2) married Eliza-beth Trenchard. Elizabeth was Bamfield's half sister, the daughter of his mother Jane Bamfylde and her second husband Sir George Tren-chard. The Church has no objection to a man marrying his grand-mother's daughter, nor to a woman marrying her mother's grandson. Jane had been very young when Bamfield was born, so that Thomas (2) and Elizabeth could well have been about the same age. What mattered much more was that this marriage amalgamated Trenchard and Chafin property.

Thomas (2) and Elizabeth needed somewhere of their own to live. Elizabeth had grown up in the lovely manor house at Charminster (it is still there) and expected a similar standard for her married life. At Folke there was father Bamfield, his second wife Mary, several small children and Thomas (2)'s brother George so the house at Folke was by now fairly well populated. It was the centre where Bamfield's pub-lic commitments were administered as well as the affairs of the estate. Chettle meantime had no resident overlord. Nicholas Dunning the bailiff had died in 1626, though his friend Robert Palmer the rector was still there. It was a very opportune time for the heir presumptive to the property, Thomas (2) to move to Chettle with his new wife and take over its management.

A manor house was built in Chettle at some time after the destruc-tion of the nunnery. No records have survived, but it is very likely that it was built in the 1630's for Thomas and Elizabeth. It would have been a satisfying way of demonstrating their standing and of spending some of their accumulated wealth. They moved there in 1635 leaving Bamfield, Mary and the children at Folke.

Their move brought them within a short distance of Wimborne St Giles where Sir Anthony Ashley Cooper (the future Earl of Shaftes-bury) had his country house. He was described as *subtile, caustic, and epigrammatical, without either diffidence or reverence, a born intriguer, though one of consummate ability.*[36] In 1639 he arranged

[36] A R Bayley *The Civil War in Dorset* 1910 p32.

that *'divers country gentlemen of eastern Dorset'* should meet together at Sixpenny Handley bowling green (three miles from Chettle) once a week. There were about twenty and they included some men who became Royalists and others who fought as Parliamentarians. They included Thomas Chafin (2) of Chettle and George Ryves of Ranston, of whom we shall hear more. Ashley Cooper described Thomas (2) as *'a personable, well carriaged man of a good estate* [who] *wanted neither understanding nor value for himself, was an enemy of the Puritan party.'*[37]

On 21 February 1642, that is eight months before the Civil War started, this group sent a Petition to the House of Commons. They listed a number of complaints including *'Distractions and fears increase among us more and more; the Kingdom is not yet put into such a posture of defence as these dangerous times require;...The very privileges of Parliament – our dear and undoubted right – have been very much impeached; and besides your Petitioners conceive themselves above others in other Counties especially endangered.'* Their special danger, they petitioned, arose from fear of foreign invasion (they bordered on the sea), the flocking together of Papists, especially at night, the decay of the trade of clothing which was the main support of the poor of those parts, and the removal of the Lord Lieutenant of the county which left them without anyone responsible for the military in the area.

This group of men, of mixed persuasions and political views, moved together at Sir Anthony Ashley Cooper's instigation, on issues that were to divide them when war forced them to take one side or the other. Complaints about the endangered ports of Dorset and the decline of the clothing (ie. wool) trade were of special concern to the Chafin enterprise.

In October 1639 Thomas (2) and Elizabeth had their first child, another Elizabeth, born at Chettle. She died two months later. Mary was born in September 1640 and Bridget in March 1643. Her mother died in childbirth and was buried in Chettle churchyard on the same

[37] Bayley op.cit. p35.

day that her daughter was baptized. Mary and Bridget both lived to maturity.

The long-standing difficulties between king and Parliament had not been resolved and by this time they were at war with each other. The English Civil War had started with the Battle of Edgehill on 15 October 1642. The political and religious controversies of the time were widely disseminated in books, songs and above all in pamphlets. The expansion in literacy meant that serious appreciation of the matters at issue was not confined to the upper echelons of society. The Roundheads, supporters of Parliament and the Puritan faith, tended to come from the towns, and those areas most affected by trade and commerce. The Cavaliers were Royalist, supported the established Church, and were more frequently to be found amongst the traditional landed gentry and their dependents. The West Country generally was Royalist though several Dorset towns such as Bridport, Lyme Regis and Dorchester were Parliamentarian, as were some of the more prominent families – the Ashley Coopers,[38] Trenchards, Binghams and Earles for example. The parishioners of both Chettle and Folke stood with their Lords of the Manor, staunchly for the king and the established Church.

The outcome of the Battle of Edgehill was indeterminate, and this set the pattern until June 1644 when the Battle of Marston Moor resulted in a clear victory for the Parliamentarians under their commander Oliver Cromwell. Robert Devereux, 3rd Earl of Essex another Parliamentarian was then on his way to the West Country. *'With slow and settled marches,... he got into Dorset about 11 June'*[39] where *'He doubts not,...of quickly reducing these parts to the Parliament service.'*[40] The southwestern peninsula was not quite the walkover that Essex was hoping, but it was a black time for the Chafins. There was a skirmish in Dorchester *'the inhabitants of which being well-affected to*

---

[38] Ashley Cooper, the first Earl of Shaftesbury, initially Royalist, turned Roundhead, and on Charles II's return was Royalist again. He changed sides yet again when James II came to the throne and was the founder of the anti-Jacobite Whig faction.
[39] A R Bayley op.cit. p194.
[40] op.cit. p195.

Parliament[41] resisted a body of Royalists who fled to Sherborne. Folke is just off the route between Dorchester and Sherborne. The whereabouts of the Chafins was certainly known, if not to the commander of the Parliamentary army, to his local recruits. They made an easy and short detour to Folke where Bamfield Chafin was captured. He was taken prisoner and sent to Exeter prison. There he died and was buried '*in the cross aisle, behind the altar*' of the Cathedral Church of St Peter in Exeter. A burial in a prestigious position in the Cathedral bespeaks an honourable dispatch and it is likely that his body was claimed and obsequies performed by Royalist colleagues. Bamfield's memorial inscription, now lost, was recorded thus: '*Here lyeth ye Body of Bampfield Chafin of Chetle in Dorsetshire Esqr. Who died in Exon the 8th Day of July 1644.*'[42]

Bamfield was fifty-three years old. His second wife survived for another sixteen years, outliving several of her children and her stepson Thomas (2). When Bamfield died Thomas (2), his eldest son by his first wife Mary Muschamp, inherited the estates. He was about thirty years old and was by then living at Chettle.

Folke had been attacked and was now under the supervision of a widow. While the men were away their homes and estates were often run by their wives. Lady Bankes is famous for organizing the defence of Corfe Castle in her husband's absence. Mary Chafin had a large household and several small children to look after. They suffered another attack by Roundheads in July 1644 a fortnight after her husband's death. The parish burial register records that '*A soldier of the Parliament side slain in the Court at Folke House was buried 22 July 1645*' and '*another soldier Will Robertson slaine in Alveston*[43] *of the Parliament side was buried 24 July 1645.*' Folke had been identified as a Royalist property and was close to the thoroughfare between Dorchester and Sherborne so was in constant jeopardy. Chettle, in its wooded hollow and with no building of note escaped the attention of marauding troops. The Chafins were still known as the Chafins of

---

[41] op.cit. p195

[42] Personal communication from Peter Thomas, Librarian of Exeter Cathedral.

[43] Alverston is very near Folke. They are now combined into the same parish.

Folke and Chettle was possibly not known to Parliamentary troops as a Royalist house. It was a safer place for a Royalist family and it is from this date that Chettle as the Chafin family home came into its own. Its capacity to provide safe haven has been a hallmark throughout its history: to dramatic effect in the twentieth century.

There were no great Civil War battles in Dorset, but the county was strategically important. Weymouth, Poole and Lyme Regis were busy ports whose shipping exchanged goods, people and news across the English Channel. Sherborne, Corfe and Portland had fortified castles, held at this time by the king. Dorset like most of the country was a kaleidoscope of religious and political ideas and allegiances. Although King Charles I was finally defeated at the Battle of Naseby on 14 June 1645 fighting continued between the opposing sides, and the Prince of Wales (the future Charles II) spent much of the following year in the West Country. During the Commonwealth (1649–1660) he went into exile in Europe and several Royalists went with him. Ralph Bankes and Edward Hyde, who were both to become associated with the Chafin family, spent much of their time outside of Cromwell's England.

Loss of life and destruction of property during the Civil War was enormous. A greater proportion of the population perished in that conflict than in either of the two great wars of the twentieth century. Many fine Royalist castles were intentionally ruined to such an extent that they could never again be used for military purposes. Wardour, Corfe and Sherborne castles, all within easy distance of Chettle, suffered thus. Corfe stands, gaunt, dramatic and accusing, but irreparable, to this day. The small rural settlement of Folke had been devastated by at least two military assaults upon it. The Lord of the Manor had died as a result and there had been an affray within the courtyard of the Chafin family home resulting in two dead Parliamentarians. Small children witnessed the blood letting of Dorset men by Dorset men. Maximum damage to property was the usual pattern. The distress was overwhelming. The Chafin heir Thomas (2) was already living at Chettle. He had come in 1635 before the war, because he and his new wife needed somewhere to live away from

Folke, which had become overcrowded, and Chettle needed the care
of an overlord. Not until his father's death ten years later did he
decide to make Chettle the centre of the estate and the family home.
Folke had been seriously damaged and held bitter memories. His
dauntless stepmother had faced the worst that the Parliamentarians
could do but nevertheless insisted on staying in her home at Folke. It
was the Civil War that changed the Chafins of Folke to the Chafins of
Chettle and the two strands of our story are from this time woven
together.

SEVEN

The Chafins of Chettle

In 1645 after nearly three years of wearying indecisiveness and alarming losses, the armies of Parliament and King met on 14 June at Naseby in Northamptonshire. Defeat and victory seem hardly appropriate terms, but the king lost so much in men and resources that his ultimate defeat looked unavoidable. But the southwest was still strongly Royalist despite the campaign of the previous year and the vigour of its Parliamentary Boroughs. So it was upon the southwest that the Parliamentary army now set its sights. There were battles at Taunton, Langport, Bridgewater and Bath. Then came Sherborne Castle, belonging to Lord George Digby, one of Charles I's advisers. Sherborne is two miles from Folke, twenty from Chettle. The Royalist commander was Sir Lewis D'Yves, half brother of Lord Digby, a stalwart who had seen action from the Battle of Edgehill onward. General Thomas Fairfax directed the Roundhead attack on the castle.

Thomas Chafin (2), now in his early thirties and a widower for two years, was at Chettle with his two little daughters, Margaret nearly five years old, and Bridget about two and a half. He and George Digby were Royalist neighbours, so Thomas was under a clear obligation to leave his children with their nursemaids and join Sir Lewis D'Yves. The siege of Sherborne Castle was made more complicated by the arrival on the scene of the Dorset Clubmen, one of whose leaders was the rector of Chettle, the Reverend Robert Rock.

The Clubmen was an organization of ordinary men and women who had seen their trade disrupted, crops ruined, property damaged and goods pillaged by armies of both sides as they moved to and fro over the countryside. No one was spared the ravages of this war. The purpose of the Dorset Clubmen was to defend themselves, their property and goods against damage that might be perpetrated by either side. They made numerous harryings to both antagonists at Sherborne, but caused particular upset to Fairfax by interrupting his food supplies and communications. Anglican clergymen were prominent amongst their leaders, partly because of their fear of Puritan influence on the church. Parliament had very recently replaced the Book of Common Prayer with the Presbyterian Directory of Worship. The status of the Church of England was being undermined leaving some Anglican clergy in a restive frame of mind. The Clubmen were an undoubted nuisance, but untrained and with clubs their only weapons, they were not a serious danger.

The sixteen-day siege of Sherborne Castle, which ended on 15 August 1645, resulted in a victory for the Parliamentarians. Sir Lewis D'Yves, veteran of many battles, was taken to London, imprisoned in the Tower and charged with treason. His trial was long delayed. He was still in the Tower on the day that King Charles I was executed (30 January 1649). The beheading of God's anointed was an event that profoundly shocked Europe. Royalists in England were terrified. Sir Lewis, after over three years in the Tower decided that the time had come for a final desperate bid for freedom. The following day, with a fellow Royalist prisoner, he is believed to have escaped in a waiting boat:[44] *'the attempt so desperate, few will believe they can get cleare away, but are either stifled or drowned.'* He did get away and lived till 1699. Thomas (2) was taken to Poole as *'a prisoner of the Governor…and very sick.'*[45] Sherborne Castle was slighted a few days later.

The Clubmen, under threat from the Parliamentary army, moved

[44] C S L Davies *Conspiracy, Kinship and Preferment.* Midland History Vol XXXI 2006.
[45] Bayley op.cit. p35.

to Hambledon Hill, making use of the ancient defensive earthworks of the Durotriges. About three hundred Clubmen were imprisoned by Cromwell in Shroton Church, some six miles due west of Chettle. Oliver Cromwell had said that they *were to be tried judicially for raising a third party in the kingdom.* On closer aquaintance he dismissed them as *poor silly creatures.*

Being no match for a trained army, their church imprisonment seems to have been sufficient to dissuade them from making further trouble for either side.[46] The Reverend Robert Rock returned to his church duties for the next thirty years and retired in 1675 – well after the Restoration.

In August 1645 the future looked very bleak for the Royalist Chafins. Parliamentarians were firmly in command. Thomas (2) was a prisoner in Poole. Mary and Bridget his two little daughters were at Chettle cared for by servants, his stepmother and her children at Folke. Men from Chettle had joined the Clubmen and seasonal work was neglected. The rector, an authority in the parish, normally looked to for guidance and wisdom in times of difficulty, had left the parish to lead the Clubmen.

Both Chettle and Folke were sequestrated, that is they were threatened with confiscation by Parliament unless they paid a stated, but arbitrary fine. In 1645 a *chief rent of £4 payable by Mrs Chafin was sequestered*[47] from Folke. The *History of Parliament* records that Thomas (2), *'a royalist commissioner valued his estate in his composition* [i.e. legal agreement whereby the creditors – in this case Parliament – agree to accept partial payment of a debt in lieu of full settlement] *at £500 a year'*[48]. Today's equivalent value is about £54,000. Sequestration was widely imposed but there was no extensive permanent seizure or reallocation of property, such as had occurred a hundred years earlier at the Dissolution. Much Royalist property was slighted and many Royalist families were brought to the

---

[46] In 1649 Cromwell put down a mutiny of Levellers (extreme Protestants) by locking them in the church of St John the Baptist at Burford. Three were shot.
[47] Hutchins op.cit.
[48] Basil Hemming *History of Parliament* 1983.

49

verge of bankruptcy. Some never recovered.[49] The imposition on Chettle was huge and reflected the condemnation by Parliament of Thomas (2) for his part in the siege of Sherborne.

Colonel John Bingham, the Governor of Poole, who was holding Thomas (2) prisoner, provided a Parliamentary sanction on 20 January 1645 [50] to enable him to make arrangements for the payment of fines in return for his freedom: '*I am willing that Thomas Chafin of Chettle shall go upon his patrol for settling his affairs as well in this county as in Surrey where occasion shall call him …I do grant him 40 days. At which time, in case he hath not made his peace with Parliament he is to return to Poole garrison a true prisoner. All are desired by this to quietly suffer him to pass…with himself, servants and horses in his own lawful negotiation,*' he wrote. The threat of long term imprisonment, with its natural menace of gaol fever (typhus) and the cruelties devised by captors, would have concentrated any man's mind, but the raising of £500 in a space of forty days was a daunting undertaking. Thomas had six weeks' parole giving him freedom to contact friends and relatives in the district. By early March he had found and delivered the £500 and six months later it was reported in the House of Commons on 21 November 1646 that '*Mr Hollis* [51] *was appointed to carry to the Lords for their concurrence … ordinances … freeing and discharging, …estates from sequestration.*' The very long list of Royalist names included Thomas Chafin and John Penruddock, a near neighbour and friend.[52]

In November 1646 he was free and returned to Chettle. Following the siege at Sherborne Thomas (2) had been a prisoner in Poole for

---

[49] A later owner of Chettle, Edward Castleman (1870 – 1946) records the unearthing of a '*small medallion… with Charles I's embossed portrait on one side and Henrietta Maria's on the other…It was a badge worn by Royalists but when Charles was defeated they buried the badge.*' Private papers of Edward W F Castleman.

[50] The year ended on 31 March until 1752. This is therefore five months after the siege of Sherborne.

[51] Denzil Holles (1599-1680) was MP for Dorchester in 1628 and between 1645 – 47. Holles was at this time a Parliamentarian, but like Ashley Cooper changed sides opportunistically.

[52] Basil Hemming op.cit.

five months. These were five busy months of the agricultural year and he had not been there to ensure that the gathering in was efficiently done. Some of his estate workers had followed Robert Rock to join the Clubmen at Sherborne, so the workforce was depleted. Agricultural historian Peter Bowden writes that *'The third, fourth and fifth decades of the seventeenth century …were probably the most terrible years through which the country has ever passed…'*[53] *'Neither contemporary nor modern economists can explain how they lived,'* writes another.[54]

Local government and trade were dislocated and men were fighting instead of growing food. Whether such harsh conditions prevailed for all at Chettle might be questioned. What cannot be in doubt is that the estate was not functioning to its full potential. For three years armies had been trampling to and fro in Dorset, though not touching Chettle, billeting themselves on families and commandeering provisions at the expense of the countryside. The Battle of Naseby had at least established Parliamentary supremacy, which resolved some ambiguities, though it was very bad news for Royalists.

Thomas (2) was a sick man and never entirely recovered his health after the fighting at Sherborne and his imprisonment. His stepmother, weary if not dispirited after events of the past two years, needed some relief from the burdens of family and estate that she had been carrying. His two young daughters wanted for maternal guidance, there was no male heir and the estate was in jeopardy. Some help, preferably in the form of a well-connected woman was needed. Within a year Thomas had found a happy solution in the form of Amphilis Hyde whom he married sometime in 1646.

His new wife was the daughter of Lawrence and Amphilis Hyde of Heale House, Amesbury. Lawrence was cousin of Edward Hyde,[55] who was to become chief adviser to Charles II.[56] As the Earl of

---

[53] J Thirsk ed. *The Agrarian History of England and Wales iv* 1967: *Agricultural Prices, Farm Profits and Rents* p 620–1.

[54] *England in the reign of Charles II* D Ogg 1934.

[55] Hutchins says his son. This is not possible.

[56] Heale House was one of several houses to give sanctuary to Charles II after the Battle of Worcester in 1651.

Clarendon and Lord Chancellor from 1658 he became one of the most powerful men in England. His daughter Anne had married the king's brother, James Duke of York in 1660, and had she lived would have become Queen of England in 1685. Her two daughters, Mary (of William and Mary) and Anne became Queen of England in turn, from 1688–94, and 1702–14.

The year following the marriage of Thomas (2) and Amphilis a son and heir was born and was baptized Bamfield, as tradition required. A daughter, Amphilis was born in 1648, and Thomas (3) arrived in July 1650.

Six months before Thomas (3) was born King Charles I had been executed and the Commonwealth proclaimed. Trade was severely disrupted and the Chafin wool business, already in decline, was further damaged. Thomas (2)'s health deteriorated and he died in 1655 in his early forties. His will reveals the secret of how he had paid his sequestration fine of £500 ten years earlier. His estate was indebted to John Ryves of Ranston for £300. His relative, George Ryves of Ranston was one of the group that had met with Thomas (2) Chafin at Sir Anthony Ashley Cooper's weekly meetings in Sixpenny Handley in the months before the war. The Ryves estate was alongside the river Iwerne in the eastern shadow of Hambledon Hill about five miles from Chettle. John Ryves was a lawyer of the Middle Temple with additional property in Southampton and London. As security Thomas (2) had *'mortgaged unto him or to some friends in trust for him all the said Manor of Chettle (except the farm of Chettle) for a long term of years yet to come.'*

Under the terms of his will Thomas (2) was able repay the sum of £80 that he had borrowed for the same purpose from his brother George who was then a merchant. He left the impossible task of balancing the books to his executors, Giles Strangeways, Thomas Trenchard, John Low, Robert Gulliford and Sir Thomas Hyde, all very well connected gentlemen: he was related to three of them. He indicates clearly how he wishes his family to be provided for (e.g. *'I give unto my daughter Amphilis the Principal of one thousand pounds for her portion to be paid at her age of one and twenty...'* and similar arrangements for his son). His will makes reference to a Deed of 21 January 1654 by which he has settled upon his four loving friends and their heirs '*all my manor and Demesne lands of Chettle*' and from the rents, issues and profits they are to raise the allowances for his children. The predicaments that are all too easy to read in this will were created, not by poor husbandry or careless management, but by the war, the disruption of trade and the dislocation of local government that it brought. Being an unswerving and conscientious Royalist from 1642 till 1660 was a great impediment.

He left a number of small bequests to faithful servants and '*all my books for my eldest son*'. Education, by the mid seventeenth century, was important both for professional advancement and for the embellishment of the gentleman's life. Books in pursuit of this endeavour were an essential appurtenance in the gentry family home. They were valuable artefacts, both materially and intrinsically and were often purchased in loose vellum form and bound, with the family crest emblazoned by the individual. It was around this time that some of the country's famous libraries were being built up. Thomas Bodley had left his collection to Oxford University and founded the Bodleian Library at the end of the sixteenth century. John Kedermister left his collection of three hundred books to St Mary's Church, Langley Marsh near Slough in the early seventeenth century. The chained library of Wimborne Minster was founded in 1686. These last two have been kept in their original state and give us some idea of the appearance and quality of the books that were bequeathed carefully from one generation to the next. They were costly items and vigilantly safeguarded.

Publishing and the book trade had been under strict control of the Ecclesiastical Court since 1559, with the Stationers' Company willingly administering its censorship for their own ends. Charles I had strengthened its powers. This inhibited the book trade in England and enhanced trade particularly with Germany and France. Book owning implied not only an education, but also considerable travel. It is evident that the Chafin family were participants in that educated and literary secular society that had grown from the Dissolution of the monasteries, flourished, particularly in London, with the dramatists and poets of the late sixteenth century and was spreading throughout England in the seventeenth. (John Ryves, Thomas's mortgagee, had a six-volume Bible, divinity and law books that were his primary concern when he came to consider his last wishes.)

Thomas paid some attention in his will to the education of '*all my children*' entrusting the undertaking to Amphilis, his wife. Amphilis came from a cultured cosmopolitan family and was quite the equal of her husband in education and accomplishments. Sons and daughters were treated even-handedly in this family in respect of bequests and education, an unusual state of affairs for many years to come.

Thomas (2) was forty-one when he died in 1655, leaving five children, starting with Mary aged fifteen and Bridget twelve from his first marriage to Elizabeth Trenchard. Mary married the rector of Folke, John Prowse and Bridget married George Strangeways, scion of a prominent local family. Of his second marriage there was Bamfield, his heir, aged nine, Amphilis eight and Thomas (3) five. The appointed trustees held the Chafin estates in trust with his widow Amphilis as head of the family.

Ten years earlier the Parliamentarians had established themselves with the upper hand, but by then their original quarrel with the king had been obscured by a proliferation of religious and political ideas for reform of church and constitution. The customary patterns and processes of government had been dislodged, but no one alternative scheme commanded sufficient support to be effective. Justices of the Peace and High Sheriffs of the County, roles in which the Chafins had taken an honourable part, were no longer appointed. Pamphlets, treatises, philosophical discourse, as well as the practical application of radical ideas abounded. The monarch's divine right to rule was deeply indoctrinated. It was a Parliamentarian who agonized '*If we beat the king nine and ninety times, yet is he king still*'. Radical counterblasts came from numerous groups. The Levellers advocated manhood suffrage: for all men? landholders only? paupers? servants? The Diggers went further, urging the common ownership of land and redistribution of wealth. In 1649 a petition for the rights of women with 10,000 signatories was presented to Parliament. There was mutiny in the army. Some of the proposals for change were allegedly inspired by visions and celestial guidance; religion was interwoven with most of the overtly secular plans. Did God speak through the king, bishops and down through a structured hierarchy or could His voice be heard by the common man – even more questionable, by the common woman? Vain attempts were made to find acceptable terms on which the king could be restored. The old order had been destroyed but a new one had not come into being.

During this period the Chafins at Chettle were debilitated and quiet. After Thomas (2) died Amphilis was the responsible adult at Chettle. She was related to a family on close terms with the exiled Charles II. Robert Rock had incurred the displeasure of Oliver Cromwell as a leader of Clubmen. Chettle and its inhabitants were deeply distrusted by those now in power and therefore vulnerable.

By 1649 the Rump Parliament was established with the right to legislate without the king's approval. Within a month Charles I had been tried for treason, found guilty and was beheaded on 30 January 1649. This act shocked the European world and isolated England. Trade, shipping and commerce suffered. The Chafin wool business experienced further damage. Two months later the monarchy and the House of Lords were abolished and in May 1649 England was declared a Commonwealth and Free State. This directly affected many friends and acquaintances of the Chafins, who were well represented in various state and civic organizations. Everyone with a grievance now had a Parliament to which complaints could be presented. There were plenty.

As King Charles I's head fell from his body his son Charles became king. Charles II took refuge in Scotland from where he invaded England, was beaten at the Battle of Worcester in September 1651 and escaped to France where many Royalists joined him. The Chafins were not among them. They stayed in Chettle, where they could at least keep an eye on their property, but it was a stringently painful time. John Bingham, Governor of Poole reported on Thomas (2) that '*since the time of his composition for his delinquency in the first war he hath lived peacefully at his habitacyon within this county and hath readily conformed himself to all orders and ordinances of Parliament.'*

With the changing fortunes of war some men changed sides. Thomas (2)'s conformation to orders and ordinances of Parliament was not because his political principles were wavering. He was no longer the *'well carriaged man of good estate'* that Sir Anthony Ashley Cooper had described in 1642. He was a sick man of very impoverished estate. He also had a new and young family that brought with it some hope for the future. His wife was related to a family on very close terms with Charles II then in exile, which caused some anxiety about further exposure. It was a time for a committed Royalist to keep out of the limelight by lying low in the wooded hollow of Chettle.

In 1653 Oliver Cromwell, who had come to prominence as a very successful military commander, dissolved Parliament and was installed as Lord Protector.

'The condition of England, as he saw it, was very ill. It was a good world for nobody but the lawyers. The overseas commerce, which was the life of the land, was crippled by piracies and by the hostility of the continental Powers. ...Hundred of thousands had been beggared, and the roads were full of honest folk turned vagrants. Trade was bad and unemployment widespread. The country gentry were in a pitiable condition, and those of them who were royalists had ... been ruined by fines and confiscations...The Church was in chaos, there was no regular provision for worship, and all the abuses of the old regime luxuriated alongside the abuses of the new.'[57]

The Chafins had been merchant mercers of the West Country for at least two hundred years. The area was reputed for its cloth industry and exports. Local sheep provided employment for shepherds, spinners and weavers, and the ships of Lyme Regis, Poole and

[57] John Buchan *Oliver Cromwell* 1941.

Melcombe Regis carried cloth to the continent and returned with wine, brandy, spices and other goods from the Mediterranean, France, the Netherlands and Spain. This trade was severely disrupted particularly after the execution of Charles I. The future King Charles II, exiled in Europe after 1651, was the focus of espionage and plots, and the south coast ports were constantly suspected of involvement. Ships that had carried wool and wine, now carried intelligence and double agents. The Chafins were dangerously close to the intrigues and conspiracies that were going on. If Thomas (2) became involved in anything to help the Royalist cause it could only be as an intelligence agent. Physically he was debilitated, but he was discerning and perspicacious, well read, a travelled man and some of his relatives by marriage were amongst the entourage of Charles II in Europe. He knew the ports of the Dorset coast intimately and his textile business gave him the necessary pretext of consorting with seafaring folk.

Cromwell allowed £70,000 for his intelligence network service, with John Thurloe 'the greatest intelligence officer that ever served an English ruler' at its head. 'His agents were everywhere...no plot was hatched in the backstreets of Brussels or the Hague...the cabinets of Paris and Madrid might meet behind guarded doors but Thurloe...had a record of their decisions.' 'There is no government on earth...more punctually informed,' wrote the Venetian Ambassador to Cromwell's England.[58] Thomas Chafin's name has never emerged in this context though his grandson George Chafin (1) intrigued with Charles II's great nephew, the Young Pretender.

Local government in the counties, which had depended upon royal appointments, ground to a halt. The local basis of military organization was largely replaced by central authority. Inevitably confusion and maladministration prevailed and Chafin power and authority as local grandees was eroded. No more did their name appear amongst the dignitaries of the county. The establishment of the Protectorate brought some of the confusion to an end, but it confirmed the eclipse of the Chafins.

---

[58] John Buchan op.cit.

In Thomas (2)'s last year his neighbour and friend, Colonel John Penruddock led a rebellion against Cromwell and the Commonwealth. Antonia Fraser writes that, in a land thick with plots *'it was only in the West that the rising showed any kind of bite, and that due to the heroic if misguided efforts of the former Royalist soldier who gave the rebellion his name – Colonel John Penruddock.'*[59] Penruddock had fought with his father and brother for Charles I in the Civil War. The family lived at Compton Chamberlayne twelve miles to the northeast of Chettle. On 15 March 1655 Penruddock led an attack on Salisbury, freed the prisoners who were held there and marshalled those who would into his militia. He turned towards Blandford to raise further troops and would have passed through or very near to Chettle. Thomas (2) was by then a dying man. He was unable to join his friend, though he no doubt offered up a blessing for the undertaking. It was another call to arms against the Puritans and in support of divinely appointed order. There was no male Chafin old enough to take part. Penruddock managed to enlist no more than four hundred men whom he marched on towards Royalist Cornwall. They were engaged at South Molton in Devon, beaten, and taken to Exeter prison. Penruddock was tried by Judge Prideaux of Plumber, a hamlet near Lydlinch, found guilty of treason and was beheaded at Exeter. He was thirty-six years old, and left three small daughters: one of them, Anne, became a Chafin wife. She would have been Thomas (2)'s daughter in law. Penruddock's sacrifice was in vain. The Commonwealth was unimpaired.

Some local men who had joined the rising were banished. Three of them returned to their home parish of Puddletown with the Restoration in 1660. The Parish Accounts record that they were welcomed back and paid one shilling. English Royalists were to be found in many continental refuges so the common soldiers would have had little difficulty in finding some sort of employment and protection. They probably spent the final five years of the Protectorate somewhat more comfortably in Europe than they would have done in England.

---

[59] Antonia Fraser *Cromwell, our Chief of Men* 1973.

Thomas (2) died in 1655 leaving Chettle, extensive estates, five young children, debts, and very little hope, in a Puritan Commonwealth, to be looked after by his wife Amphilis and his stepmother Mary. Maybe he also left a functioning spy network with Amphilis keeping the contacts, as his legacy of hope for a return to prescribed order.

Thomas (2) had moved to Chettle in 1635 with his first wife Elizabeth. Life had then looked full of promise. There was a new manor house and a pleasant parish, there had been a year or two of good harvests and the wool trade was going reasonably. The twenty-five years that followed had cost England very dear in men and property. Chettle was surrounded with ruined castles, houses, homes and fortunes. Chettle was undamaged but mortgaged. Many friends and colleagues had fled abroad in 1649. Church services had been altered, social life as the Chafins knew it had disappeared, hunting was restricted, food was short, the Cromwellians were in power and this state of despair was to last another five years.

EIGHT

The High Noon of the Chafin Family

At Chettle in 1655 were the surviving Chafins, Amphilis, by then about thirty-three years old with her three children, Bamfield, eight, Amphilis, seven and Thomas five, her two step daughters Mary, fifteen and Bridget, twelve. At Folke there was Mary Chafin, second wife and now widow of Bamfield then in her fifties and her two sons George, a merchant, aged twenty-five and Edmund, twenty-four. They faced five more anxious and penurious years under the Protectorate.

The Decimation Tax, introduced in the late 1650's, confiscated a further tenth of all property belonging to Royalists. Then in September 1658 Oliver Cromwell died. His years of military dictatorship – high minded, puritanical, egalitarian in origin, but in practice repressive and punitive – came to an end. His eldest son, Richard took his place: his incompetence quickly earned him the name Tumbledown Dick. He resigned after eight months. This was a year of very great anxiety with no effective leadership. Government at central and county level quite lost its way: it became known as the Summer of the Great Fear.

Chettle had in the past several years become accustomed to feeding itself. Fare at the manor house was not noticeably different from that in the cottage. There were few imports and trade with other towns was made difficult by the general disorder created by the hordes of vagabonds and homeless. Far from London and quietly isolated, Chettle was surviving at not much above subsistence level.

At the beginning of May 1660 Parliament voted to restore the king. To general relief, and in some quarters rejoicing, at the end of the month Charles II returned to London with Edward Hyde (by then the Earl of Clarendon) as his chief adviser. Royalists could breathe somewhat more freely. The great republican experiment was at an end.

The Royalist Chafins and Chettle did indeed rejoice. Amphilis now had a relative in a central position at court (Edward Hyde was her second cousin). There was very little money, but the gnawing fear of the preceding twenty years had abated. The dowager Mary Chafin, Amphilis's mother in law, died in the same month as Charles II returned to England. The property at Folke passed to Bamfield, Thomas (2)'s elder son and was held in trust. Mary's son Edmund stayed at Folke and was for the rest of his life a good friend and adviser to the younger members of the family – Uncle Edmund was constantly called upon. Bamfield the heir was then fourteen, so the responsible adult at Chettle was Amphilis. Into this fatherless, war weary and dislocated family came the Bankes family.

Sir John Bankes, Charles I's Lord Chief Justice of Common Pleas had bought Corfe Castle in 1635. His busy life kept him away from Corfe, and from 1642 he was with the king and his exiled court in Oxford, where he died in 1644. His wife Mary was left to look after Corfe Castle, which was ruinously sacked by Parliamentarians in 1646. Ralph Bankes (1631-1677), their son, was an exile in Europe during the Commonwealth. He returned to find that the contents of his home had been plundered and the great Norman stronghold that had guarded the gap in the Purbeck Hills for over five hundred years was slighted beyond all hope of restoration. He was betrothed to Jane Mary Brune of Athelhampton. Their marriage had to be delayed until they had somewhere to live.

Corfe Castle, where they would have expected to make their home, had been destroyed in 1646 when Ralph was fifteen. Thomas (2) and Amphilis Chafin, then living in their manor house, which was less than twenty years old, often discussed their local Royalist friends who had been forced to take refuge abroad. It is more than likely that they considered offering help to the young Bankes when the war should be over. Thomas (2) inserted a clause into his will which gave Amphilis *'full power and free leave to dwell and be in my manor...the garden and orchards thereof, sufficient room always being left and reserved for a tenant.'* This clause looks tailor made for the returning exile Ralph Bankes. It protected Amphilis from the smirch of impropriety in having a young man who was not a relative as a tenant, and would have reassured the trustees. It is an indication of the planning that was going on between exiled and homebound Royalist families. The grateful tenant took up residence in the manor house at Chettle. Ralph was knighted shortly after his return in 1660 and early in 1661 he and Jane Mary Brune were married in the church of St Martin's in the Fields in London. He attempted to recover furniture, carpets, tapestries, and building material that had been taken from Corfe for the embellishment of several houses belonging to local Parliamentary grandees. He stayed in Chettle for about six years from where he supervised the building of Kingston Lacey into which he and his family moved in 1665.

Sir Ralph was Member of Parliament for Corfe for most of his life and was a member of the Privy Chamber, the chief governing body for the Stuarts. He and Sir Edward Hyde were centrally placed when the Restoration Settlements were made. These settlements attempted to re-establish the Church, and the county gubernatorial functions, on lines similar to those before the great upheaval. They also compensated Royalists for sequestrations, fines, the Decimation tax and so on. It was a complex and exacting undertaking. The Chafins had lost two lives and a great deal of money. Amphilis had one member of the Privy Chamber living in her house, and another was her cousin to whom she could make her personal pleas. She exploited these contacts for the benefit of her family and for the parish of Chettle. Within a year or two the standard of living in the manor house was improving, and signs of betterment in the parish followed.

Chettle of the seventeenth century was no bigger than it is today. The presence of the dazzling Bankes family made a formative impression on the fatherless Chafin children. Sir Ralph was *'part of the cultured circle which Charles II attracted to the court at Whitehall which included Sir Peter Lely.*[60] Lely was the court painter, generally kept busy with commissions to record for posterity Charles II's numerous mistresses. One portrait of Sir Ralph Bankes by Sir Peter Lely hangs in the Guildhall Art Gallery. The hair of his luxuriant wig flows over his shoulders, and his rather small figure is enveloped in voluminous silk robes. His left arm leans nonchantly upon a classical pillar and his somewhat fleshy face has a haughty thoughtful gaze. Another in the Yale Centre for British Art shows him in a rural set- ting in rich russet clothing of similar style with the head of a large hound by his right hand. A painting of Lord Clarendon (Edward Hyde) shows him with a similar flowing headpiece, rather stout, a stiff little moustache but otherwise clean-shaven, and wearing a heavily embroidered gown. The rich fabrics, commanding posture, the hauteur of expression and opulent background convey wealth, confidence and influence. These were formidable men with whom Amphilis was associated. (A painting of Amphilis is said to exist but its whereabouts have been lost.)[61]

Sir Ralph was, like his father, a lawyer and was kept very busy, first with the Restoration Settlements and then after 1666, with another swathe of legal work in connection with property ownership follow- ing the Great Fire. Sir Christopher Wren's design for a new London took no account of previous boundaries. Wren's family lived nearby at East Knoyle in Wiltshire and he was using the local Portland stone for his buildings. He and Sir Roger Pratt, the architect of Kingston Hall (now called Kingston Lacey) were part of the influential and intellectual circle that impinged on Chettle.

In 1662 the two elder children of Thomas (2) and Amphilis died, leaving the younger son Thomas (3), then aged twelve, as heir to the Chafin estate. The deaths of both siblings occurred at about the same time, which suggests some infection as the cause. Several years of undernourishment must have taken their toll and it is perhaps sur- prising that the youngest child survived. This was the fourth Chafin

[60] Anne Sebba *The Exiled Collector* 2004 p11.
[61] Edward Bourke Personal communication.

generation in which reproduction only just kept ahead of loss. Thomas (3) was a much-treasured child. His older half sisters were by then married. In that same year the Bankes had their first child, a daughter Mary, who was baptized in St Mary's Church by the Reverend Robert Rock. So Thomas (3) was the only child in the manor house, except for the new baby.

Sir Ralph was the dominant male in this small community and the one to whom Thomas (3) naturally looked for fatherly guidance. He was however very busy. As an MP his attendance at the House of Commons was a necessity, particularly in the Parliaments called in the years immediately after the Restoration. His travels to Europe to see the latest that art and architecture had to offer were frequent. But he was building his new house to a very grand plan indeed and needed to inspect progress. When he was in Chettle, conversation to which the young Thomas was party, ranged over politics, travel, fashion, architecture, painting and affairs at court and in London. It was a vibrant and distinguished company, though for a few years after the war there was no great wealth.

The money for the building of Kingston Lacey came largely from an inheritance of Sir Ralph's wife Jane. Despite her contribution however serious debts accrued. Thomas (3), intelligent, growing up in a house with cultivated, literate companions, reared in his early years to a necessary frugality, watched and learned. As he grew to manhood he husbanded the resources of his estate and never embarked on any grand building scheme or other flagrant display of status. He cultivated a somewhat detached, self-deprecatory humour and looked with rather mocking eyes at the foibles of some of his contemporaries.

On 19 December 1665 Ralph's youngest sister, Arabella was married to Samuel Gilley Esq. of High Hall, a fine house about a mile and a half from Kingston Lacey, at St Mary's Church, Chettle. Arabella's parents were both dead so it fell to Ralph to make arrangements for his sister's marriage. There had been a vigorous reaction to the Puritan spirit of the Protectorate and this marriage provided an occasion to celebrate the reinstatement of local Royalist families. This was another ceremony performed by the Reverend Robert Rock who had been leader of the Clubmen at the Siege of Sherborne. Those unhappy and painful days had been thankfully forgotten with rejoicing and feasting and something for everyone in the parish. Royalists were by this time regaining their funds, possessions and their places of authority in the community.

Amphilis had been diligent in carrying out her late husband's wishes for the education of their children. Thomas (3) graduated from Magdalen Hall Oxford at the age of sixteen and he was at this early age taking over some of the management of his encumbered estate. Amphilis, advised by trustees and no doubt helped by Sir Ralph Bankes, guided him, and together they began the restoration of the confidence and prestige of the Chafins of Chettle. Thomas (3) was not particularly interested in ostentatious spectacle, but he did pay careful attention to his affairs and exerted his influence through national and county public positions.

Lord Shaftesbury (previously Sir Anthony Ashley Cooper) of Wimborne St Giles had acquired the rights of part of Cranborne Chase and therefore had superordinate authority over the landholder. The rights of the Chase gave him freedom to maintain and hunt deer regardless of who held the land for agricultural purposes. By the late seventeenth century arguments about the relative rights of the landlord who worked and depended upon the land and the Chase Lord who owned the deer that competed with domestic animals for pasturage, damaged boundary markers and so on, were becoming increasingly knotty. Ever since Norman kings had abrogated the ownership of Chase deer to themselves, their rights had been resented but by this time aspirations for agricultural improvement began to complicate the matter. The Royal Society had been chartered by Charles II in 1662. One of its aims was to bring scientific principles to bear upon agriculture. Some of the more forward-looking landowners were improving their crop yields and improving the growth of animals. Land values were increasing and the changes that heralded the Agricultural Revolution were under way. Shaftesbury was looking greedily at nearby property and a very young landlord would have presented quite a temptation. Shaftesbury had supported Cromwell but changed sides and in 1672 became Charles II's Lord Chancellor. His undoubted ability was widely recognized, but very few people trusted him. Thomas (3), destined in 1681 to be appointed to the esteemed position of head ranger of Cranborne Chase, had an altercation with Lord Shaftesbury '*brilliant subtle and arrogant founder of the Whig party*' in 1671/2. Shaftesbury had deprived Thomas of the customary use of that part of the Chase known as Alderholt Walk and a lodge associated with it. Shaftesbury was suspected of planning more general encroachments on the land. Young Thomas (3), then about twenty, wrote him an exquisitely polite but firm and reprimanding letter.

'My Lord,

I am spiritually sensible of those favours your Lordship was pleased to vouchsafe me, and I therefore now return my hearty thanks for all. I confess it a singular bounty that your Lordship entrusted Burches Stoole Walk to my care, which I humbly conceive I have not unworthily discharged, since I have observed your orders in all respects. I [will] not mention in the first grant the small encouragement I received myself, nor my entrance upon a Walk almost destitute, nor your Lordship's retrenchment of keepers fees and consequently advancing wages from the ranger [*i.e. Thomas had to pay the wages himself*]. But since you descend to tell me that you repaired the Lodge at your own charge, with all humility I return, that those very reparations required, and had amendments; and yet the house requires a third hand to repair it to the full…. As to my claims and pretensions I presume to stretch them no further than to what my right invites me; and your Lordship who is a great patron of law and property, might justly place me in the lowest class of the softest heads, should I on easy terms part with anything my ancestors have enjoyed as their right and I receive from them as mine… Immediately after receipt of yours, I delivered up the possession of the Lodge and Walk into your servants hands, and am abundantly satisfied with your pleasure therein. If your Lordship thinks me worthy to execute any of your other

commands I shall very gladly obey them; for notwithstanding my charge is removed, my resolution is fixed; and that is ever to continue as My Lord, Your most obedient humble servant
Thomas Chafin.'

This is one of the very few Chafin letters to have survived and is quoted in his grandson William's *Anecdotes*. Thomas (3), seething at being deceived and cheated by Lord Shaftesbury nevertheless expresses himself with controlled clarity before a social and political superior. Many men with more years and experience than Thomas (3) were extremely wary of the duplicitous Shaftesbury. This letter portended great promise. The exchange also demonstrates the uneasy relationship between the holder of the land and the Lord of the Chase whose position was that of representative of the Crown. Despite the fact that the property was part of the Chettle estate Shaftesbury had rights in respect of maintaining and hunting deer which meant that Thomas (3) had to '*observe*' Lord Shaftesbury's '*orders in all respects*'. Difficulties between the two parties became more and more acrimonious over the next one hundred and fifty years until the overlordship of the Chase was brought to an end in 1830.

In July 1674 Thomas (3) married Anne, the youngest of three surviving daughters of John Penruddock. She had been a year old when her father was executed in 1655 for leading a rebellion against Cromwell. The Penruddock property of Stoke Abbas Manor was divided between the three girls, five twelfths of it coming to Thomas and Anne. Stoke Abbas Manor is about thirty-five miles west of Chettle, a few miles inland from Bridport. In 1681 Thomas (3) was appointed ranger, that is the senior administrator, of Cranborne Chase, the hunting rights of which were by this time enjoyed by Mr Freke of Shroton.[62] The Frekes and Chafins were related by marriage so this was a family appointment. For centuries the monarch had appointed a local Lord Warden to administer and protect the royal

[62] His daughter married a Pitt and this family were therefore forbears of the Pitt Rivers family.

interests in the Chase. Queen Elizabeth had appointed Henry Herbert, Earl of Pembroke, of Wilton, and King James I had made his much valued Lord Treasurer, Robert Cecil, his Lord Warden, elevating him at the same to Viscount Cranborne. The Lord Wardens eventually became independent owners and they in turn created their own appointees to manage their affairs. Thomas (3) held the post until his death. It passed to two more members and stayed with the Chafin family until 1766.

Thomas's ten years as head ranger for the Chase was interupted in 1685 by further military excitement. It was in that year that Charles II died, and as he had no legitimate heir the crown passed to his younger brother James who had become a Catholic in 1671. (James's first wife, Anne Hyde, second cousin of Amphilis Chafin, had by then died and been replaced.)

The prospect of the country reverting to Catholicism caused widespread concern. An illegitimate son of Charles II, James, Duke of Monmouth was encouraged by his Protestant supporters (of whom Lord Shaftesbury was one) to return from exile to claim the Crown. He landed at Lyme Regis, a town with a long-standing reputation for religious dissent, on 11 June 1685. Several thousand supporters joined forces with him as he marched though Dorset to Bridgewater.

Monmouth, who had a fine reputation as an experienced soldier, had undertaken a prolonged visit to the West Country in 1680, five years before, to gauge and encourage support for such a venture. The enterprise was geographically limited to Dorset and Somerset. Whatever misgivings the local landowners might have had about James II and the religious question, few of them supported Monmouth. Some took themselves into voluntary exile thereby avoiding the decision as to which side to take. The Chafins had not done this during the Protectorate and did not do so now. The rebels have traditionally been dismissed as '*The Pitchfork Rebellion*,' poor farmers and peasants with little to lose. Daniel Defoe described them at the time as men '*who live well… the working trades, who labour hard but feel no want, and the ordinary country people, farmers etc., who fare indifferently.*' Whether Monmouth relied on the hard working and respectable or whether it was the rougher elements who came to his support is a matter still debated.

Thomas Chafin (3) summoned his militia and marched to Dorchester to join others in defence of the Crown. Despite any preoccupation he may have had about the risks and dangers of battle he shows himself concerned about the welfare of his wife and children. Anne with their latest baby, Bridget aged three weeks, was almost certainly staying with her mother at Compton Chamberlayne. Five days after the Duke of Monmouth's landing at Lyme Regis he wrote to Anne from Dorchester, on 16 June 1685. Dorchester men were mainly in support of Monmouth so Anne would have been anxious for news.

'My dearest creature. I am very well soe far on my journey...My cos Strangways was killed as he was takeing horse. Major Stiles saved himselfe in a plat [*i.e. garden plot*] of kidney beans: Mr Churchill of Muston saved himselfe by running up into the garrett ...We've a great army against them ...I don't here of any more killed, gentle or simple, of our side; but of the rebels 2 or 3 killed and 2 or 3 and twenty taken prisoner. I was forced to take Collington[*one of the family servants*] knowing no other soe fitt: therefore if you be pleased to come home you must send to Chettle either for Will Horner or Will Lambert. Horner and the colt would draw you home almost as well. I have Thomas Clements and the gardiner, well armed, with me. Give my service to all my friends and blessing to the brattes and let Nancy take true love from her deare Tossey.'

Thomas had clearly gone to join the militia in Dorchester in a hurry and taken with him the most able of the servants at Chettle. One of his officers, Strangeways (his half sister Bridget's husband) had been killed and two had to go into hiding – one in an attic and the other in a patch of kidney beans – not a promising beginning.

Five days later King James II wrote to the Duke of Beaufort who was at Badminton about twenty miles from Bristol concerning the threat that Monmouth presented to the City of Bristol. It was then the busiest port on the west coast of England, and second only to London. The King gave instructions for the defence of Bristol.

'The preservation of Bristol being a matter of great importance I have directed the Duke of Somerset to joyne with you with his militia… there is a bridge at Keinesham halfway between Bathe and Bristol. I would have you by all means to break the same immediately. Upon receipt hereof which will in great measure delay, if not hinder their passage that way. James II'

The bridge was not destroyed but the Duke of Monmouth was turned back by Royalist forces when he reached it. Monmouth attacked the Royalist army very early on the summer morning. Despite the advantage of making a surprise attack the rebels were defeated by a better organized force. Monmouth was finally defeated a few miles east of Bridgwater at the Battle of Sedgemoor on July 6 1685. That morning Thomas (3) wrote again to his wife after the battle

'Monday about 7 forenoon July the 6 1685
This morning about one o'clock the rebels fell upon us whilst we were in our tents at Kings Sedgemoor with their whole army: we had for about an houre a briske fight, but at length away they ran. Wee have lost but few men and as yet know but of one comrade killed. We have killed and taken at least 1000 of the rebels. They are fled to B'water;… 3 loads of arms have we also taken. My service to cos. Lowe. I thanke God Almightly I am very well without the least hurt; soe are our Dorsetshire friends. I am thyne only deare Tossey.'

The following day he wrote

'Tuesday July the 7th 1685 Wee have totally routed the enemys of God and the King…'

Monmouth was captured at Horton five miles north of Wimborne while trying to make his escape to the coast. The Monmouth Ash now marks the place of this final downfall. He was committed for trial by Sir Anthony Ettricke, Recorder of Poole, whose tomb can be seen in the Trinity Chapel at Wimborne Minster.

The Battle of Sedgemoor was a resurgence of the Civil War, but this time the Chafins were on the winning side. Thomas (3) joined other victorious Royalists who made their way to London. He dispatched another letter, dated 16 July 1685, to his wife from Greene Street, London, the address he used when summoned to London on Parliamentary business. Stuart London was still a small place and Greene Street was about one and half miles to the northwest of Whitehall with open parkland between. It would have been a convenient place with stabling and a short carriage drive to St James's Palace and Whitehall. London was extending to the west although the really fashionable part of London was still between the Strand and the river Thames. It was now a little over a month since Thomas (3) had left Chettle.

'…The king gave us his hand to kiss… The whole company gazed on us as somewhat extraordinary and enquired who we were…Mr Chaldecott had an hundred guineas given him by the king for riding post with news of Monmouth's being taken, by which it may be gathered tis better riding post with good news than fighting. Those who had their bones broke will want such a sum I doubt; though the King ought to be served without reward, and shall for ever be so by me …I hope to be at home on Saturday sennight. The late Duke of Monmouth's head was severed from his body yesterday morning at Tower Hill about 10 or 11 forenoon. Lord Grey will soon be there too. Blessing to the bratts. Soe farewell, my dearest deare Nan quoth Tossey.'

Grey was reprieved, but along with Monmouth went many of the plebeian rebels. King James II had appointed George Jeffreys as Lord Chief Justice and he was dispatched to the West Country to try Monmouth's supporters who had been captured. Jeffreys was admired for the acuteness of his thinking in civil cases, but as a criminal judge was notorious, even in those harsh times, for his brutality. The

Bloody Assize that sent so many to the gallows left an indelible mark of bitterness upon several market towns of Somerset and Dorset. It is inconceivable that any resident of Chettle was amongst the rebels. They were all estate workers bound in loyalty to the Chafin family. Many weavers in the area whose standard of living had deteriorated since the Civil War had joined with Monmouth. Their corpses were not allowed to be taken from the gallows where they swung sere and ghastly for months.

The Chafin family were clearly in the ascendant. Thomas (3) was thirty-five, he had taken on various public roles and he was captain of the militia. The Bankes family had vacated the manor house of Chettle in 1666 and it was rapidly filling up with little Chafins. Trade and commerce had recovered and with it the family's woollen export business. Agricultural improvements were under way in the country, though at Chettle itself the medieval strip and furrow system inhibited major advance. Each man tilled several separate strips in open fields, and was content to continue to do so. The indifference to agricultural improvement was born of ignorance. Members of the Chafin family were the only inhabitants of Chettle to be aware of some of the changes being initiated by a few big landholders. The strip system was inefficient as a man's total acreage might be spread over a large area and as each strip was relatively small much of the work had to be done by hand.

King James II had received Thomas (3), although as he wryly remarks, his fighting was accorded no financial value though riding (safely) with good news was royally valued at one hundred guineas. He had gone to London direct from the battle without returning to Chettle: as he writes 'the whole company gazed on us as somewhat extraordinary.' Social demarcations were pronounced in dress, deportment, speech and demeanour. A member of the upper ranks of the gentry would in more measured times have arrived at court for an audience with the king suitably attired, shod, bejewelled, peruked and waited upon. Thomas (3) had on several occasions in the recent past attended the House of Commons as he was Member of Parliament for Poole in 1679, 1681 and 1685. As captain of the militia, with more than a month of active service, punctuated by periods of great excitement and fighting he probably arrived looking a bit the worse for wear. From his self-deprecating remarks about the event he obviously found it rather amusing that folk should gaze and enquire who he was. Back in Dorset such ignorant questions would never have been asked. With the Restoration this was a family growing in wealth, self-confidence and recognition.

The House of Commons papers record that on 9 February 1688 Thomas Chafin Esq. was *'duly elected to serve in this present convention for the Town and County of Poole'*, and that Mr Trenchard and Mr Chafin *'when they were made Freemen of the said town gave £50 apiece to the Use of the Town for their Freedom.'* Elections were corrupt and raucous though the franchise was limited to a narrow stratum of property owners. Nevertheless a Royalist candidate could not be complacent about Poole, a port of international standing whose merchants and burgesses were given to independent views and could not be relied upon by a Royalist. If this fifty pounds was a thank-you we may be sure that expenditure on bribery beforehand exceeded it.

The Parliament of 1688 was the last one of the reign of James II. He had modified his autocratic ways not at all since Sedgemoor and the birth of a son at St James's Palace on 10 June 1688 to his second wife Mary of Modena brought the ever-simmering anti-popery to boiling point. England in the seventeenth century was in no mood to consider the prospect of a Catholic dynasty on the throne. Parliament invited James's elder Protestant daughter of his first marriage to Anne Hyde to return to England to become queen. On November 5 1688, three years after the Battle of Sedgemoor, and on the eighty-third anniversary of the Gunpowder Plot that had attempted to assassinate James II's grandfather, she and her husband William of Orange, with his large army, arrived from the Netherlands, landing further west along the coast at Brixham in Devon.

The local militia were summoned. On 5 December 1688 a meeting was called in Dorchester. Two regiments were to be raised, one under Thomas Erle of Charborough and the other under Thomas Strangeways of Melbury. Thomas Chafin was one of Erle's captains and wrote to him as *'your most affectionate brother'*. Another Sedge-moor was threatened. On this occasion James II did not put up a fight but fled on 12 December and finally left England on 23 December. The regiments were dismissed to their homes, taking their uniforms with them. They were to stand by in case of need. Some of the estate workers and Thomas (3)'s servants from Chettle were involved. They returned to the village with stories of their recent adventures and no doubt warnings of dangers to come. That James, with French help, would invade was always a possibility.[63] For the next sixty years the risk of a Jacobite uprising, instigated from France, was never far away: it was never far below the threshold of Chafin consciousness either.

William and Mary made a well-managed and miraculously peaceful entry to London to become joint monarchs. The new King and Queen accepted the Bill of Rights that limited royal power in favour of Parliament. This *Glorious Bloodless Revolution* thus achieved much of what had been attempted by the confrontation between Parliamentarians and King Charles I in 1642 that had led to so much bloodshed, grief and waste.

In supporting James II at the time of the Monmouth Rebellion Thomas (3) had written *'the king ought to be served without reward, and shall for ever be so by me.'* In the House of Commons he was derided as an *'obnoxious Tory'*. He was proud to hear such a term. The Chafin family always believed deeply in a prescribed God-given order of human life and society, and his estate workers were of the same mind. This was a family never far from the fret and turbulence of public life and consistent in its conservative views, lagging a generation or two behind social and economic change that inspired new political thinking over six generations.

Thomas (3) was Member of Parliament in December 1689 for Dorchester and in 1690 and early 1691 for Hindon. He was also JP for Dorset from 1678–1688 and captain of the Dorset Militia from 1688 till his death. His busy public life provided many opportunities

---

[63] B F P, CAS/83.

for impressing upon the ordinary folk of Dorset the rightness of his philosophy.

Thomas was also proud of his growing family. Fecundity had not been a characteristic of the Chafins, but he and Anne had a quiverful of children, eleven in all. Three had died in infancy, two in their twenties, three in their thirties and three survived into old age. The average length of life of these eleven children was about thirty-five years – considerably longer than for previous generations and a reflection of improving social conditions. There was enough food, life was much more comfortable and the shocks and griefs that had marred the second half of the seventeenth century were things of the past. Several of the West Country families were reunited in amity and had reasserted their readily assumed authority as the ordained leaders of men.

The *brattes* to whom Tossey had sent his blessings from his battle travels were Thomas (4), who was ten, Bamfield, nine, Anne, four, Mary three, Arundel who was ten months old, and Bridget of a few weeks. Rachel and George (1) were born after 1685. George was born in 1689 and he was christened privately very soon after the birth. This usually meant that there was some immediate doubt about the child's chance of survival. George however lived for seventy-seven years and fathered at least eleven children so any initial frailty was temporary.

On 5 January 1691 while in the House of Commons Thomas (3) complained of feeling ill. The next day he made his will: the witnesses were Chettle residents, so he had made the journey from London. Eleven days later on 17 January 1691 he was buried at St Mary's Church, Chettle, a victim of smallpox, the epidemic disease that had been increasing in incidence and virulence since about 1680. King William lost both his mother and his wife, Queen Mary to smallpox.

The two men credited with observations and discoveries that eventually brought this disease under control[64] were not yet born. It

---

[64] It was eventually eliminated from the world in 1979 – except for specimens in a few laboratories.

was commonplace knowledge in dairying areas that some degree of protection against smallpox was conferred on workers who handled cowpox-infected cattle. This empirical observation had led to attempts at control by intentional exposure to cowpox by inoculation. In 1717 Lady Mary Wortley Montague had her five-year-old son inoculated. The two young daughters of the Prince of Wales were inoculated in 1722 on the instruction of Sir Hans Sloane, then President of the Royal College of Physicians.[65] By the 1760's advertisements were appearing in the Salisbury Journal. The *'Suttonian Method of Improved Inoculation'* and inoculation by a local surgeon, Mr Lardner *'at the commodious Beach House Christchurch, one and half guineas'* were advertised in the Salisbury Journal in 1769.[66] Benjamin Jesty, dairy farmer, acquired more lasting fame by being memorialized on his gravestone in Worth Matravers churchyard, twenty-three miles due south of Chettle as *'An upright and honest man, particularly noted for having been the first person (known) that introduced the Cow Pox by inoculation, and who, from his great strength of mind, made the experiment from the cow on his wife and two sons in the year 1774.'* Smallpox was with justification much dreaded. Schemes for its control and cure were widely debated and promoted, as the extracts from the contemporary press testify. The international accolade for the discovery of smallpox inoculation goes however to Edward Jenner (1749–1823) a practising doctor from Berkeley in Gloucestershire. He performed the same procedure twenty-two years later in 1796, with scientific erudition and a treatise to back it. Both Jesty in Dorset and Jenner in Gloucestershire lived in dairying areas. No other burial in Chettle in 1691 is recorded as due to smallpox. The village inhabitants would have had, in the course of their daily lives, intimate contact with cattle.

Thomas (3) was the most sophisticated of the Chafins up to this time. His tutelage in the Restoration circle of Sir Ralph Bankes and

[65] H D Traill (Ed) *Social England* 1896 p52.
[66] *Salisbury Journal and Weekly Advertiser* 6 February 1769. By a curious coincidence Henry Castleman and his wife Emma moved to the Beach House, Christchurch in about 1850.

his friends, his education at the knee of his mother and at Oxford had taken him away from the daily life at Chettle. The humble folk of Chettle secured an immunity against the virus that brought his life to an untimely end. He spent quite a lot of time in London and the death rate in the metropolis from infectious disease was always high.

Thomas (3) had come into his estate when it was burdened by debt and during a regime inimical to a Royalist family. In the thirty-six years since then the country had been transformed; so had Chettle and the fortunes of the Chafin family. Thomas (3) had done much to secure Chettle's position in Cranborne Chase against the predations of Lord Shaftesbury. He had, with the help of the Restoration Settlement been able to pay off the mortgage to the Ryves family. At his marriage the estate was enlarged with the Penruddock property and Thomas (3) had also bought additional land. He had taken advantage of the support given by the Government of Charles II to the woollen industry, to improve the flocks and to keep the spinners and weavers employed. Woollen cloth from the Chafin estate was exported from the ports of the south coast.

He left a thousand pounds (present day equivalent approximately £26,000) to each of his five daughters and a farm for each of the younger boys, Bamfield and George. Thomas Clements, the servant in Chettle who had accompanied him to fight the Duke of Monmouth received £30 and the tenancy of a property (probably a small farm or holding) for his lifetime. This would give a man of servant status an opportunity to gain a measure of independence and a toehold on the slippery ladder to social betterment. There were other modest bequests to his employees in Chettle. His heir Thomas (4) was then only sixteen, so trustees were again appointed and given 'full power' over '*all my farms and manors... in the Parish of Yarlington,...manor of Knowles ...Wales...Queen Camel,...North Eggardon, ...Stoke Abbott...Lidlinch ...Pimperne Mead.*' Some of this property had come into the family with Anne Penruddock, and he also refers to property he had bought. The estate had been saved from the havoc created by the war and its aftermath. There had been thirty years of reasonably favourable economic and political circumstances. Many

Royalist families however never recovered their losses. This family had the resilience, restraint and initiative that carried them through. Thomas (3) did not forget the people of Chettle who had stood by him so valiantly in hard times. In his will of 6 January 1691 Thomas makes provision for a child or children yet unborn, his wife being *'with child at this present'*. The possibility of twins had crossed his mind. (The records are ambiguous but two previous children, Jane and Henry James, may have been twins.) Sadly, this child was *'dead born'*. The doubly bereaved Anne was in her late thirties and was left with eight young children. Her Penruddock relatives were at Compton Chamberlayne and certainly maintained contact. Thomas (3) had appointed three trustees *'putting sure confidence in them that they will manage the trust put into them to the best advantage of my family.'* Nevertheless it is never an advantage for an estate to be nominally owned by a child.

For country gentlemen with middling sized estates the Restoration period was a good time for recovery, but new methods of land improvement required capital investment. Chettle was poised for recovery. Wisdom, determination, a long view, some appreciation of events beyond the shores of England, and available capital were some of the ingredients needed to carry things through. Thomas (3) had shown himself to be astute and far seeing. There was real promise that the Chafins of Chettle would become a secure dynasty of the West Country alongside the Pitts and the Arundells. The smallpox virus confounded these hopes and brought the upward trajectory to an abrupt halt. There were four more owners of Chettle. For a variety of reasons – some within, several beyond the control of the individuals concerned – from the early eighteenth century the trend was generally downhill.

Decline

William and Mary had been joint monarchs for just over two years when Thomas (4) became Lord of the Manor of Chettle. At the national level the old rancours between Royalists and Parliamentarians were giving place to the more civilized conduct of the emerging Tory and Whig parties and the Crown was more open to Parliamentary influence. The Chafin family would always be for the King, but there was now a greater chance that their allegiance could be expressed in words and argument, not battles and bloodshed. Thomas (4) had been ten at the time of the Battle of Sedgemoor. His Uncle Strangeways had been killed but it was the Bloody Assize of Judge Jeffreys that had made the bigger scar on the West Country. Many simple men who had come forward to support the Duke of Monmouth had been condemned to a barbarous death or transported. It was an appalling and beastly punishment that had even disgusted some of the West Country Royalists with its inappropriate ferocity. Thomas (4) doubted whether many of them had properly understood what they were called upon to fight for, or the dangers they risked. Many of the nobility and gentry who had encouraged rebellion had fled to safety when Monmouth arrived. The ignorant rabble had been left with no proper leadership. No man from Chettle had been for Monmouth, but each knew well some of the families in the district who had paid the very high price that had been exacted by King James II's Chief Justice. Thomas (4) was proud of his father's part in the Battle of Sedgemoor but he worried about the way Judge

Jeffreys had dealt with these simple fellows. Forty years earlier Cromwell had called some of their fathers and grandfathers who joined the Clubmen *'poor silly creatures'* and sent them home. It would take centuries for this communal wound to heal. The hardships and grief it had left made local social and political life more tortuous and touchy. Thomas (4) knew that when the time came for him to take his place in one of the governing positions customarily held by a Chafin he would have to proceed with caution and not make too much of his family's past association with King James II.

The troublesome Lord Shaftesbury had died in 1683 and Sir Thomas Freke now held the Lordship of the Chase. He was a friend, and a distant relative so affairs of the Chase could be dealt with more agreeably. The woollen business was satisfactory, though the competitive mills that would eventually undo the southwest were setting up in Yorkshire. Acts of Parliament designed to encourage the woollen trade had been passed during the reign of Charles II. A corpse for burial, for example, had to be shrouded and the coffin lined with wool. Failure to do so incurred a fine of £5. Parish burial records from this time show how effectively this legislation was implemented, for most record *'buried in wool'*. The great markets of the world were kept open for the trade. Spinners and weavers in the locality of Chettle were kept busy. The working day was thirteen hours long and young children joined the work force, not the primary school. It was a very favourable time for men who held land that was good sheep pasture. Some landowners were experimenting in new ways of growing things but the novel methods had not yet been tried on the Chafin acres.

In 1691 Thomas (4) became the hopeful young Lord of the Manor of a large property, at a time when land values were rising, in response to agricultural improvements, and England at last seemed reasonably settled politically. He was sixteen years old, so for five years the trustees under the terms of his father's will had legal authority. The trustees were Sir Thomas Freke, his great uncle Edmund Chafin of Folke, and Uncle Maurice Borland of Standlynch, who had married his mother's sister, a Penruddock daughter. They had all known the family for years and held affectionate memories of the father of this young brood. Their responsibilities were considerable. They endeavoured to maintain the estate as a profitable enterprise, and to see that Thomas both continued his formal education and became properly equipped to take over the full responsibility of his estate when he turned twenty-one. They did a good job for, despite the disadvantages of youth and inexperience the momentum initiated by Thomas (3) continued for several years to come.

At home in the manor house of Chettle in 1691, with their mother Anne, were Thomas (4) aged sixteen, his brother Bamfield aged fourteen, five sisters aged between four and twelve and little brother George just two. Thomas (3) was sorely missed as father, husband, friend and much-respected Lord of the Manor. He had left them well provided, and had taught by example and precept self-reliance and responsibility in the stewardship of property. The promising prosperity built up since the Restoration had been overshadowed for a while by Thomas (3)'s untimely death but the family was resilient and resourceful. Within a year or two Thomas (4) was able to discuss estate matters with the bailiff with some authority, and with the help of Uncle Edmund was learning about the export business. After a suitable period of mourning the daily and seasonal round at the manor house and in the parish of Chettle was back to normal.

Mary, Thomas (4)'s eldest sister became interested in the culinary arts and began collecting recipes that she used. She has left us her book of over two hundred recipes collected between 1698 and 1719 that gives us a glimpse of domestic life at the manor house of Chettle.

Several cookery books and collections of recipes made by others had been published in the second half of the seventeenth century, based mainly on the grand banqueting at the French and English courts, where a variety of exotic imports were used to supplement home grown fare. For over a hundred years some member of the Chafin family had been going regularly to London on government business, socializing and dining with the court circle. London affairs were discussed in the family and Mary aspired to bring to Chettle some of the pleasures of the table that she heard about, though her book is a more homely affair and appropriate to a country based life. Every family had to ensure adequate sustenance from mainly local fare and it is likely that there were quite a lot of records of this kind kept in the gentry and more comfortable farming houses where literacy was by now the rule. Mothers taught their daughters and they made notes of their successes and failures. Mary was probably not unique in being a collector of vernacular recipes but the survival of such a record is rare.

The family ate well and entertained friends liberally as their status required. Some recipes are from acquaintances. Lady Lear and Lady Napeir (sic) provide instructions for making biscuits. Mrs Rupe, Mr Cary and Mrs Ann Way make their contribution. Claret, brandy and sweet herbs are frequently used ingredients. Preserving with the help of vinegar and salt was of special importance to offset each winter's dearth.

Many domestic animals were killed at the beginning of winter to reduce the demand for fodder. Before the days of the freezer, salting, drying and smoking were applied for the preservation of meat and fish. Icehouses were coming into vogue by the late seventeenth century, though Chettle kept to more traditional methods. With the exception of wine and brandy most of the ingredients were derived locally. If this little book of collected recipes is a guide, the family had a high protein, high fat diet with plenty of alcohol though relatively few vegetables. The humbler folk of Chettle would have had a more restricted, and farinaceous diet, with locally produced cider in place of claret. Both manor house and cottage tables would have been affected by the seasons, for they were all heavily dependent on the plants and animals whose environment they shared.

The modern introduction to the book describes their house in Chettle (that is the one that preceded the present mansion) as

'an Elizabethan house... The kitchen would either have opened directly from the hall or have been a separate building. A large number of other outhouses would have provided for all the wants of what was virtually a self-contained community. The family and their servants brewed and baked, they churned and ground the meal, they bred up, fed and slew their beeves and sheep and brought up their pigeons and poultry at their own doors. In all this the women of the family played a vital part; wool and flax spinning, needlework of all sorts, embroidery, cooking, curing, preserving, wine-making and the preparation of herbs and medicines were all their responsibility... Gardens were small and functional, largely devoted to herbs, and the importance of domestic remedies for common ailments is shown by the number of potions that Mary included.'[67]

Mary had started her cookery book when she was nineteen and her marriage to William Clutterbook was planned, in 1698. He was a seafaring man from Exeter and owned a trading ship or ships. English foreign trade and shipping doubled between 1700 and 1780, but the little inlets of the south coast had for years been associated with smuggling. Tobacco had been brought into Cornwall in contempt of the customs officers for most of the previous century. As various Customs Acts sought to raise revenue on imports, so smuggling not only became more lucrative but its products were increasingly in demand. The Clutterbook and Chafin paths had probably crossed during Thomas (3)'s time when the Chafin cloth exporting business was getting under way again, with Clutterbook drawn into the family economy to deal with the trade in Europe. He was clearly deriving benefit from the expansion in trade and dealt in both legal and illegal business.

He and Mary lived in Chettle for the first nine years of their marriage and four children were born to them there. They needed their own house and by 1709 William was able to buy the manors of Pucknowle and Bexington from the Napier family. These two villages on the Dorset coast provided him with secluded port facilities for some of his shipping business and also gave him the coveted status of landowner so that he could take his place amongst the governing gentry in the county. In 1712 he became Sheriff of Dorset and as a

[67] Mary Chafin *Original Country Recipes* (Reprint Macmillan) 1979.

land tax paying squire his name appears as a contributor to the public celebration to mark the accession of Hanoverian King George I to the English throne in 1714. Pucknowle became well known as a smuggling centre. Bexington is still a very small coastal hamlet with Pucknowle in its immediate hinterland. A glance at the map shows how convenient these two places would be for the purpose – about midway between Bridport and Weymouth, away from the prying eyes of civic authorities. This marriage of Chafin and Clutterbook began the diversification that led, in the late eighteenth century, to the residents of Chettle becoming largely dependent on smuggling for their livelihood. The immediate benefit to Mary was that she could include some of the exotic ingredients that she had learned about from court recipe books into her own cooking.

Bridget, her younger sister married Thomas Haysome of Weymouth who was in the business of quarrying Portland stone. It was about thirty-six years since Christopher Wren had started using this material, conveyed by sea to London, for his grand rebuilding programme after the Great Fire. Thomas Chafin (3) and Christopher Wren had been well acquainted. They had been MP's together and there were trading links with the Haysome family. These two Chafin marriages confirmed pre-existing commercial links, and were part of the Chafin network so important in building up a prosperous family undertaking.

The youngest sister, Rachel lived to be fifty-six. She was eighteen, and the only daughter still living at home when her mother died. As so often happens to single daughters she took over the household on her mother's death and by the time she was able to relinquish the task maybe the chance of marriage had passed her by. She ran the household for her brother Thomas (4) till he died and then for brother George (1) until he married in 1715. She always had 'a room' in Chettle House, where she lived comfortably with her own servant. She had twenty-four nieces and nephews, eleven of them under the same roof as her at Chettle, the rest within reasonable distance. Miss Rachel Chafin lived quietly, devoted to them and to the small community in which she lived.

Rachel had been left £1000 by her father, and her elder brother Thomas bequeathed her a further £1000 in 1711. She died in 1743 and still had the capital sum of two thousand pounds to leave to her several nieces and nephews. Her investments would have generated about £100 a year. It was reckoned a gentleman could live comfortably on £300 a year so Rachel had a modest but adequate income. Her younger brother George married in 1715 (he was by then the Lord of the Manor) when she gave place as chatelaine to her sister in law. In addition to various benefits to her relatives Rachel left in her will the curious bequest of five pence to William Feltham. There was a large family of Felthams living in Chettle: the sixth of nine children was William, then five years old. He was perhaps a young favourite. Richard Bannister, a trustee, was left *Five Pounds to purchase a silver plate for the use of the Communion Service at the Parish Church of Chettle.* She was buried by the Reverend Charles Dobson, who as rector at Chettle for fifty-seven years was the longest serving in the whole recorded period from the year 1210. She had been six years old when her brother Thomas (4) had appointed him to the living in 1693. There were complaints about his excessive drinking which at one time came to the ears of the Bishop, though there is no evidence that his imbibing had any deleterious effect on his position in the church. The two rectors who followed Dobson at Chettle can reasonably be suspected of involvement in smuggling, as we shall see later on. The proclivities of these three men of the church point, as does much else, to Chettle becoming a focus for one of the major smuggling enterprises of the south coast during the eighteenth century.

The family, the trustees and the parishioners of Chettle all had an interest in making a success of Thomas (4)'s young ascendency. The poverty, discomfort and conflict of the war years would be long remembered and was one of the spurs to new endeavour. The labouring men and women of the parish expected no riches but hoped for enough to feed and clothe their families, to live a peaceable life and to die a natural death. The momentum created by Thomas (3) carried them forward, and the reign of Queen Anne (1704–1714) was generally contentedly peaceful. The estate and the reputation of the Chafins prospered and at the age of twenty-three Thomas (4) was elected Member of Parliament for Shaftesbury – a position he held from 1699 to 1701. From 1702 to 1711 he was member for Dorset. The fathers of marriageable daughters in the district had him earmarked.

When his mother died in 1705 Thomas (4) had a fairly simple wall monument in memory of his parents and their large family placed in St Mary's Parish Church at Chettle. Many of the parish churches of England are beautified by sixteenth and seventeenth century alabaster and stone monuments made to proclaim the status and attainments of gentry families. These were made at great expense and were no longer fashionable, but Thomas (4) was proud of his father's achievements and his mother's forebears. He wanted Chettle and all who visited it to appreciate them and the Chafin family. The family memorial commissioned by Thomas (4) in 1706 was moved into its present position on the right of the chancel arch when the church was rebuilt in the 1850's. Thomas (3), Anne and their eleven children are all named. Seven of the children were alive when the memorial was made. George (1), the youngest, then a youth of fifteen, lived to look at his own memento each Sunday that he attended service for the next sixty years.

This memorial is quite a lesson in the politics of the period. Overtly a list of members of the family, it gives, on closer examination, some plain hints about the prevailing attitudes and values of the early eighteenth century, and how Thomas (4) wished to present his family to the world.

There is no mention of Thomas (3)'s exploits at the Battle of Sedgemoor, nor of his presentation to King James II. Local sensitivies had been coloured by the Bloody Assize that had followed the battle. Thomas (4) had no wish to remind the local population of the Chafin allegiance to the architect of that cruelty. The Royalist credentials of the Chafins are more agreeably presented by Colonel John Penruddock, maternal grandfather to the eleven children, who had been executed for his leadership of a Royalist rebellion during the Protectorate in 1655 more than twenty years before any of them was born. His credentials as a brave anti-Cromwellian Cavalier are declared. This selective presentation of family history by Thomas (4) served also to ingratiate the name of Chafin with those who held the reins of power in 1705.

Thomas Chafin (3) had fought for Roman Catholic autocratic anti-Parliamentarian James II at Sedgemoor. James was deposed by his Protestant daughter and her husband William of Orange, who ruled with the support of Parliament. A limited and Protestant monarchy replaced the autocracy for which Thomas (3) had fought. Whig and Tory arose from the ashes of the Parliamentarians and Royalists of the seventeenth century. Whigs were in the ascendant for almost all of Thomas (4)'s life. His father, Thomas (3) had written to his wife from Sedgemoor in 1685 *we have totally routed the enemy's of God and the King*. By 1705 those enemies ruled in Whitehall. They remained a dominant force in English politics till the accession of George III in 1760.

This modest memorial in the parish church is an eighteenth century public relations exercise which attempts to obscure from the ruling party the allegiance of the Chafin family to James II, and to distance themselves in the eyes of the local population from Judge Jeffreys. At heart they were Jacobites still, and they maintained a connection with the exiled family of James II. Looking back fifty years to John Penruddock in this public memorial is a subterfuge to disguise their continuing allegiance to an exiled cause.

Thomas (4) never married. He died at the age of thirty-six, after months of incapacity. He made his will on 14 March 1710 declaring that he was *sick and weak but of sound and powerful mind.* There is no mention in the will of Thomas (3) to suggest that his heir was deficient in any way. Whatever made him *sick and weak* in 1710 occurred in adulthood. A disabling accident – a broken and infected bone seems the most likely possibility. Carriage transport was becoming popular by the early 1700's but Thomas (4) would have made most of his journeys on horseback. Riding and agricultural accidents accounted for numerous deaths as the coroners' records of the time testify. Some would have inflicted long term disability

Thomas (4)'s death is a critical point in the panorama of the Chafin story. In 1711 the property passed from the first-born to the eleventh-born. Thomas (4) the first-born and heir had been subject to expectations and discipline directed to his future responsibilities. He had known sixteen years of Thomas (3)'s plans and achievements and his father's guiding voice was seldom absent from his ear. This was followed by five years of tutelage by the trustees of the estate. The attitudes of obligation to dependents, of stewardship of property for future generations and accountability to a higher authority were firmly indoctrinated. When Thomas died the estate passed to his youngest brother George, the eleventh child of the family, then just twenty-one years old. His only recollection of his father was from stories he had heard. He retained no whispered directions in his mind for he had never heard them. George had escaped the rigours of birth order discipline experienced by his elder brother, and he was just old enough to be independently free of trustees.

Thomas (4), in writing his will, listed property in several counties and then, impatiently, as if there was too much of it to remember, *'in any other county or counties, Parish or place whatsoever within the Kingdom of England.'* The Chafin estate was very large and it now passed to George the youngest, eleventh born and only surviving son of Thomas (3).

To his married sister Mary (Clutterbook), Thomas (4) left £10 *'to buy her mourning'.* It was customary for the head of the family to arrange his mourners and provide for their appropriate attire. There were two unmarried sisters. To Bridget he allocated £50 and to Rachel *'as much money as will make up her present fortune to the sum of £2000'.* Bridget already had marriage prospects (to Thomas Haysome) so her needs would have been seen to be smaller. Thomas (4)'s steward John Lane and various servants received bequests in recognition of their loyal service.

Thomas (4) had inherited from his father a property that had been much improved since the Civil War. He had maintained his inheritance, rather than improved it. There had been no marriage to bring land to the family, and the estate had concentrated on woollen exports rather than agricultural impovement. At the time when his young brother took over in 1711 the Chafin fortunes hung in the balance.

Primogeniture has disadvantages for a large family. It is inequitable, and risks drowning all but the one. The great advantage is that it keeps an estate as an integrated whole. Several recent surveys of the health and ability of children show that first and only children are on average healthier and more intelligent than their later born siblings. This suggests that primogeniture is a system well adapted to maximize the chance of an inherited property going to the most capable.

George (1) (1689–1766), the last-born had been delicate at birth and deprived of fatherly guidance when he was two. He grew up in an affectionate and lively family. When he was fifteen his mother died and his nearest companion was his sister Rachel, then seventeen years old. His elder brother Bamfield had by then died and his eldest brother Thomas (4) fifteen years his senior, head of the family, Member of Parliament, a man of the world, was too busy to spend much time with him. He was probably thoroughly spoiled by his older sisters, the household servants and the parishioners. For a few years he had most of the benefits and none of the responsibilities of the son of a well-to-do family. He spent four years at Winchester College and was a student at Oriel College, Oxford. Then, at the age of twenty-one he became head of the family. Sister Rachel stayed to keep house at the manor. Bridget married and moved to Weymouth.

In 1715 George (1) married Elizabeth Sturt. Her father Sir Anthony had bought the manor of Horton, six miles southeast of Chettle, in 1696 from the Uvedale family. (It was a predecessor, Mr Uvedaele, High Sheriff of Dorset who had issued the original charter transferring Chettle to Thomas Chafin (1) in 1572.) Elizabeth's grandfather was a successful London merchant who had been victualler to the navy and an Alderman of the City of London. In his dealings with the navy he would have met with Samuel Pepys, who was secretary to the Navy Board and surveyor general of the Victualling Office in the 1660's and 70's. This was one of the many families buying country properties with their city wealth acquired after the Restoration: the upwardly mobile generation of the seventeenth century. This was another advantageous marriage in which the political influence of the Chafins was joined with the business acumen of the City of London merchant's family.

Queen Anne had died in the previous year and German George I came to the throne. He was also the ruler of Hanover, spoke not a word of English and initially showed no great interest in his new country. The Jacobites in Scotland took this as an opportunity to bring back the son of James II. The uprising was restricted to Scotland and was fairly quickly quelled. George (1) Chafin was sufficiently occupied with his marriage not to get involved. His name however was sent to the Pretender, Charles Edward Stuart in 1721 as a potential supporter in the event of a further Jacobite invasion. George (1) Chafin was described as 'tres puissant en vasseaux.' It was claimed that the many workers in the woollen industry on his estates could be called upon to join him. A second more serious invasion from Scotland came in 1745. Louis XVI was supporting the Pretender Charles Edward and there were grave anxieties about the possibility of invasion from Catholic France. Fears of a Jacobite insurrection were not dispelled until 1746 when the Scottish troops were finally and decisively defeated at the battle of Culloden Moor. The Jacobite invasion from Scotland in 1745 got no closer to Dorset than Derby so George Chafin was not called upon to fulfil his pledge.

Dorset was famous for its sheep that did so well on the chalk uplands. Defoe writing in 1724 claimed that 600,000 sheep were farmed in the Dorchester region: 'the herbiage on these downs is of the sweetest and most aromatic plants, such as nourish the sheep to a strange degree.'[68] The spinning and weaving enterprises that constituted the woollen business of the West Country thoroughly infiltrated the rural economy. Spinning was, in the main, a cottage industry carried out by women and children. Weaving was more centrally organized, and done by men in manufactories in the towns, though

[68] Quoted Cecil N Cullingford *History of Dorset* 1980.

still on a domestic scale. Woollen exports were keeping their pre-eminence as the most important source of national wealth. George (1) was sharing in the prosperous times that prevailed during the reign of Queen Anne. England was still predominantly rural, divided into large land holdings each made up of several parishes where the parish dignitaries, the rector, the yeoman farmer or the bailiff kept affairs running smoothly on their patch. Chettle was one of many parishes of the Chafin property. It was special in that it had the Lord of the Manor in residence.

Near neighbours of the Chafins were the Pitt family, cultured and cosmopolitan. They set extravagant standards and their eccentricities sometimes went beyond the bounds of tolerable behaviour. There were five George Pitts in succession between 1630 and 1828. The second of them became Lord of Cranborne Chase in 1714 and the third was an almost exact contemporary of George Chafin (1). George Pitt (1690–1745) and George Chafin (1689-1766) became close friends. George Pitt came into his own as head of the family and Lord of the Manor in 1720 at the age of thirty. These two young men moved as one. Pitt made Chafin one of the trustees of his will. No greater sign of friendship and respect can be found.[69] Together with Anthony and Humphrey Sturt (George (1)'s father and brother in law) and Robert Lowe he was required under the terms of Pitt's will to *'yearly raise and expend a sum not exceeding £100 for the education and schooling of all the children.'*[70] He also made him a grant of land.

The Pitt family was older and its wealth more deeply established. This friendship was one of the temptations to extravagance that beset George Chafin (1). He had to live up to the standards of a friend and colleague who had a deeper pocket. George (1), delicate and pampered made his youthful and unexpected debut as head of a family into a society that became increasingly bent upon conspicuous expenditure, gambling, field sports and drinking. The energies of the previous generation had been absorbed with repairing devastation,

---

[69] DRO D/SEN/3/3/1/5.
[70] DRO D/SEN/3/3/1/5 Will dated 28 February 1727.

getting trade and exports running and life functioning comfortably. George (1) was a beneficiary of his father's diligence, but he had inherited little of the capacity for it. He was comfortably off and his marriage to the wealthy Elizabeth Sturt added to the several prevailing invitations to indulgence.

Many of the houses, parks and gardens developed at the time stand as a memorial to the taste and refinement, as well as the wealth of their owners. They were built in the eighteenth century to provide an improved standard of comfort, a suitable setting for furniture, paintings, porcelain and other household artefacts as well as creating a powerful symbol of prestige for the family. In addition, the interests and refinements that were dependent upon urban life were getting easier of access for Chettle. The Salisbury Journal, one of the earliest of local papers, started publication in the 1730's. It provides a view of the interests of the local populace and the expanding culture and entertainment being made available in the city sixteen miles away.

The houses and gardens being built were a drain on many a pocket. Building costs were only the beginning. Maintenance and upkeep were daunting. The great Vanbrugh house of Bubb Doddington in Tarrant Gunville, the adjacent village, which cost £140,000[71] to build, was demolished less than fifty years later. No tourists came to help defray burdensome costs. The Doddingtons (Lord Melcombe) buckled under the strain. All that remains of this great building effort is a set of kitchen quarters and an ornamental archway.

With the help of the fortune his wife had brought to the family, George (1) set his hand to the building of the fine house at Chettle that stands there today. Nicholas Pevsner describes it as 'a plum'. Most architectural authorities now seem agreed that it was designed by Thomas Archer, who lived fairly nearby. He had been engaged by George Pitt to design his house at Kingston Maurward, near Dorchester. If George Pitt had a new house George Chafin would need one as well.

---

[71] The present day equivalent is about fourteen and a quarter million pounds.

To carry out the design of Thomas Archer it is likely that the Blandford building firm of Thomas Bastard and his two sons was engaged. A *Country Life* article suggests that George Chafin 'a Londonising squire', perhaps had a plan drawn up by Thomas Archer, to whom St John's Smith Square, St Paul's Church Deptford and St Philip's Church in Birmingham (now the Anglican Cathedral) are attributed, with the work carried out by a local firm.[72]

Chettle House was completed for the Chafins in about 1725. It symbolized the Chafin achievements of the previous one and a half centuries. Like many men of the *middling sort* they had acquired property that had been purloined from the Catholic Church; they had supported the crown and risen to be counted in the ranks of the elite of the southwest of England. They could count the Trenchards, Hydes and Frekes amongst their relatives. The Pitts, Bankes and Arundells were neighbouring landowners. George Pitt was Lord of Cranborne Chase and George Chafin (1) MP its chief administrator appointed to keep the Chase 'in a flourishing state until the general dissolution of all things'.

The house was the centre of a large estate. It dwarfed most of the buildings for miles around but was not out of proportion with George (1)'s conception of his estate, his family and himself. He was the fifth generation of a family that had weathered all the setbacks of the seventeenth century, had risen triumphant into the eighteenth. His large family promised a hopeful future. They would all be married into suitably aspiring families and the Chafin name and influence would spread commensurately. The fine baroque rose pink mansion symbolized their achievements and signalled their ambitions.

The family, by then consisting of George (1), his wife Elizabeth, their son and heir George (2) born in 1717, five other children and Rachel, George (1)'s unmarried sister, moved into this splendid mansion with much rejoicing. Five more children arrived; the last was William, born in 1731. There were fine rooms for entertaining and

[72] Geoffrey Webb *'Chettle House Dorsetshire' Country Life* 6 October 1928.

the Chafin energy, directed for years to the seasonal demands of the land, and to fighting when the king required it, could now be expended on more pleasurable pursuits.

George (1) had not been reared to an understanding of how the comforts and privileges of his life were generated. He had seldom been denied anything and consequently had little practice in the art of calculating how to overcome obstacles and difficultes. As a youngster he had made the happy discovery that a smile achieved more than a scowl. As few demands were made of him he saw no reason to change this and developed little in the way of self-discipline. He grew up to be a pleasant and easygoing man. No one would have described him as a strong character, but the circumstances of his life did not call for such a quality. He was somewhat vain and could be frivolous. His new house at Chettle fed his vanity. It was the talk of the county and he heard little but praise for it.

George and Elizabeth had eleven children. George (2) their first-born was born in 1717. There is a local story that his father, thinking to help the boy avoid the perils of too soft and comfortable an up-bringing, had him reared by a local shepherd for the first few years of his life. It may have improved his physical stamina though whether it had a similar enhancing effect on his cognition is doubtful.

George (1) was elected as Member of Parliament in 1710, 1715, 1722, 1727, 1734, 1741, and 1747. His ownership of land was a necessary qualification and the franchise was limited to the 2,400 men who were freeholders of land above a certain value. The *great popularity* attributed to him on a wall monument in St Mary's Parish Church, needed to extend no further than that landholding elite to secure a successful election campaign. Between the ages of twenty-one and fifty-seven he periodically took his place and attended the House of Commons when summoned. On his first election he was presented to Queen Anne who *from their common relationship to the Hyde family, addressed him as 'cousin.'*[73] There is a locally told story that George rode the one hundred and twenty miles horseback to

[73] David Ellis Chaffin unpublished paper *Chaffin* 1973.

London in one day. By leaving in the early morning he could reach his house in Greene Street and be at the House of Commons by four o'clock in the afternoon.

In the Salisbury Journal in July 1747 George Chafin and George Pitt announced to *'the Gentlemen, Clergy and Freeholders of the County of Dorset: Gentlemen: Having had the Honour at the General Meeting held at Dorchester on Monday 29th June to represent this County in the ensuing Parliament we entreat the favour of your appearance at Dorchester on Wednesday the 19th of this last, the day appointed for the election. Your most obedient servants George Chafin, George Pitt'*

It was to be George (1)'s final election.

His eldest son and heir, young George Chafin (2) had friends, like his father, who could claim a more elevated background. Eight miles to the north of Chettle is Wardour, home of the long established Arundell family. During the Civil War the Arundells had been Royalist. Blanche, Lady Arundell had organized the defence of Wardour Castle as Lady Bankes had done at Corfe Castle, and with a similar result. Almost a century had passed since those distracted days and Wardour Castle remained a ruin, but a new residence had been built nearby. Henry, who was to become the 7th Lord Arundell was born on 4 March 1718 so was a few months younger than George (2).

George (1)'s friend George Pitt had a son – another George – of about the same age.[74] These three were children when Chettle House rose to dwarf the church and every other building of the parish. Twenty-two miles to the southwest was the Pitt family's new house at Kingston Maurward.

George Chafin (2), George Pitt and Henry Arundell grew up in a world replete with riches and pleasures and they were all three heirs to their respective estates. Older and wiser generations knew that present comforts were neither acquired nor maintained without constant vigilance, but these three young men had experienced no hardship.

---

[74] George Pitt 1721-1803. He became the first Lord Rivers.

There were several paths to financial ruin in the early eighteenth century. Unwise or greedy investment had come very publicly to grief with the South Sea Bubble of 1720. Support of a losing political faction was very risky. George (1) had followed the political allegiance of his forebears and an offer of support had gone to the Young Pretender. His help was never called for and his interest in this direction probably never came to the notice of authority. Then there was gambling, the scourge of the day.

> '...expenses of gambling and of sport, as well as a noble zeal for building and for laying out gardens and planting avenues, burdened estates with mortgages which proved a heavy clog on agricultural improvement and domestic happiness. Immense sums of money changed hands over cards and dice.'[75]

George Chafin (1) and (2) could have provided the data for this comment of Trevelyan's.

The early eighteenth century was marked by a general indiscipline across the classes. The satirical paintings of Hogarth and much of the Restoration drama portray some of the social dysfunctions. The Chafins in common with several other families in the area were spending money they had not had to earn, and there was much conspicuous expenditure. Clothing, jewellery, household decoration, garden display, as well as entertaining – dinners, card parties, and dances – were all brought into the service of display, of letting friends and neighbours know of the taste, wealth, education and sophistication that the family had attained. One of the joys of Chettle House was that it provided a family setting for entertaining and an elegant social life. Gambling was the great excitement of the times. It reached frightening proportions with stakes so high that estates were changing hands overnight. It had become such a problem during the reign of Queen Anne that legislation had been passed to the effect that a debt incurred through gambling could not be enforced through the

---

[75] G M Trevelyan *Social History of England* 1942 p314.

courts. That protected novices and simpletons who were tricked into high stakes. For the wealthy sophisticates it was irrelevant. It was a matter of honour that no debt was ever reneged upon. Social ostracism would have been the result.

In 1738 George (2) had his twenty-first birthday. It heralded disaster for the Chafin family and for Chettle. The disaster is recorded, but what caused it is not. From what we know about the Chafin family and the values, behaviour and style of life in the early Georgian period it is not too difficult to look back through two hundred and seventy years to reconstruct what happened.

An evening party was arranged for George (2). Chettle House was still rather a novelty so the local gentry were pleased to accept their invitations to see for themselves how the Chafins of Chettle were getting on in their mansion. George (2)'s friends George Pitt and Henry Arundell were pre-eminent amongst the gathering. Young Pitt was only about seventeen years old, but self-confident, rather aloof and very much in control of himself. The young Arundell and Chafin, both twenty-one, engaged in a lot of good-natured banter with each other. There was supper during the early part of the evening with innumerable toasts. French brandy was in plentiful supply. Uncle William Clutterbook from Pucknowle had brought a cask or two. After supper the tables were cleared and most guests settled for cards and dice. In their fine new house it was only right that the fashionable trends of London should be followed where *'gaming is become so much the fashion amongst the Beau Monde, that he who, in company should appear ignorant of the Games in Vogue, would be reckoned low bred and hardly fit for conversation.'*[76]

There were a few rash wagers but nothing dramatic until late in the evening when George (2) and Henry Arundell became very intense. Several friends had gravitated to their table to watch their risky play. With an audience they both became bolder with their stakes. This was George (2)'s birthday celebration and he was being rather brash and noisy about the Chafins of Chettle. Arundell's good

---

[76] *The Compleat Gamester* Richard Seymour 1754.

nature of the early evening seemed to have waned somewhat and given place to a calculated determination. The cooler Arundell became the more flustered Chafin got. The evening's drinking had affected them in quite different ways. Henry disliked Chafin's comparison of the Arundell home built near the wall of the old Wardour Castle with Chettle House. Chafin history would never compare with the long pedigree of the Arundells. The banter about old nobility and new money hardened into unfriendly insults. The onlookers heard the mounting stakes, some with complacency, some with amusement and a few with alarm. This was not a game, but a deeply personal and deadly struggle. George (2) then staked the value of all the Chafins' *'several Manors Lordships Hereditaments and premises with the Appurtenances situate in the County of Devon, Dorset Somerset Wilts, Southampton and Cornwall.'* He, Henry Arundell and all the onlookers knew that this was almost all of the Chafin property, their wealth, their livelihood, their existence, their legacy from Queen Elizabeth. What was George (2) thinking of? Where was George (1)? The card was turned. Henry Arundell had won. The stake was so large that it could only be raised by realizing almost all of the Chafin property. Until that could be arranged the *'several Manors…'* were now held by Henry Arundell. It was the end of George (2)'s birthday party. It was the end of the Chafin family. It was very late and George (1) had already retired to bed.

The next morning George (2) faced his father. Neither man considered for a moment invoking the legislation that could make this gamble unenforceable. Honour required that the debt should be paid. But all the property that George (2) had staked was feudal and could not be sold.

On 26 January 1738[77] a Deed was granted to Thomas Sleigh on behalf of the Right Honourable Lord Arundell. The Agreement was that *'for a term of four hundred years…* [he held] *the several Manors Lordships Hereditaments and premises with the Appurtenances situate in the County of Devon, Dorset Somerset Wilts Southampton and*

---

[77] The year ended on 31 March until 1752.

Cornwall.[78] The feudal property had been mortgaged to Lord Arundell, and the Chafins were left with the parish of Chettle, their new mansion and nothing else. It was not enough to support the family. This Deed of Settlement (of 25/26 January 1738) was drawn on in 1739 when it was directed that George Chafin and John Webb (trustees of the Settlement) raise £20,000 for the portions of the younger sons of Henry Lord Arundell, Thomas and James Everard.[79]

Sir Anthony Sturt, concerned for his daughter, George (1)'s wife, and their children, embarked with his son Humphrey on a campaign to protect them from the destitution that faced them. Under the terms of the Marriage Settlement between George Chafin and Elizabeth Sturt signed in November 1713 Elizabeth and her assigns were to have an annuity of £600 for eighty years to be administered by Sir Anthony Sturt and his son Humphrey, i.e. Elizabeth's father and brother. The Sturts, anxious above all to salvage something for Elizabeth and the children sought an Act of Parliament to change the status of the property from feudal to allodial. Allodial property was held in absolute ownership, free of feudal ties and obligations and could be sold. The agricultural improvements that were to change the face of rural England and end the feudal land holding system were only just beginning. Enforcing a change of this sort by legislative fiat was a protracted business. The Sturts, in prefacing their approach to getting an Act of Parliament through, claimed that George (2) *'through inexperience was prevailed upon… To part with his estate of inheritance without any valuable consideration paid.'*

The family moved out of Chettle House. Henry Lord Arundell leased *'Two acres… with the Manor of Tollard Farnham'* to George Chafin Senior and George and William his sons.[80] It was *'all that close of pasture commonly called Flodways otherwise Gowre Close late in the copyhold tenure of Charles Green deceased.'* The Green family had been long established in Chettle and Charles had died in September 1735 at the age of seventy-three. The availability of Tollard Farnham

---

[78] PRO Prob.11/946 Image ref. 284 Attachment to the will of George Chafin (1).
[79] Hampshire & Swindon R O 6M80/E/T/215 1739.
[80] Hampshire & Swindon R O 6M80/E/T/215 1739.

Manor came at an opportune time. Chettle House, no longer afford-able, was let to John Carver, a well-connected gentleman who died prematurely by falling from his horse when he was returning from a hunting dinner at Farnham Inn to Chettle. (He is commemorated in Ashmore Church.) The Chafins became copyhold tenants of Lord Arundell and moved in to Tollard Farnham Manor. It is doubtful if a Chafin ever again inhabited the glorious mansion built to promote their name and image.

The Sturts achieved their Act of Parliament in two bites, one in 1748, the second in 1757. Under these two Acts the Chafins were obliged to sell *'unto any persons who shall be willing to purchase for the best price that can reasonably be got'*. George (1), who had been described in 1721 as *'tres puissant... et des sentiments tres elévés'* and as having *'multitude presque innombrable d'ouvriers dans les manu-factures de laine,'*[81] was by 1749 impoverished.

Under the requirements of the two Acts the property disposed of was extensive: in Dorset the hundred[82] and manors of Alton, Alton Westbroke, Holleborne, Holeborne Estbroke, Westbroke; lands in Hartley Wintney and Farnham, Trinsham, Windlesham, Bursted, Godalming; in Somerset the manor and advowson of Whateley, Knoll (which had been mortgaged for £6000) *'besides other lands for as much more.'*

The trustees were able to pay all debts except a mortgage to Sir William Napier for £3,000 on which there was due £4,293 principal, interest and costs. Elizabeth had her annuity of £600 in accordance with her marriage settlement and the children were saved from penury. George (1), then nearly fifty, withdrew from public life. Lord Egmont wrote of the Dorset members in his election survey of 1749/50 that *'one of them cannot stand again being ruined in his affairs.'*

This had the making of a considerable West Country scandal. The Civil War and the Parliamentarians had put this family to the test for

[81] Romney Sedgwick *The House of Commons 1715–1754* HMSO 1970 p 540

[82] A hundred was an ancient territorial division meaning a hundred hides. A hide was land that would support one family and its dependents.

eighteen years and they had survived with dignity and with their principles intact, but in 1738 it was felled by George (2) when he *'had but just attained his age of twenty one years'*. The Reverend John Hutchins, the eighteenth-century historian of Dorset, who was a near contemporary and knew the Chafins, makes no reference to the radical change of circumstances that would have followed. The Acts of Parliament achieved by the Sturt family refer only to *'debts'*.

On 4 November 1763 George (1) wrote a simple four sentence will, the nub of which is *'I give, devise and bequeath to my son George Chafin the Younger all my Real and Personal estate whatsoever and do nominate and appoint him executor of this my will.'*[83] No local squire or loving friend was called upon to witness the signing or to act as trustee. Difficulties arose over the granting of probate and there was an unusually protracted delay of two and a half years after George (1)'s death.

George (2) died childless and intestate in 1776 without having administered his father's will.

There had been eleven children born into the family of George (1) and Elizabeth, at least six of them still living in 1738. Elizabeth, on her marriage to George (1) in 1715 had brought considerable wealth to the family that was now sacrificed. Whatever furies were unleashed in 1738 were seemingly kept under close control and out of the public eye.

The friendship between Chafin and Pitt remained strong. In 1763 George (2) received *'An Annuity for my own life and benefit…Wholly issuing out of freehold land and tenements and hereditaments belonging to George Pitt of Stratfield Saye … being in the Parish of Cowfield and Whiteparish'.*[84] On George (2)'s death this was transferred to his younger brother William Chafin.

For five generations the Chafins had worked, traded, managed their interests, defended their rights and governed their community successfully. They had been welcomed as evenly matched negotiators

---

[83] P R O Prob 11/946.
[84] Bank of England Archives F/12/34.

in the marriage markets of the well bred. Their fall just preceded the onset of the Industrial Revolution and the difficulties for agriculture that followed. The ingenuity, energy and above all, political and economic circumstances that would have favoured recovery, were things of the past.

All the inhabitants of Chettle and many spinners, weavers and sailors were dependent upon the Chafin enterprises. The cloth workers would have found employment with the new landowners, or emigrated. The parishioners of Chettle found their boundaries much contracted. They were no longer part of a large prosperous estate, but downcast servants of a disgraced and impoverished family whose humiliation they shared even if they could not fathom the reason for it. For many years incomes had been supplemented along the south coast by illegal imports. George (1)'s Aunt Mary and Uncle William Clutterbook had owned ships and property in Bexington and Pucknowle, well known locally as a place for getting continental delicacies at bargain prices. As the eighteenth century progressed the government put import duty on an increasing number of goods thereby making smuggling more likely and more profitable. The hoped for recovery in the parish did not occur. There were no more jobs for the cooks, carpenters, gardeners and grooms. The Chafin family had moved out of the mansion. As the scale of the catastophe gradually seeped into local consciousness, so did plans for survival by new means. It is from the middle of the eighteenth century that smuggling, centred on Chettle begins to surface. Deprived of their customary way of earning a living, the residents of the parish turned to this lucrative contraband trade.

Like his parents, George (1) had eleven children. Five had died. The survivors were utterly dispirited by their great change of fortune. None sought a spouse amongst the influential families of the locality. Anne was born in 1724, lived till she was seventy-eight, and never married. Her sister Elizabeth married the rector of Whately in Somerset. The Chafins held the advowson of Whateley until its enforced sale after 1748. Elizabeth's value in the marriage market was much tarnished by her brother's folly, and maybe the Reverend John Floyd was offered the living on condition that he supplied Elizabeth with a husband. John and Elizabeth Floyd had three children, Thomas, Elizabeth and Ann. John Floyd maintained a friendship with two other rectors, William Chafin and Morgan Coker.

Another daughter of George (1) married William Dolling, a tenant on the Chettle estate.[85] William Chafin the eleventh child, born in 1731, went into holy orders, did not marry, and lived to be eighty-seven.

George (1) died in 1766. The wardenship of the Chase, held by the Chafins since 1681 was not renewed. His successor was not worthy. His two surviving sons, George (2) and William retained one symbol of their past prestige – a pack of fox hounds that were kept for twenty-two years. Fox hunting in the area had become popular after the Civil War though it did not entirely replace deer hunting until the mid nineteenth century.

George (2) joined the Dorset Militia and became Colonel of the Regiment. He was said to have excelled in all kinds of field sport and was described as *'very good company'*.

The 7th Lord Arundell who had gambled so successfully with George (2) died in 1756 at the age of thirty-eight. The second Act of Parliament enforcing the sale was not passed till 1757, so it was his son Henry, the 8th Lord Arundell who was the beneficiary of the sale. He had a new Palladian mansion built at Wardour in 1766 and at about the same time had a fine full-length portrait painted of himself by Joshua Reynolds.[86] The remnants of the Chafins looked on, thinking of what might have been, but for one act of folly. George (2), returning from a visit to see the new Wardour mansion, fell from his horse at Win Green and broke his spine. Win Green is a local beauty spot, precipitous and rough, where a horse might well stumble, but George (2) was a very experienced horseman. He was taken home and died within a few days.

The Chettle Estate, without any of the extensive property that had

[85] B F P Chettle Court Book 11 November 1711.
[86] The portrait now hangs in the Dayton Art Institute Ohio USA.

been important for generating the wealth of the family, passed to his younger brother, the Reverend William Chafin.

George (2) left no will but in August 1777 the '*Administration of the goods, Chattels and Credits of George Chafin… was granted to the Rev. William Chafin, the natural and lawful brother and only next of kin of the said deceased…*'[87]

[87] B F P CHA/11.

William Chafin and his Anecdotes

William Chafin was forty-five when he, being the only surviving male Chafin, became a reluctant Lord of the Manor in 1776. He was the eleventh child of George (1), who had been the eleventh child of Thomas (3). The likelihood of an inheritance finding its way to that birth position where primogeniture prevailed was remote. William's inheritance, now limited to the parish and estate of Chettle, was fraught with problems that would have taxed a man far more conscientious and diligent than himself.

The population of England was growing and moving into the towns. Home-based textile production that had been so important in the West Country was giving place to factory work dependent on machinery in the north of England. Forward-looking landowners were increasing their acreage by enclosing common land, and improving crop yields and animal husbandry to meet the food needs of the nation.

Land at Chettle was still in medieval holdings: strip lynchet, ridge and furrow. It was part of the three hundred and eighty square miles of Cranborne Chase, the area of Dorset and Wiltshire more or less enclosed by a line encompassing Shaftesbury, Salisbury, Ringwood and Blandford. The difficulties of the parish of Chettle became entangled with the increasing troubles of Cranborne Chase. This was still held by the Lord of the Chase, as had been determined by William the Conqueror seven hundred years before. The crown had retained the right to hunt and maintain deer regardless of who held and farmed the land. Only the monarch's appointees or representatives could avail themselves of the pleasure of the hunt and the good meat that resulted from a successful chase.

In time, the monarch had appointed members of the nobility as Lords of the Chase. Queen Elizabeth had appointed the Earl of Pembroke of Wilton, and James II had created Robert Cecil Lord Cranborne when he became Lord of the Chase. By this means the monarch abrogated much of the responsibility for local maintenance without forgoing any hunting rights. The local Lord of the Chase was expected to entertain the royal entourage from time to time. This might have been a burdensome demand, but brought inestimable benefits in status and influence. It also created ambiguities of ownership and boundaries: other local aristocrats looked with jealous eyes at Lord Cranborne and disputes arose between lord and lord in a way that would have been unthinkable, and possibly treasonable, between lord and king. *'The peculiarity* [of the Lords of the Chase] *was that they could legally impose restrictions of an obnoxiously "medieval" character on other landowners whose properties lay within the established boundaries of the Chase.'*[88] The territorial boundaries as well as ownership, access, rights and duties were largely matters of tradition, common law and general acceptance. From the eleventh century the unstable equilibrium between royal overlord and local landowners had been increasingly challenged. By the eighteenth century persistent irritations, sometimes breaking into open and rancorous dispute, arose from confusion between Chase and landlord rights. A Chafin had been chief ranger of the Chase from 1681 to 1766. It had been one of his duties to enforce the rights of the Lord of the Chase as against the landowner, or holder.

The last generation of Chafins – George (2) and William – almost exactly spanned the eighteenth century. George (2) was born in 1717 and his youngest brother William died in 1818. Eighteenth-century changes in food production, preservation and transport reduced the pressing need for access to good meat, but deer hunting became

[88] Desmond Hawkins *Cranborne Chase* 1980. Hawkins is an authority on the wider and complex issues of Chase history.

The Castleman farmhouse in Hinton St Mary was built in 1685 for the yeoman farming family. William Castleman (2) was born here but never followed his father into farming.

William Beale's box tomb in Chettle churchyard. It was used in the 18th century to hide contraband brought in along the south coast, via Wimborne.

St Mary's farmhouse, Chettle.
The home of Robert Rogers and
his family from 1834–1880. The
Rogers family were the main
farmers of Chettle.

Edward Castleman (2).

Mary Dean, Mrs
William Castleman.

Mrs Fuidge.

ABOVE LEFT: Esther Bourke (1904–1967), niece of Edward Castleman (3). She came to Chettle with her children in 1939, fell in love with it and saved it as her great-great-uncle Edward Castleman (1) had done a hundred years earlier.

ABOVE: Edward Castleman (3) (1870–1946). He was badly wounded at Gallipoli. His interest in fox-hunting consumed his time and energy.

LEFT: Edward Castleman (1) (1800–1861) He saved Chettle Estate from being sold off.

Cranborne Chase Keeper's hat and truncheon.

Mrs Anne Castleman (1799–1883), wife of Edward (1), grand-daughter of Isaac Gulliver. She held complete authority over Chettle until her death.

William Castleman (1766–1844). Lawyer, banker and land-agent of Wimborne. He made a fortune that enabled his son Edward (1) to purchase the Chettle Estate in 1847.

William Castleman (1766–1844) with two of his grand-daughters, Emily and Elizabeth.

Alice Roe, Esther Bourke's mother.

The great smuggler, Isaac Gulliver (1745–1822)
and his wife Elizabeth, a Chettle girl.

Chettle House.

Chettle Church.

The Keeper's Cottage in 1892. The cottage was built by Edward Castleman (1) in the 1850s to enhance the sporting facilities in Chettle.

The Keeper's Cottage as it is today.

symbolic of landholding rights. Poaching and deer stealing still incurred harsh penalties; differential access to venison was important for the maintenance of a hierarchical social structure. The spread on the dinner table was as important as the vote in influencing power, and as bitterly fought over in rural England.

William's education and experience had not prepared him for the challenges. He was born in Chettle House and had lived there for the first seven years of his life where he could just remember affluent pleasures, an affectionate family and good company in the house for evening entertainment, or occasionally splendidly dressed ladies coming to drink tea with his mother. Then he recalled family conclaves with tears and solemn faces. They centred on his beloved brother George (2), but his enquiries only brought more tears and he was generally shushed away. His father had become more and more morose and spent a lot of time in London. Grandfather Sturt occasionally visited but then everyone became terribly gloomy. William had been summoned home from school when he was fifteen or sixteen because there was no longer enough money to keep up the family standards. The servants went and the family all moved out of Chettle House, which was let to a young man with a lot of horses. William had sufficient of an allowance, thanks to the efforts of grandfather and uncle Humphrey Sturt, to enable him to go to Cambridge where he took Holy Orders. He returned to Chettle as the rector for twelve years from 1756 till 1768. His father had held the advowson so it was a happy arrangement whereby he could return to the place he loved, get a modest living from the tithes of the copyhold tenants, and take his place in the community that had supported the Chafins for nearly two hundred years. He was then appointed to the living in Lydlinch about fourteen miles to the east of Chettle from 1768 till 1818. He rode there on horseback for Sunday service for fifty years.

Hunting engaged his enthusiasm as nothing else could. He and George (2) kept their own pack of hounds. He was a model of the eighteenth-century foxhunting parson.

He gradually came to understand how the Chafin domain and

influence had been lost. Everyone in the locality knew that the family had been ruined and for a few months in 1748 the speculations were rife at every alehouse, dinner table and hunt meeting, but none had been able to confirm their guesswork. A few good friends were loyal and George (2) and William had made themselves agreeable enough to keep a semblance of their social world. They had invitations to dinners, card parties and suppers but as they were unable to reciprocate, these had become, by 1776, rather infrequent.

Lord Rivers was Lord of the Chase and William had managed to maintain a relationship there, if necessarily an obsequious one. Lord Rivers' cousin, William Pitt was Prime Minister and was created the Earl of Chatham in the same year, 1766, that George (2) became Lord of the Manor of Chettle. It was painful to think how far the paths of Pitt and Chafin had diverged since they were roistering young men together.

Neither George (2) nor William had found women of their class who were willing to marry men of such tarnished substance. Other girls had been willing surrogates and there were a few children for whom modest provision had to be made, but there was no legitimate heir. William and George (2) had sometimes talked over who would be the sole survivor. Each hoped it would be the other, though with George's fourteen years seniority it had always been assumed that he would die first.

The eighteenth century was a time of improving agiculture. Land values in England almost doubled between 1700 and 1790. In 1768 Arthur Young's report of his *Six weeks tour through the Southern Counties of England* was published. This promoted the merits of improved farming methods. In Norfolk, the New Husbandry was increasing output sometimes fourfold in a few years. The enclosure movement reduced woodland, common and waste ground, replacing them with fields, hedges, walls and roads. Cottagers were deprived of their customary access to common land for fuel and grazing which was causing a lot of social unrest. These troubles had an additional dimension in the small communities of the Cranborne Chase as Chase law interposed a further layer of authority based on an outmoded

tradition, over and above the landowners and farmers. The protected deer competed with sheep and cattle for food. They and their
hunters might destroy or damage money crops, trees and hedges.
Neither gentry nor cottage dweller had any formal means of redress,
nor had they any right to a venison pie on their dining table.

In 1745 the Lordship of the Chase passed to George Pitt (1721–
1804), boyhood friend of George (2). The improving aspirations of
landlords within the Chase were firmly resisted.

A *Survey of Crown Woodlands* carried out in 1792 reported that
there were twenty-two forest or chase areas remaining in England.
They epitomized feudalism in an age when England was becoming
an industrial nation. Lord Rivers held tenaciously to the ancient
monopolistic right to maintain and hunt deer. That the area is still
one of peace and tranquillity, farmland and birdsong can in part
be attributed to the brakes that were applied during the eighteenth
century, when much of England was becoming industrialized and
agricultural practices changed. The effect at the time was very different. Tempers were roused to violence and bloodshed by the damage
and depredation caused by the deer and the outdated laws that
continued to protect them. The ancient privileges inherent to the
Lordship of the Chase were exercised with little acknowledgement
that the circumstances that had given rise to them had long since
gone. They were challenged on all sides. The area became infamous
for deer poaching and stealing. The spinneys, hidden pathways and
quiet hiding places known to local men who became deer stealers,
were of the greatest value to the smugglers who landed their contraband along the coast between Poole and Weymouth, and needed safe
haven for their goods and persons. Cranborne Chase became the
haunt of smugglers as well as poachers. There was a robust disregard
for many of the requirements of civil order. But it was not only the
underclass involved in thieving and smuggling who broke Chase
law. The lines were drawn, not between cottager and aristocrat,
but between royally appointed hunter and agricultural improver.
The Ashleys and Arundells were amongst those who campaigned
for disfranchisement of the Lord of the Chase, and undermined

his authority whenever opportunity offered.

Many landowners and farmers were irked by the overweening behaviour of the Lord of the Chase and there were serious moves afoot to abolish the ancient lordly rights. An open letter to Lord Rivers from a committee of local landowners as early as 1791 had argued that the patent injustices supported by Chase law were contributing to community breakdown and lawlessness.[89] Several issues were woven together in this vexatious controversy – boundaries, the 'ownership' of deer and other animals, their right to feed in various areas and the means of social control. Who, for example, was entitled to employ a keeper? What authority did one landowner's keeper have over an employee of the Lord of the Chase? These labyrinthine matters have been carefully documented by Desmond Hawkins[90] and have a bearing on Chettle both through the Lord of the Manor and through the parishioners. The Lord of the Manor of Chettle had always been to some extent under an obligation to the Lord of the Chase. It is doubtful if the nature of the obligation was ever precise or precisely specified. Changing times, conditions and different personalities would have modified requirements and expectations. Some of the parishioners were involved in the illegalities that were marring the area. The eighteenth century was feverish with changing attitudes and practices.

William Chafin had no stomach for change. Those changes he had experienced had been for the worse. He looked to the past and contemplated his forbears with pride. From the time of the Wars of the Roses they had been amongst the leaders of men in the West Country. But he could not look forward. Alarming changes were taking place. The old well-tried practices were giving way to new that he did not understand. A man called Hargreaves had just invented a machine to speed the work of carding, which the Chafins had been skilled at for three hundred years.[91] New methods of spinning and weaving were taking employment away from Wiltshire and Dorset.

[89] Desmond Hawkins op.cit.
[90] op.cit.
[91] James Hargreaves invented the spinning-jenny in 1764.

Farmers in the east of England were trying to make the land do too much. Their ideas were spreading to Dorset and causing unrest. In Chettle men were content with their holdings of strips of land and with the crop rotation system with a regular fallow period that had served for centuries. Times were often hard for them, but with William's surreptitious support they were eking out a living with the help of the contraband trade. He was pleased with some of the proceeds of the trade himself, but on occasion, if the excise men visited the village, he had to put on a Sunday face and support the king's laws.

William Chafin was no improving landlord. His relationship with the land was as a consumer rather than a producer. He had no money for improvements in any case. He loved the Dorset countryside and hunting above all else. His experience of both, and his classical education opened social doors that his poverty would have closed to him. He fully supported Lord Rivers' determination to keep the Chase as a hunting ground.

When William was fifty-six the French Revolution started. The turmoil that followed frightened all of Europe. There was widespread anxiety that England would follow revolutionary France and overthrow the established order. Edmund Burke's *Reflections of the Revolution in France* had appeared in 1790 deploring the lawlessness and violence of the revolution, and promoting conservatism, inheritance and tradition. Thomas Paine's counterblast, *The Rights of Man* was published the following year.

The disturbances on Cranborne Chase resonated with those across the English Channel. Both stemmed from resistance to an ancien regime of tradition and privilege. The prospect of local grievances getting quite out of hand was terrifying. Several men had already lost their lives in confrontations between excise men and smugglers, between Chase keeper and poacher. There was no police force. The militia were called out if the local constables were unable to quell a riotous assembly. Men were finding it difficult to get enough employment and they were all too ready to join an affray. Several publications were issued between 1791 and 1818 on the very hot topic of the history, disputes and boundaries of the Chase. William feared what might lie ahead and made his contribution to the debate. He used the subject to promote his anti-revolutionary views in a little polemic he called the *Anecdotes of Cranbourne Chase*. It is the only Chafin record, apart from a few letters, that survives.

It purports to recount the history of the Chase based on *'oral tradition only, and the received opinion for ages.'* He frequently reminds his readers that he has had seventy years experience of hunting in the terrain and has been personally present at a number of events that he describes. The first quarter of the *Anecdotes* is written in support of that part of the established order he knew so well – the royal and aristocratic traditions of Cranborne Chase.

He alludes to the French Revolution as *'the levelling system which was so fatal in another Kingdom, which ought to be thoroughly reprobated in this, and every the least tendency towards it most cautiously attended to and averted.'*[92] His declared aim is to *'promote harmony, friendship and good neighbourhood'* which he believes can best be achieved by perpetuating the ancient Chase traditions. He sides with Burke in supporting tradition, fearing that the movement of one stone would bring the entire edifice tumbling.

The neighbourhood had become scandalously disharmonious during William's lifetime. His hope for *'harmony, friendship…'* etc was the pipe dream of an old man whose own world had been demolished. Chettle and Cranborne Chase accommodated deer poachers and smugglers, excise men and lookouts, keepers and crooks. Many went armed, violence erupted and murders were not unknown. The *Anecdotes* give us a vivid picture of illegalities committed by every class of society whose life and concerns centred on Cranborne Chase. Law breaking by the nobility and gentry he recounts with approving amusement as in the case of Lord Castlehaven (one of the Arundell family). The latter and his friends, including George (2) and William Chafin, having dined together, captured a buck from a nearby field, but a keeper arrived *'to carry away the deer*

---

[92] William Chafin *Anecdotes of Cranbourne Chase* 1818.

as being the property of Mr Pitt'[93] who was then the Lord of the Chase. *'We all stand here as criminals and plead guilty: what are the damages to be paid?'* asked Lord Castlehaven. £15 to the poor of the parish and a bottle of claret for the keeper settled the matter.

When William's father George (1) was Ranger for the Lord of the Chase he discovered that a wealthy landowner, Bubb Doddington (later Lord Melcombe) had appointed his own game keeper who was found with gun and dogs, beating for game. George (1) warned him off but he was found doing the same thing a few days later. George (1) promptly shot the three dogs. Doddington challenged George (1) to a duel. He went to *'the expence of buying a sword'* but when Joseph Bankes, his second, met Doddington to make arrangements he had cooled down. The three of them dined together and *'spent a very jovial day together and were good and social friends ever after to the end of their lives.'*[94]

These conflicts involving social equals were settled amicably, but confrontations that lacked the oil of social familiarity took a different course. Four men from Donhead with guns were found by two Chase keepers in Bursey Stool walk, close by Chettle. One was captured and gave the names of two of his companions. The three were convicted at Dorchester Assizes and transported for seven years.

Open warfare between keepers and deer stealers prevailed during much of William Chafin's life. He gives several accounts of keepers meeting with deer stealers in which both keepers and thieves sustained serious injury – sometimes lethal. Keeper Tollerfield was murdered near Fontmell on his way home from church on Easter day, and another at Fernditch met a similar end.

In May 1738 William Harcourt, the keeper of Copley Lodge, met some deer stealers with their dogs and nets. The confrontation led to Harcourt being killed. Richard Frampton, the first person arrested was not charged. Nearly two years later Henry Wheeler was sentenced to death at Salisbury Assizes. On 31 March 1740 he was *'executed at five o'clock in the morning at Fisherton Gallows and from*

[93] op.cit. p19.
[94] op.cit. p12.

thence carried near to the place where the fact was committed on the road that leads from hence to Blandford and there hanged in chains in a Gibbet erected for the purpose. He was stubborn to the last, and declared himself innocent of murder though he did not deny being in company.'[95]

That Chase boundaries were somewhat imprecise had mattered little for centuries. In the conditions of the eighteenth century they had become matters of dispute. Whether the Chase extended into Wiltshire on the east, and to Chettered Walk on the west had become contentious issues. Similarly the question of what wild life came within the ambit of Chase law – deer only, or all undergame? The third vexation was fencing (i.e. enclosing) of land within the Chase. Lord Rivers removed the fences erected by the landlord. The *Anecdotes* cites two court cases, both of which found in favour of Lord Rivers. William's *Anecdotes* give a glimpse of both the social malaise in and around Chettle, and his apparent blindness to the inequities that gave rise to it.

Twelve years after William Chafin died the Lord of the Chase was disfranchised by Act of Parliament, thus bringing to an end over seven and a half centuries of royal and aristocratic privilege. The landowners had, under the terms of the agreement, to pay compensation to Lord Rivers, and it was treated as a secular tithe.

We also get a glimpse of William's own divided personality. He was rector of the parish and like many an eighteenth-century squarson seemingly found no difficulty in combining his church duties with an intense interest in field sports, and a hearty participation in the bibulous social life that was so much part of contemporary gentry existence. For sixty years he had publicly wagged a reproving finger from pulpit and bench, but was himself complicit in some of the illegalities. He gives us hints of his privately held views through the traditional device of attributing opinions to *'a friend'* or *'the person…whom I well knew in the early part of my life.'* Through this literary construction of his alter ego we learn of his *'natural taste for*

[95] *Salisbury Journal and Weekly Advertiser* Tuesday 18 March 1740.

poetry, and Milton ...his favourite author.'[96] Milton, anti-Episcopalian and anti-monarchist was hardly to be openly confessed as a favourite by a Church of England parson and last scion of a Royalist/Tory family. He also quoted *'passages in Hudibras, an admired author in another style.'* Hudibras is a three part satire by Samuel Butler (1612–1680) attacking both Presbyterians and secular tyranny, particularly as practised by the republicans during the Commonwealth. The third section of Hudibras is largely devoted to Anthony Ashley Cooper, the first Lord Shaftesbury (1621 – 1683), founder of the Whig party and considered by many of his contemporaries as an unprincipled but very clever turncoat. John Dryden (1631–1700) satirized him in Absalom and Achitophel:

'A name to all succeeding ages curst;
For close designs and crooked counsels fit,
Sagacious, bold and turbulent of wit,
Restless, unfixed in principles'.

With his successor and namesake, the sixth Lord Shaftesbury, a powerful Whig grandee, living close by, discretion demanded that an admiration for Hudibras be attributed to an acquaintance.[97]

William Chafin can have felt little pride in the condition of his estate as his life was reaching its end. Chettle had fallen into disrepair and dereliction, the parishioners were making ends meet by smuggling, but he has left us an intimate account of the pursuits and pastimes of the village and the Chase that he knew so well. It is his political credo. Slightly below the surface he has also left a discernible record of the discomfitures and incongruities experienced by a reluctant Lord of the Manor, powerless to fulfil his obligations

William Chafin died in August 1818. He was buried at Chettle by

---

[96] op.cit. p75.

[97] In the Catalogue of the Sale by auction of the contents of Chettle House on 25 and 26 July 1946, Lot 492 included *HUDIBRAS 1750*. The first edition of *Hudibras* was published in stages between 1663 and 1668. The later edition in the sale was published when William was seventeen. Perhaps he had bought it as a student.

the rector Philip Rideout, whom he had first appointed curate at Sixpenny Handley more than a half a century earlier.

The Napoleonic Wars that followed the French Revolution had been over for three years, but they were not followed by harmonious prosperity. In 1815 the Corn Laws, which prohibited the import of corn until the homegrown reached 80 shillings a quarter, were enacted. This did something to secure the income of landowners, though it affected the price of bread of the labourer for whom there was no minimum wage. Industrial developments in the north of England created an alternative labour market that kept wages up in that part of the country. The southwest was losing its home industries so the labour market was depressed. Machines were being introduced by the agricultural improvers. Threshing machines were taking the place of hand flailing. Fire setting and destruction of machinery manifested local distress amongst the landless poor. Punishments were severe, usually transportation to Australia for seven years. Several well-publicized events occurred in Sixpenny Handley, the village three miles away. The population of Chettle kept out of the limelight but their plight was no less.

This is how things stood when William Chafin died. The story of the Chafins had not quite come to an end. In pursuit of raising money for his private pleasures William had secretly made an illegal and perfidious transaction in 1807 that was to inflict further immeasurable damage on the already ravaged Chettle for another forty years.

ELEVEN

Chettle on Trial

When the obsequies for William Chafin were over in 1818 a London man, Abraham Henry Chambers, aged fifty-three, a London banker of Bond Street appeared in Chettle to claim his place as Lord of the Manor. There were about a thousand acres of farmland on the Cranborne Chase, an unruly and disreputable area at the time, a hundred year old mansion in need of repair, a derelict church, twenty houses and a population of about one hundred and ten.[98] Many men with long family experience of agriculture and deep roots in the land were floundering; it was not a good time to take over a failing estate. Chambers had made money as a banker and theatre entrepreneur.

Chambers was described by one of the parishioners as *'a very small excitable man who used to ride a horse in one day from London.'*[99] He had a considerable network of financial and property connections in many parts of England and was a man on the make. The Napoleonic wars had provided opportunities for the quick-witted and the expansion of industry and agriculture required money for investment. Lending banks were not always well run and bankers not well regarded. He typified the nervous, loquacious, snappy little city gent, rather despised by the ponderous, measured, taciturn village dweller. The possession of a landed estate for Chambers was confirmation of

[98] Figures from the enumeration Return to Parliament 1801.
[99] George Chafin (1) had a similar reputation which seems to have served as a character yardstick.

a coveted status, though he was not well apprized of what he had taken on. Chambers and Chafin were both financially unethical, but had little else in common. Chafin was tall and handsome (his picture hangs in Chettle House), knew everybody, and every inch of the land. He was well read, decadent, completely unprincipled, and fitted the caricature of the eighteenth-century foxhunting parson to perfection.

In May 1807 William Chafin had allegedly sold the whole of the estate to Chambers and six colleagues. Chambers had, as he believed, bought the estate by an Indenture of Feoffment with Livery of Seizin. This was an ancient ceremony for the conveyance of freehold lands. Under an Act of Henry VIII every bargain and sale of freehold lands was required to be registered either in Westminster or in the county of the sale. The sale of Chettle in 1807 had not been registered and nor was the land freehold. *'Ingenious lawyers...discovered a means of evading this statute so that transfers of land again became secret, the bad effects of secrecy were experienced once more,'* wrote A L Smith of the eighteenth century.[100] (The first Land Registry Act was passed in 1862.) This sale had not been registered. It had been kept a private transaction between Chafin and Chambers while Chafin lived. It had been negotiated by Thomas Dashwood, Chafin's attorney and for many years land agent of Chettle. The deception was maintained by Chafin who continued to preside, or to hold court, as Lord of the Manor at the Court Baron. This was the forum where copyhold tenancies were arranged and the reciprocal obligations that went with them agreed. It was a manorial assembly of medieval origin that met for the transaction of business *'according to the custom of the Manor'* on a regular basis. The tenants came to pay homage to their lord and parish affairs were allocated. The maintenance of pathways, boundaries, ringing of pigs and impounding of stray cattle were amongst the matters attended to. The Court Baron was the administrative office of the estate.

It was important that the nature of the transaction to which Chettle

[100] H D Traill (Ed) *Social England* cf p215 1896 p119–120.

had been subjected was not revealed until after William's death. He was now an old man for whom change was anathema, and he had acted illegally. The area in which he lived was in turmoil with a distressed agricultural population spoiling for trouble at every attempt to modify customary rights, or at the introduction of any modernizing methods. A landlord from London, Abraham Henry Chambers, would not have been welcomed. So to preserve his last years in tranquillity and in good relations with the inhabitants of Chettle he retained all the outward behaviour customary to his position. William was seventy-six when this deal was done and an unspoken assumption was undoubtedly that the necessary charade would not have to be kept up for more than a few months. William, however, lived for another eleven years. They were years that put a severe strain on the patience of both joint manorial lords. A very elderly resident, Andrew Rideout, interviewed in 1902 by Edward W F Castleman (1870-1946) referred to Chambers as *'Squire Chambers'* so he was acknowledged by the inhabitants as the governor on the spot, not a distant London banker. Chambers was very proud of his role as Lord of the Manor and fought for years to retain it. But while Chafin was alive it was politic for him to keep in the background.

Chambers' colleagues in the acquisition of Chettle were four of his banking partners, together with Robert Frome, a Chafin relative who had been rector of Chettle from 1776 to 1782, and Elias Lane. The Lane family had been associated with Chettle for many years. John Lane had been steward for Thomas (4) in 1710. Elias himself had been a servant of William Chafin and became bailiff of the estate for Abraham Chambers. He died in 1834 at the age of sixty-eight and is buried in the churchyard. (His widow remarried, transferring his property to her second husband, as we shall see.)

Neither Chafin nor Chambers was above sharp practice, and they irritated one another. It was inevitable that they quarrelled about their relative rights and responsibilities. There were various fines that Chafin had to pay Chambers between 1807 and 1818 including one for £1400 for preventing his using, or having access to, the property.

The years from 1807 to 1818 were not harmonious, but worse was to follow.

By the end of 1818 the inhabitants of Chettle knew that they had a new Lord of the Manor. Chambers was settling into his position of country squire and attended the Court Manor of 1820 and 1824, receiving homage and arranging parish business. Thomas Dashwood was there as surveyor and Elias Lane as bailiff.

In September 1824 Chambers' banking business was in difficulty and he sought a loan from the Bank of England, providing Chettle as security. Chambers was proud of his status as Lord of the Manor and anxious that there should be no record of this mortgage arrangement. Mortgaging the family estate was behaviour incompatible with the landed gentry status to which he aspired. He was assured by the Bank of England's solicitors, Freshfield and Kaye, on 30 September 1824 that *'There will be no record of it as Dorset is not a Register County and when the money is repaid the mortgage will be returned to you and may be destroyed…'*[101] An *'ingenious lawyer'*, that is Dashwood, had indeed by-passed the legal registration requirement.

Five weeks later in November 1824, Chambers and Son went into liquidation, closed the doors of their bank and *'stopped payment'*. Banking practice was not well developed and many small lending banks got into difficulty. On 19 November a Commission of Bankruptcy was issued against them and five assignees were appointed to manage the affairs of A H Chambers. They were Richard Groom, Francis Bernasconi, Ralph Garrett, William Leonard and John Richardson. As the Bank of England held the deeds of Chettle these five men (or their replacements) became, in effect, Lord of the Manor and they are recorded as attending the Courts Baron from 1826 till 1846. Their interest in the estate extended only to its financial value. For the first time in its long history Chettle was at the mercy of men with no interest in the land or in the parish. Thomas Dashwood, lawyer of Sturminster Newton and land agent for Chettle was always present and would, by virtue of his local knowledge and expertise,

[101] Bank of England Archive, F 12/34.

have wielded disproportionate influence. Chambers had had the benefit of his estate for four years. He did some tree planting, appointed a gamekeeper and a rector, the Reverend John West, who was to make a big impression on the parish and the locality.

By the end of 1824 the Bank of England had on its hands one of the many lending banks that was failing. For security it had an estate in a condition of advanced disrepair; land upon which it depended was in the doldrums, and the working population of Dorset was mutinous. Freshfield and Kaye, the Bank of England's solicitors, were anxious to wash their hands of both Chambers and Chettle with all speed. In December 1824 they requested the map and survey of Chettle from the Governor of the Bank, *'our object being to sell the estate as soon as maybe.'*[102] They were to be sadly disappointed. Instead of selling Chettle, recouping the loan debt and closing the Chambers file they embarked upon years of legal wrangle. Seeming misunderstandings, delays and incompetence by the various legal firms involved, exacerbated the undoubted difficulties. The parish of Chettle was left to its own devices. The experienced farmers became the backbone of the community. As most of the agricultural labourers were illiterate rumour and anxiety prevailed while men in London disputed, for their own gain, over the disposal of the land upon which the parishioners depended.

The estate was auctioned in July 1826. According to the Castleman/Bourke family, the present owners, their forebear, William Castleman, bought it, but a dispute erupted over the title and aborted the sale. The dispute arose for two reasons. First, Chettle was still feudal property and was not therefore saleable. Secondly there were some Chafin relatives who might have been able to establish a claim to it. William Chafin had had two married sisters both of whom produced children. These matters had to be looked into.

Meanwhile Chambers had petitioned the Lord Chancellor appealing against the bankruptcy. *'I require you not to part with the possession of the title deeds of my estate at Chettle,'* he wrote.[103] He had

[102] op.cit
[103] op.cit

private resources, but the stronger ground for appeal was that he was owed money by John Symmons that would, if paid, enable him to repay the Bank of England and reclaim Chettle.

In 1822 Symmons had signed a Warrant of Attorney acknowledging a debt of £50,791.12s *'for so much money borrowed at the suit of Abraham Henry Chambers'.*[104] The assignees appointed to manage the affairs of the Chambers banking business wanted the Bank of England to *'issue a writ ... against the goods of Mr Symmons for the amount due ... to the Bankrupts'.* The Governor of the Bank of England would have none of this. He did not, he replied, *'expect... the powers of the Bank should be used against the property of Mr Symmons.'* He recommended that the assignees take the securities into their own hands. They did not. John Symmons, Gentleman of Knowle, was then over eighty years old, and not entirely in command of his affairs. The assignees were reluctant to tangle in this way with a frail old man whose faculties were crumbling.

Things rumbled on, as nineteenth-century legal cases were wont to do and Chambers had to wait till 1831 for his appeal to be heard. On June 24 the Lord High Chancellor, the Right Honourable Henry Baron Brougham and Vaux, pronounced that Chambers was *'duly found and declared bankrupt'.* Chambers went to a debtors' prison and John Symmons died a little while afterwards. The Bank of England claimed on Symmons' estate to offset the Chambers debt.

Two years later Symmons' son, Charles Augustus John Symmons brought a Bill of Complaint against the Bank of England. The Bank had taken considerably more from the Symmons estate than was owed by Chambers to the Bank. £6371.19s.11d due as interest on the sum taken in excess was *'to be paid on Saturday 1st February 1834 between 11 and 12 o'clock at the Office of the Chapel of the Rolls in Chancery Lane'.*[105]

Furthermore, the Master of the Rolls ordered the *'transfer by the Bank of England of the Securities in the Chettle Estate to the represen-*

[104] op. cit.
[105] B F P CHA/12.

tative of the late Mr John Symmons... for securing to them the Claims against Mr Chambers.[106]

John Swarbreck Gregory was the solicitor acting for Symmons, and the deeds of Chettle, sealed by the Bank of England, were duly transferred to him at his office at Messrs Adlington, Gregory and Faulkner, at number One Bedford Row. The firm still exists as Gregory, Rowcliffe and Milner and in the same house between Holborn and Chancery Lane. The deeds of Chettle were held, for the Symmons family, by the solicitors for the next thirteen years. The parishioners of Chettle were part of an area which has been described as suffering the *'most squalid and depressed living standards to be found in England'* at the time. They were powerless and had only the haziest idea of what the future might hold for them. After this settlement, unsuccessful attempts were made to sell Chettle in whole or in part. The estate did not emerge from this imbroglio for another thirteen turbulent years.

Chambers spent many years in a debtors' prison. His daughter wrote an impassioned letter to Sir John Reid, Bart. MP, Governor of the Bank of England in 1840, complaining that her father had been in prison for the past thirteen years, despite the fact that he could have paid the debt. She lists objections to imprisoning people of seventy, particularly emphasizing the risk of suicide. She prays that a *'Clause will be added to the English law and that I shall not continue the wretched agonized being I now am'*.[107]

Abraham Henry Chambers died in 1853, aged eighty-eight. He was then living at The Cottage, Park Place, Paddington – now just to the north of Westway, where the A40 brings its unending stream of traffic into London. He made his will in 1849 leaving his all to his son and daughter. He did not die a poor man but Chettle is not listed amongst his bequests, as he had so passionately hoped.

This episode in Chettle's story dramatizes the meeting of ancien regime with new money, of deep tradition of the land with urbanization: a microcosm of the travails of England, then occupying much

[106] B of E Archive, op.cit.
[107] B of E Archive, op.cit.

of the time and energy of the government. The immediate trigger for this protracted legal case was a bank failure, which could have been settled expeditiously. The delay was caused by the feudal status of the property that the Bank held as security. Sir Anthony Sturt and his son Humphrey had taken twenty years in the mid eighteenth century to get the necessary Acts of Parliament through to change Chafin lands from feudal to allodial in order that the debts incurred by George Chafin (2) could be paid. Landowners dominated the legislature until the Reform Act of 1832 and the majority were not disposed to consider changes to their domain. Legislation, which ushered in the end of feudal tenancies, was under discussion at the time that this case was in process. The first Copyhold Act was passed in 1841, possibly informed if not inspired by the Chettle proceedings.

After twenty years of legal argument the ancien regime had most of the winnings. William Chafin had illegally bought himself eleven years of financial benefit. The Symmons family (Gentleman of Knowle) held the deeds of the Chettle Estate. Abraham Henry Chambers had lost the property and spent several years in prison. Overtly he was punished for mismanaging his banking business. His real offence was his affront to feudal interests and the great landlords of England who still had a near monopoly of power. He was disciplined for his hubris in bringing his money to breach the ancient laws of feudal inheritance and to expect homage from the venerable institution of the Court Baron.

Further afield in Dorset, beyond the disorder and uncertainty of this abused estate reviving spirits were emerging. Where change had overwhelmed the Chafins, for the new men it provided risk-fraught opportunities for innovation, experiment and establishing new paths to advancement. A yeoman farmer of Hinton St Mary, William Castleman (1) changed his age-old family calling and became a land agent. His son William (2) trained as a lawyer and started a local lending bank to which William Chafin might have turned. To have used a local bank would have exposed the Reverend William Chafin to the risk of embarrassing revelations about the state of his affairs. He was no doubt proud of his long family history and Castleman was a newly rising professional from a yeoman background. Class sensitivities in 1807 were acute, and bankers were certainly not considered gentlemen. Castleman in any case, acutely aware of local conditions, may have been more cautious than Chambers in his dealings with William Chafin. Castleman was one of a band of local rising stars to whom we must now look for the fashioning of new conditions, and the revival of hope in the locality and at Chettle in particular.

TWELVE

William Castleman (1) and (2)

For many years gentlemen stewards had managed the Chettle estate. Richard Moore, born about 1750, a trained attorney with a legal practice in Sturminster Newton Castle had come to Chettle as a young man in 1773. George Chafin (2) had then been Lord of the Manor for seven years. The estate was not in good shape when he took it over and he had done nothing to improve it. He had not administered his father's will. His mother's family the Sturts, and his brother William, his sisters and their husbands agitated constantly about the state of affairs at Chettle. Richard Moore was a great help and when he retired in 1811 his younger partner Thomas Dashwood took over and managed things in William's last years, throughout the time of Abraham Chambers and his bankruptcy until 1847.

Moore and Dashwood of Sturminster Newton were exemplars of the specialized profession of land agent or steward that had grown up in the eighteenth century. It had evolved from the manorial reeve who had been responsible for the day-to-day running of the feudal estate. Geoffrey Chaucer's reeve of the fourteenth century was an old carpenter and 'a churl'. The reeve was a higher servant usually elected by the villagers from amongst their own number. By the eighteenth century many stewards were independent men of good education, and appointed by the landlord. They made regular inspections of their employers' land, buildings, walls, drainage and timber, dealt with complaints from tenants and neighbours, negotiated buying and selling and arranged leases. They often had some legal training.

The employers of this new professional class were sometimes absent, incompetent or not particularly interested in the task of land management that they had inherited. In such circumstances the steward often had not only to execute policy, but also to make it on behalf of the landlord. It was a powerful and influential position, with little except the personal integrity of the steward to ensure the landlord's best interests. Though of higher social status than Chaucer's reeve, the popular reputation of the nineteenth-century land agent bore close resemblance to the description of his forbear in *The Canterbury Tales.*

'No auditor could gain a point on him…
Feared like the plague he was by those beneath;
He had a lovely dwelling on a heath
Shadowed in green by trees above the sward.
A better hand at bargains than his lord
He had grown rich and had a store of treasure
Well tucked away, yet out it came to pleasure
His lord with subtle loan…'[108]

Moore and Dashwood between them supervised the affairs of Chettle for seventy-four years from 1773–1847. William Chafin made them executors of his will. To Dashwood fell the task of mollifying the disinherited Chafin relatives and of holding Chettle together through three decades of turmoil. William Chafin had left two nieces an annuity of £400 each, but as he had secretly sold all his property there was nothing available with which to meet these bequests. In March 1820 Dashwood negotiated an agreement with Chambers to pay them. When Chambers became bankrupt in 1825 Thomas Dashwood effectively ran the estate on behalf of the assignees appointed by the Commission in Bankruptcy.

Moore and Dashwood's seventy-four years at Chettle were some of the most difficult in the history of British agriculture. The loss of

[108] Geoffrey Chaucer *The Canterbury Tales* translated into modern English by Neville Coghill Penguin 1951.

the American colonies in 1783 and the French Revolution six years later disrupted trade and commerce, changing the patterns of demand for homegrown food. Between 1815 and 1846 the question of agricultural protection divided England. The growth of industrial towns producing textiles, mainly in the north of England, depressed the woollen industry in Dorset. The new machinery coming into use was the target of the Luddites who perceived it as the cause of their unemployment and distress. Luddite behaviour had spread to agricultural districts and machinery introduced to increase production was broken up. The Corn Laws, introduced after the Napoleonic Wars, kept the price of corn up for the landlords. It also kept the price of bread up for labourers. The resulting hardship was the cause of much of the disturbance in Dorset. For almost exactly the same period that Moore and Dashwood held sway at Chettle, the Castlemans, of Hinton St Mary and Wimborne Minster, who were to become so important to the story of Chettle, were stewards of the much larger Dorset and Somerset estate of Lord Uxbridge.[109] The William Castlemans, father and son, followed by Henry and Edward of the third generation, managed the Dorset and Somerset part of Lord Uxbridge's very large property from 1781 till 1854.[110]

Castlemans had been in Hinton St Mary and adjacent villages for at least as long as the Chafins had owned Chettle: steady prosperous yeomen copyholders on the large Freke estate.[111] Thomas Castleman, husbandman of Hinton St Mary, who died in 1584, was a prosperous working farmer. Samuel Castleman, a descendant of Thomas, was a blacksmith who died in 1653. Both were men of some substance with

[109] Sir Henry William Paget (1768-1854) became Lord Uxbridge on his father's death and was created Marquis of Anglesey in 1815. To avoid confusion he is referred to as Lord Uxbridge throughout.
[110] The managerial role on several of the large estates in the area was an important one. One of the Ashley Coopers managed Viscount Cranborne's property. Baker, the agent for Lord Portman has left a permanent mark on London with Baker Street running from Portman Square to Regent's Park and intersected by Blandford Street, Dorset Street, and Melcombe Street.
[111] Copyhold was a feudal tenancy, usually for a period of two or three 'lives' arranged at the Court Baron and recorded in the manorial roll. See Chapter 13.

property and money to leave to friends and relatives. A substantial farmhouse of Castleman's, built in 1685, is still inhabited today. There are memorial tablets in the church porch commemorating two branches of the eighteenth-century family and another memorializing William (1), his wife Anne and their son James who died in infancy. This was erected by their surviving son William (2). These memorials are simple and undecorated signifying a respected and useful role in the village but without any pretension to grandeur.

The yeomanry had a reputation for hardworking reliability and resourcefulness and they were unfettered by the gentlemanly prohibition against working with their hands. The Castlemans were model yeomen. During the seventeenth and eighteenth centuries they were important people in the village, subordinate with the rector only to their landlord. By the mid seventeenth century the men in the family probably had access to an education. A school had existed at Sherborne eight miles away, attached to the monastery, since the fifteenth century and had been re-opened as a Protestant establishment in 1550 in the time of Edward VI. There was also the sixteenth-century Queen Elizabeth Grammar School at Wimborne. Literacy had been spreading since the introduction of the printing press to England in 1472 though it was slow to find its way into rural areas. As dignitaries in the parish the Castlemans were conscious of the need to be able to keep records and accounts. Their ability in this respect would have been of benefit to the Lord of the Manor who probably encouraged, perhaps subsidized, an education for the boys.

The Frekes, Lords of the Manor at Hinton St Mary[112] and the Castlemans are both commemorated in the church, so they worshipped together and would have known each other well. Large landowners relied upon local men to ensure the smooth running of the parishes within their estates. The rector and the yeoman farmer were indispensable village dignitaries, the backbone of the parish

---

[112] The Freke estate passed by marriage to George Pitt, and eventually became part of the Pitt Rivers estate.

vestry administering the Poor Rate,[113] maintaining law and order and generally leaders of their community.

In 1780 Lord Uxbridge needed an additional agent to manage part of his Dorset and Somerset estate that he had just inherited. Some of this estate had been in Chafin hands before they were obliged to sell. It was property that the Uxbridge family did not need and had little interest in. *'I know nothing of the locality,'* his heir wrote forty-five years after the family had inherited. Lord Uxbridge owned about eighty thousand acres in Staffordshire, London and North Wales (where he made his home). Part of his newly acquired property surrounded Hinton St Mary and another part rather neatly encircled Chettle. Lord Uxbridge was distantly related to the Freke family, and it is likely that he consulted a local contact about an area with which he was unfamiliar. A yeoman farmer, trusty, reliable and literate, had the necessary qualities and perhaps Freke was pleased to recommend an elderly tenant who was, like all the agricultural community, facing hard times. At the age of sixty-six William Castleman (1) took on new work and responsibility and became the steward of 1314 acres of Uxbridge property at Stalbridge Weston, which was about six miles distant from his home. At just this time fifteen miles due east of Stalbridge Weston, the impoverished William Chafin of Chettle was looking fixedly backward to a mirage, pondering only the means of his own pleasurable survival.

William Castleman (1) had not married until 1764 when he was fifty. His wife Anne Vining was thirteen years younger. Their one surviving child William (2), born in 1766, was fourteen when his father embarked on his second career as a steward. It was a precarious time for tenant farmers, but a steward's salary was predictable and often quite generous. Large landowners were enclosing land and using machinery to maximize productivity. Tenant farmers were therefore in jeopardy. It is quite possible that William Castleman (1)'s new job was negotiated in exchange for his agreement to allow his tenancy on the Freke estate to lapse. A steward for the Stalbridge Weston property

[113] The Elizabethan Poor Law of 1601 required each parish to provide for its indigent parishioners in their own homes by raising a rate on the land of the parish.

had to keep accounts, record tenancy agreements, and negotiate sales of farm produce. William (1)'s attainments enabled him to appreciate the world beyond his immediate boundaries. He aspired to a higher standard of life for his only son. He and his family had been tenant farmers for generations but he saw that the old ways were going and that new paths to earning a living had to be explored. His is a small part in the story of Chettle, but he broke the age-old direct dependence on the soil. At the age of sixty-six he became an agent and was paid a salary by Lord Uxbridge. He paved the way for his son William (2) to become an independent professional man and for his grandson Edward to become the owner of Chettle.

As elderly parents William Castleman (1) and Anne doted upon young William (2) and provided every opportunity for him to fulfil their ambitions. In due time he came to have plenty of his own. His acute intelligence was combined with a resolute determination. Generations of practical experience of the many tasks of farming were bred in him. Ploughing and tilling, milking and sheep shearing as well as the whims and cruelties of nature were instinctively understood, as were man's efforts to tame them and maintain control. Family experience as a member of the parish vestry, the administrative hub of the village, required thought for the elderly, the poor and the children, as well as for the better off who were paying the poor rate and the tithe. Balancing the books was an important function of the parish vestry. The intimate though respectful association with one of the great landowning families provided a wider national, perhaps international perspective. William Castleman (2) was well blessed in his modest but varied, kindly and stimulating background.

He never took over the farm. As he was an only child, a good education for him was well within reach. William (2) was able to train as a lawyer. He became a prosperous and wealthy nineteenth-century lawyer, banker, land agent and landowner. He was the local coroner for many years, clerk to an Enclosure Commission, a school governor, a member of the Corporation of Wimborne Minister and had a surreptitious interest in smuggling.

In 1789, when he was twenty-three he married Mary Dean in

Wimborne Minster and moved from Hinton St Mary. He and Mary established themselves in Wimborne where he started in practice as an attorney. An announcement appeared in the Salisbury and Winchester Journal on 16 June 1792 to the effect that *'Messrs Dean and Castleman are dealing with conveyancing.'*

His father died in the same year, after twelve years as steward. Lord Uxbridge then made several changes of staff on his Dorset and Somerset estate but William (2) was concentrating on his legal business and did not immediately take over from his father. He was employed initially as an occasional legal consultant for Lord Uxbridge.

William (2) commissioned Jeffry Wyatt[114] to design Allendale House that became the family home in Wimborne. Jeffry Wyatt had worked with his uncle James Wyatt on the restoration of Hereford, Lichfield, Lincoln and Salisbury Cathedrals. Jeffry Wyatt built additions to Sidney Sussex College, Cambridge and was responsible for the restoration of Windsor Castle. William (2), not yet thirty years old was aiming high.

By 1800 William (2), attorney, aged thirty-four had many interests. He had a growing family and was developing his legal practice in Wimborne. He was founder-partner in the Christchurch, Wimborne and Ringwood Bank and maintained an interest in the thousands of acres of agricultural and residential property in Somerset and Dorset where his father had first ventured to a new career. He was involved in the management of the Kingston Lacey estate just to the north of Wimborne Minster and he had a finger in many local pies.

Chettle with its legal and financial problems was located within William Castleman (2)'s geographical sphere of interest. There were several reasons why his attention was increasingly drawn to the place. By 1800 it was plain to the entire neighbourhood that Chettle was going downhill, that William Chafin was getting old and had no interest in maintaining his family inheritance and that he had no direct heir. Gossip and rumour, even possibly hard fact related over the dinner tables of Dorset by Thomas Dashwood, increased the

---

[114] He was knighted in 1828 when he became Sir Jeffry Wyatville (1766–1840).

fascination that Chettle had for the ambitious and energetic William Castleman (2). He was acquiring all the trappings of worldly success that the Chafins had been shedding. William Castleman (2) was building a reputation for sound judgement and careful hard work; his coffers and the nursery at Allendale House were both filling up.

His first child, William (3) was born in 1790 at Hinton St Mary in the house where he, William (2) had been born twenty-four years earlier and his father William (1) fifty-two years before that. The child's baptism in the village was a family and village event. This was the only grandchild that William (1) lived to see as he died in 1792. There were nine more children, all born at Allendale House and baptized in Wimborne Minster. Four died before they were five years old, and three when they were about twenty.

William (2), despite several attempts, never acquired Chettle but he built up resources and cultivated opportunities that enabled his eldest surviving son Edward to become the freehold owner of the estate after his death. His envious ghost, if such exists, must surely haunt the fields and woods around the village, and we must digress for a few pages to consider the character and spleen of this remarkable man who was pivotal to nineteenth-century Chettle.

The legal practice that William (2) established was to become the mainstay of the family. Several mutations notwithstanding, it exists to this day as Meesons of Ringwood. His legal work brought clients to his door who needed loan capital for development projects in local enterprises – agriculture, shipping and trade. Their needs inspired his second venture. In 1800 with partners William Dean and George Adams he set up the Christchurch, Wimborne and Ringwood Bank. Dean was thirty years older than Castleman and had been a surgeon. As senior partner he probably contributed the larger share of capital. Castleman however provided invaluable legal advice.

At the beginning of the nineteenth century banking was not a well established, nor a properly regulated practice. There was increasing need for loan capital in the area to finance agricultural improvements, but the principles of its administration had not been formulated.

Everyone was learning as they went. Land was being enclosed, much voluntarily, but by legislative fiat where local agreement failed. The resulting enclosures created our modern field system in place of common land and the medieval ridge and furrow strip system that had lasted for a millennium. The landowning beneficiaries of enclosure needed capital to plant hedges and trees, to ditch, make gates, drain their land and buy machinery. With the anticipation of increasing production by say 10% they could afford to borrow from a local bank at 5%. The banking and finance system depended on human judgement in a relatively novel field. Landowners and farmers were stepping away from traditional practice, innovating in ways that were often quite experimental. Land and labour were recognized as the *honest* essentials for making a living. The contribution of capital, lent at interest, though no longer either criminal or sinful as it had been until the early eighteenth century, was neither well understood nor were its practitioners entirely trusted; with good reason. Circulation banks issued paper money to represent the gold coin deposited with them. Each piece of paper was a *Promise to Pay*, that is, to return the gold coin, and worked well only so long as lenders had confidence that there was enough gold coin available in the vaults should they need to call upon it. Bankers had little to guide them as to the safe relationship between their gold deposit and the amount of paper promises they could make. The value of the harvest, ever subject to unpredictable weather conditions, disease and insects was the crucial element in the equation. Miscalculations by both borrower and lender were inevitable and the early part of the nineteenth century saw many bank failures.

William (2) had a rare combination of attributes that gave him advantages in this risky field. He had a deep understanding of the land and its potential. The community of East Dorset was small enough for him to know both lenders and borrowers personally and he had a discerning eye for incipient success or failure. His weighing up was seldom found wanting and he had a realistic confidence in his own judgement. He was an astute man of business in the constantly shifting conditions that prevailed.

William Dean, the senior partner of the Christchurch, Wimborne and Ringwood bank, had purchased over a thousand acres of land at a little over one pound an acre as a result of the Enclosure Commission's allotment of land upon which part of Bournemouth now stands. His daughter, another Mary Dean, married William Clapcott. Dean died in 1810 and left his share capital and interest in the bank to his son-in-law, William Clapcott.[115] All went smoothly for eight years and then William Castleman (2) withdrew his capital and resigned from the bank in 1818, the year that the Reverend William Chafin of Chettle died.

Bruce writes that disagreements over banking practice between Castleman and Clapcott lay behind this,[116] but William Castleman (2) had had his eye on the dying Chafin and the Chettle property and was in readiness to purchase if the opportunity arose. By September 1818 Abraham Henry Chambers was revealed as the new owner of Chettle. Castleman had an alternative scheme for applying his capital. He lent it to William Clapcott and this loan was secured on property belonging to Mary, Clapcott's wife. By 1827 Clapcott owed Castleman £10,400 and was being pressed for repayment. Bruce writes '*Castleman played a seemingly unscrupulous role*'[117] in this loan. There was not much chance that the loan would be repaid but Clapcott was rash and imprudent in the management of his affairs, and also in the management of his wife's property, over which, from the day of her marriage, she had no jurisdiction. Castleman had perhaps hoped to acquire Mary Clapcott's property that secured the loan, but William Clapcott avoided this by re-mortgaging his property to Samuel Bignold, a Norwich banker and lawyer and also Chairman of the Norwich Union insurance company. The £10,400 was returned to the Castleman coffers. William Castleman (2) was certainly acquiring a portfolio of property and had made a few

---

[115] William Castleman (2) married a Mary Dean. William Clapcott married another Mary Dean whose father was partner in the Christchurch, Ringwood and Wimborne Bank. The forbears of William Castleman (2)'s wife have not been traced.
[116] George Bruce op.cit. p56.
[117] George Bruce op.cit.

unsuccessful attempts to get Chettle included in it. It is doubtful whether he was motivated by anything more than a straightforward desire to exchange money for property at the time. His father William Castleman (1) had been a young man, a copyholder of Thomas Freke, relative and fellow Lord of the Manor to the Chafins at the time of their fall. The lure of the cachet of becoming Lord of the Manor in their place cannot be discounted, but it was not to be.

William and Mary Castleman were then, in 1826, both sixty-one, and their three remaining sons, all destined to be lawyers, were twenty-seven, twenty-one and nineteen, and the family legal practice seemed secure. William (2) had been running a banking business for ten years and although he had withdrawn from the firm, he continued to make extensive personal loans at interest throughout his life. His third important professional pursuit, the management of the Uxbridge estate had been gathering momentum. After his father's death in 1792, he had become legal adviser for the Somerset and Dorset estate. There were many difficulties. Lord Uxbridge and his son Lord Paget[118] had little interest in their Somerset and Dorset property, above the fact that Milborne Port, a Rotten Borough, provided a convenient vehicle whereby Paget became a Member of Parliament. They left the management of the land, which so intimately affected the population, to a succession of agents two of whom were distinctly crooked. Robert James, agent from 1803–1809 let land illegally which led to every tenant in Manston, Stalbridge, Marnhull and Henstridge being turned out.[119] He was followed by George Cox who over a five to six year period defrauded the estate of between £6–7,000, which was about ten percent of the entire Uxbridge income. Ownership of land was a sine qua non to political power, and in this instance it led to the land being poorly managed and the

[118] Paget, who became 2nd Earl of Uxbridge on his father's death, was described by Richard Holmes in his biography of Wellington 2003 as 'probably the best cavalry officer in the army'. He was Wellington's second in command at Waterloo where he famously lost a leg.
[119] H Kaines Diary of a Dorset Farmer Dorset Year Book 1928.

borough of Milborne Port being exploited. The political fabric of the early nineteenth century was shabby and outdated.

William Castleman (2) was brought in initially to sort out accounts in preparation for a Chancery Suit against George Cox, the fraudulent agent, in 1814. In that same year he took on the management of the Dorset and Somerset estate as principal agent and stayed until he died thirty years later. The day-to-day running of the law firm in Wimborne could be left to colleagues and subordinates. His second son (another William – the firstborn died in infancy) coming up to twenty years old was assisting him. Nevertheless it was a formidable undertaking.

He followed two unsatisfactory agents, estate records were in disarray, and he was often obliged to make far-reaching decisions with little opportunity to confer with his employer. John Sanderson, followed by Thomas Beer were the principal agents for the entirety of the Uxbridge property in Wales, Staffordshire and London and in them he found supportive, if sometimes critical, senior colleagues.

In 1815 the Battle of Waterloo, at which Lord Uxbridge lost a leg, finally brought Napoleon's ambitions to an end. The troubles that had been mounting in agriculture were more intractable; distress and unrest increased in the post war period. *'Throughout the nineteenth century the Dorset agricultural labourer was associated with about the most squalid and depressed living standards to be found in England, and the most embittered class relations.'*[120] The Castleman family were personally removed from the pains and privations, but they could not be oblivious to them. Coroners' Court records of the period show how precarious agricultural life was. A common ending was to be *'accidentally run over by a wagon'; 'killed by a blow from the arm of a threshing machine'* or *'thrown from a cart and killed'*, and these sudden deaths occasioned little comment. Self-hangings and drownings constituted part of the retinue of human despair that came William Castleman (2)'s way when he sat as coroner. He investigated *'unnatural, sudden or suspicious death'* as had been the coroner's duty

---

[120] K D M Snell *Annals of the Labouring Poor: Social Change and Agrarian England 1660–1900*. Cambridge 1985 p387.

since 1194, and for which the sole qualification was to be a landholder. In December 1815 his own young son William died just before his twenty-first birthday.

The adversities that faced William Castleman (2) nourished the strengths within him. In his forty-eight years he had edged his way upward through the formidable class demarcations of the time, from son of a respectable yeoman farmer to become legal adviser, and to some extent confidant, to one of the great aristocrats of the nation. Castleman was no Jude the Obscure, hammering frustratedly on the closed doors of privilege, nor did he fall into the trap where Abraham Henry Chambers had come to grief, of affronting landed interests with new money. He knew the landed elite too well. He was a rare phenomenon of early nineteenth-century England who knew from practical daily experience the life patterns, attitudes and expectations of the very rich and of the very poor. He neither doffed his cap to one, nor patronized the other, but perceived their dilemmas in the setting of the rapid changes that were taking place. Nor was he slow to pick out, from this kaleidoscopic scene, opportunities for the betterment of himself and his family. He shared with many in England at the time a foreboding that revolution on the recent model of France was threatening, and this coloured his response to overtly destructive and unruly behaviour. The quiet management of risqué opportunities was however something of which he approved and practised.

A letter from William Castleman (2) to John Sanderson in October 1826 gives a picture of the local difficulties.

'Lord Anglesey's [Uxbridge] audit commences next Wednesday. The result I fear will be bad. The wheat crop has been generally good, but the [? hand] crops have almost universally failed. The drought during the summer has much reduced the Grazier's as well as the Dairyman's profits. Wool can only be sold at ruinous prices to the Grower. Store sheep and lambs by sale of which the Corn farmers in this neighbourhood generally pay the Lady day rents have been sold at upwards of 30 percent less than last year and the Poors (sic) Rates are increasing.

The turnip crop has generally failed and the Crop of hay as well as of Straw has been very short. The manufacturing Districts in Somersetshire have not yet shown any sign of revival. This is as gloomy a statement as the greatest enemies of the country could wish for. I forbear to mention the political causes which seem to me to have contributed to this state of distress – those arising from the State of the seasons are beyond our control.

I have had for several years but very little new building and not any considerable repairs on the Estates under my Agency. [*We have*] kept some carpenters constantly employed at weekly wages in general repairs … I believe this was a good plan, not that I think much was saved to his Lordship by it, but it fixed the persons thus employed who were votes completely in his L'ship's interest.'[121]

One of the major political causes of distress to which Castleman alludes was the Corn Laws, and his '*forbearance*' was because the topic was so intensely divisive. In 1844 a meeting was called in Sturminster Newton '*of the Tenantry…to counteract the RUINOUS INTENTIONS of the Anti-Corn Law League.*' Twenty-nine names from sixteen villages of Lord Uxbridge's estate subscribed. Castleman wrote to the main agent, '*Have the goodness to inform me whether it is his L'ships wish to promote the object which the subscribers have in view?*' William Castleman, in the last year of his life was feeling more acutely than ever before his divided loyalties. The Corn Laws periodically starved the poor and raised the spectre of revolution. Their repeal would signal the end of the great agricultural enterprise of England. The juggernaut of industrialization and population growth moved glacially and irresistibly along forcing the government to a decision. It came a year after William's death when the Corn Laws were repealed.

William Castleman's stewardship of the thousands of acres of Uxbridge land gave him unparalleled opportunities for enhancing his intelligence about Chettle and the various illegal enterprises that

[121] DRO D/ANG/B5/61.

latticed the Cranborne Chase. Farnham, Sixpenny Handley and Gussage St Michael were within the Uxbridge property and all within a ten-minute horse ride from Chettle. Sixpenny Handley was quite closely associated with Chettle. They had often shared the same vicar and had boundaries in common.

Numerous recorded disturbances took place at Sixpenny Handley, and were therefore within the purview of William Castleman (2). Agricultural machinery was destroyed, a boy was sentenced to three months in prison and *'to be privately whipped twice'* for fire setting. For years the entire population seemed to be constantly spoiling for trouble and riots were sparked at any hint of infringement of customary rights. In 1819 Castleman and Lord Rivers' agent forbade their tenants their annual hunt because it was the day of the Manorial Court (Court Baron) at Sixpenny Handley.[122] Riots followed, demonstrating that disruptive restlessness was not the monopoly of the landless labourer and had spread to the better off of the parish. A man called Adams of Sixpenny Handley was imprisoned for six months for *'shrouding'*[123] a tree. Castleman wrote to Lord Uxbridge recommending that he be released after a month as he had a wife and four small children. Adams' family would inevitably have become a charge on the Poor Rate, which was raised from the landowners and farmers. Castleman's experience with the parish vestry of Hinton St Mary had taught him the political necessity of minimizing this charge, so his motives may not have been entirely benevolent, but this event exemplifies the frequently observed difference between Castleman's austere legalistic public face and his seemingly more considerate and constructive private activity that arose from his appreciation of both sides.

There are a few allusions to William Castleman's lack of straightforwardness. John Lowe, a fellow attorney who worked on the Dorset and Somerset estate wrote on one occasion that Castleman worked more for his own benefit than for his lordship's. John Sanderson, Uxbridge's principal agent, having suffered two untrustworthy

[122] DRO D/ANG/B5/25.
[123] i.e. destroying the roots.

agents (James and Cox) at the Dorset and Somerset property was particularly vigilant over discrepancies or careless accounting. Castleman did not escape criticism either from Sanderson or the tenants. One anonymous source described him as *'worse than Bo...te'* (Bonaparte) and another recommended that the exorbitant salaries of agents would be better in the pockets of distressed tenant farmers. William Castleman (2) was the recipient of letters from *'Captain Swing'* the leader of a seditious organization that had national ramifications. From Sixpenny Handley he wrote threatening to *'burn his house down, blow out his brains'* etc. But Castleman stood resolute.

Castleman publicly affected a tough line with tenants. Small tenant farmers often found it difficult to raise the necessary capital for land improvements, and were therefore at a disadvantage in the market place and were unable to pay their rents. They sometimes absconded taking their stock with them. Castleman took the role of uncompromising agent for his landlord, and did his utmost to seize their property as compensation. Behind the scenes however he showed himself fully aware that agricultural failure was a structural problem not a personal defect. He advised John Sanderson that distraining goods was a *'greater evil than submitting to the accumulation of arrears.'*[124] Uxbridge however was ambivalent: *'I very much distrust my Dorset and Somerset tenantry ... If I could separate the unfortunate from the designing I should be ready to make sacrifices, but I am sore by having been plundered and tormented,'* he wrote.[125] Distinguishing between the deserving and undeserving poor, between the sturdy beggar and the genuinely afflicted, is a ubiquitous and ageless problem. And to make matters worse Uxbridge had had two untrustworthy agents. Nevertheless Castleman wrote in 1844, *'The rents have been better paid than I expected. Crops of corn very deficient and this, added to the decrease in the value of Dairy goods has caused several and severe losses. I know from the Marquis of Anglesey's [Lord Uxbridge's] universal kind and generous feeling towards his tenantry that I shall not be censured for extending indulgences.'*

[124] DRO D/ANG EC 1815.
[125] DRO D/ANG EC 1815.

As a liaison between landlord and tenant the steward was inevitably the butt for criticisms each had of the other. Castleman often had to make decisions under considerable provocation and his lordship's opinion, although fully and carefully given in writing, was never available promptly. Castleman was in a vulnerable position. He was undoubtedly ambitious for himself and his family. The decisions he was often called upon to make had far-reaching implications. He never dissociated himself from the agricultural workers of the area, though his education, his responsibilities and his successes put him at a considerable social distance.

In 1830 serious rioting was spreading. As yet there was no police force. Special constables, recruited ad hoc from the upper echelons of the parish – the tenant farmers, tradesmen – usually handled local troubles. Hardship pinched very keenly in small agricultural villages and in several, men were refusing to be sworn in as constable. They were unwilling to come to the defence of the landowners by raising their hands against impoverished neighbours. An anonymous writer pleaded with Lord Uxbridge to *'lower ... rents...let your steward immediately summon your tenants and cause the proper enquiry as to what they may with justice require.'*[126] Lord Melbourne, Home Secretary in Grey's Whig Cabinet wrote to Uxbridge, who was about to be installed as Governor of Ireland, asking *'Is there nobody you could send down to rally your tenants ?'*[127] Uxbridge sent his eldest son who knew nothing of the locality. He met a group of tenants in Milborne Port, on 29 November 1830, provided refreshment of bread and cheese and beer, bells were rung and the band played and he departed, leaving Castleman to take the brunt. Castleman was absolutely set against any concession to rebellious labourers. *'Marauders should be put down or we shall very shortly have them for our masters,'* he wrote,[128] reflecting the widespread anxiety that England was in danger of following France into revolution. Facing an angry crowd and taking the testament in his hand he took the oath and was sworn in

[126] DRO D/ANG/EC 1830 3.
[127] DRO D/ANG EC 1830 2.
[128] DRO D/ANG EC 1830 2.

as a special constable saying that he did not wish to involve others in personal danger that he was unwilling to face himself. This persuaded all but a few to enlist as law enforcers. They were provided with staves, there was some talk of training and uniform and the nearest troop of Lancers at Blandford was alerted. In December 1830 seven men were arrested in Stalbridge. They were bound over to keep the peace: a remarkably lenient disposal. George Eavis from Henstridge, just over the border in Somerset was transported for seven years for destroying a threshing machine. A week later Castleman met some of the men involved in the disturbance and then left for a meeting at Uxbridge House in London. No record of the meeting has been found, though what followed is clear. When William Castleman (2) returned to the business of the Uxbridge estate, farm rents were reduced, employment was stimulated through improvement schemes of drainage, hedging, ditching, road laying, repair of buildings and the planting of oak and elm saplings. Possibilities for the employment of women and girls at the local glove factory were explored and Castleman wrote of *the necessity of purchasing Hennings glove factory.*[129] This was not achieved until 1836 and may have been helped by the marriage of Martha Jane Henning to William's son Charles in 1832.

A scheme for improving labourers' accommodation on the estate went into operation quite quickly. A group of ten houses with an acre of land attached was built in Stalbridge, at the cost of £1065 5s 1d.[130] *'They have gardens to each giving an average of 49 perches to each. The total ground occupied being about 3 acres 0 p 35 rods.'* The first of these houses was rented on 5 November 1832. The total rent in 1838 was £138 18s 2d. The declared intention was to continue the building programme if this should be a success. The immediate criterion of success was the restoration of *'peace and tranquillity.'*

William Castleman (2) was kept extremely busy after the riots, organizing men into employment and getting plans for drainage, planting and land improvements. Revised tenancy agreements had

[129] DRO D/ANG/B5/36.
[130] DRO D/ANG/B5/61.

to be made and all would have absorbed hours of work.

A few years later Henry Castleman wrote on behalf of his father to Thomas Beer, then Uxbridge's main agent, reporting on the result of '...*the allotment system which has been in operation for some time...with the greatest benefit to the Poor. In these numerous lettings (the rent of which considerably exceeds per acre what would be paid for the same land if let as part of a farm). You have seen by the accounts that scarcely a farthing is ever lost, but the rent is paid with thankfulness on the day appointed and the holdings, though trifling find some employment for the agricultural population and prevent them from spending their time and money at the Beershops. There is some trouble in first setting out the land and from the great number of tenants it takes some time to collect the rents and keep the accounts but this my father does not regard* [does not mind], *the benefits to both parties being so obvious.'*[131] William Castleman (2) was of that small minority who believed that labourers, given the opportunity for productive work would take it in preference to rioting and destructive behavour.

The Uxbridge property that Castleman was looking after encircled Chettle, which was at this time in the hands of the Bank of England. No record of riot or disturbance at Chettle has been found. The population was so small that any insurgent would have made more impact by joining with a larger village. Castleman was not only courageous in stepping forward as special constable, he was resourceful and innovative in arranging to meet and discuss the event with the rioters when tempers had cooled. The prevailing fear of the time had initiated repressive legislation and sentences were often cruel. The fairly typical response of the governing class was not to listen but to flog and transport. That seven men involved in the Stalbridge riot were bound over to keep the peace (that is, freed on condition that they cause no more trouble) is nothing short of astonishing. The scheme for improvement that was agreed at Uxbridge House depended on an intimate knowledge of local conditions, which only Castleman could have possessed. It is to him that the coherent plan

[131] DRO D/ANG/B5/61.

144

for investment and stimulation of employment must be attributed. A week before the riot there had been a vestry meeting in Wimborne where it was decided that *'men out of employment to be sent to Hinton Moor and Pills Moor to drain and improve ... William Castleman to advance money to the overseer.'* [132] A year later Castleman was *'compelling...tenants to contribute to this necessary work'* [by raising their rents] and urging others to do likewise. *'In considering this subject you will not treat it merely* as pounds shillings and pence,'[133] he wrote. *'You will not throw out of your consideration the fact that the whole of the Agricultural population of this neighbourhood was ... in a state very little short of riot.'* William Castleman had handled the ugly situation competently and had instituted a private taxation system for the relief of the poor, which the more affluent paid without demur appreciating what he had achieved.

In 1822 Lord Uxbridge was seeking loans. Castleman did much of the negotiating and by 1824 had arranged loans amounting to £34,750. After Castleman's death in 1844 his estate lists the Marquis of Anglesey (Lord Uxbridge) as the largest of twenty-five debtors. He owed the Castleman estate £9,600.

William did knowingly take risks when he lent his own money, but made careful assessment of the borrowers' reliability. They were recorded as Good, Doubtful or Bad debts. Lord Uxbridge was never other than Good. Lord Ashley (Shaftesbury) was assessed as Bad.[134] He lived at Wimborne St Giles, eight miles from Wimborne, so perhaps his request for a loan was hard to refuse. Castleman, son of a tenant farmer, had been lending his own money to two of the great landlords of England, both with estates of thousands of acres.

There is no doubt that Castleman derived benefits from the Parliamentary enclosures of common land that were taking place. The Commissioners for an area decided what land should be taken out of

---

[132] DRO S 235/C/12.
[133] Castleman claimed £14 1s 3d from Sherborne School. The Governors, who had never been consulted, 'cannot, nor will not object to repay.' They were only too grateful that an explosive situation had been so well handled.
[134] ORO PAR/17/9/F1/1.

common use for enclosure. They could then arrange for its sale. John Wickens Esq. was appointed Commissioner for Enclosures at Corfe Mullen, two miles from Wimborne in 1807. Notice of the first meeting to be held at the King's Head, Wimborne was placed in the Salisbury Journal and on the Corfe Mullen parish church door. Mr William Castleman, Attorney at Law was appointed Clerk to the Commissioner and Messrs Fryer, Andrews and Co were appointed bankers.[135] Four years later in 1811 the banking partnership of Fryer, Andrews and Co. was dissolved and the Dean, Castleman and Adams Bank, then in business for less than a year, was appointed in its place. Ann Fryer, William Fryer, John Andrews and John Clapcott, shareholders in Fryer, Andrews and Co. made immediate complaint to the Commissioner, with an appeal to the General Quarter Session of the Peace. They charged that the Commission was not competent to make such an appointment; that the meeting was not properly summoned; that the decision was against the votes of the majority and that it was irregular and improper because the Clerk of the Commission was one of the partners in the Bank. Summoning the meeting and recording votes would have been the task of the Clerk and these complaints were clearly directed at Castleman. As Clerk to this Enclosure Commission he had access to privileged information about land that would become available, and was in a favourable position to negotiate its purchase. He acquired property at Corfe Mullen at some time or another as it figured, amongst much else bequeathed to his sons, in his will.

Between 1810–1812 William Castleman with William Clapcott as his agent bought the St John's Estate in Hartwell, Northamptonshire for £12,000.[136] Over the next fifteen years by a process of purchase and exchange and taking '*the opportunity provided by inclosure to consolidate*' he acquired three freehold farms with a total of 419 acres with at least one manor house.[137] The Duke of Grafton was developing

---

[135] DRO D/CRL/G/1.
[136] NRO ZB 135/13/25.
[137] Philip Riden (Ed) *Victorian History of the Counties of England: Northamptonshire* 2002 pp182,183 and 345.

some model farms in the area. Castleman developed a relationship with him and exchanged some land with him for their mutual convenience.

William left this Northamptonshire property to his son Henry from whom it passed to Henry's wife Emma. On her death she left it to trustees, who sold it in 1896 to a local farmer.[138] The M1 motorway now borders this land opposite Salcey Forest.

Wimborne, where William Castleman (2) lived and had his attorney's office and his bank between 1810 and 1818, was sited eight miles from Chettle. Both Wimborne and Chettle were part of the hinterland of the thriving smuggling enterprises of the south coast. The many inlets of Poole Harbour with its miles of coastline were difficult for the excise men to patrol. Hamworthy, only four miles from Wimborne was close enough for smugglers to get their contraband unloaded and away within an hour. They relied on accomplices who could provide accommodation, horses, money and a legitimate front. George Bruce suggests that bankers charged very high rates of interest of 20 to 25% for loans to smugglers,[139] thereby benefiting from the illegal trade. The Dean, Castleman and Adams Bank in Wimborne was one of many potential points of contact between William Castleman (2) and the most famous of all smugglers, Isaac Gulliver. During the early part of his life Gulliver kept on the move, never in one place long enough to be caught, but when he aspired to legitimacy he settled for Wimborne, his financial and psychological home. Residents in the area who did not benefit from smuggling were few and far between, though the evidence is almost always circumstantial. William Castleman (2) was well acquainted with the great smuggler Isaac Gulliver. Their names appear together on several legal documents. Castleman was witness, with two of the clerks of his law firm, to Gulliver's lengthy will, which he almost certainly helped him draw up. He may, as Bruce suggests, have lent money at exorbitant rates of interest to the smugglers thereby benefiting indirectly. Maybe his dining table displayed an urbanely cosmopolitan

[138] *Victorian History* op.cit. p183.
[139] George Bruce *A Fortune and a Family* 1987.

range of food and wine, possibly his wife was elegantly accoutred with lace. Wimborne was on a direct route from the inlet of Poole Harbour at Hamworthy to the turnpike road to Salisbury and London, and would have provided a convenient entrepôt. It was quite widely agreed, even amongst the more orderly elements in society, that excessive duty on goods that were available across the English Channel at a fraction of the legal price in England was an invitation and an encouragement to smuggling. All classes of society were involved in some aspects of the illicit trade in the late eighteenth century.

By the second decade of the nineteenth century, while the Napoleonic Wars were still going on, William was in his forties, and was accumulating a lot of money. He had income from his law firm, his private lending arrangements, his fees as agent, as coroner, as Clerk to the Enclosure Commission and probably from smuggling. He had acquired hundreds of acres of land in Northamptonshire and Dorset and he knew that his skill in valuing land, timber, orchards, and a standing field of wheat had very few equals. His assessment of a horse for heavy work, for hunting or breeding was valued in the neighbourhood. His capacity for judging the richness of soil by crumbling it in the palm of his hand was something he had learned from his father. He could spot an ailing ewe, a swarm of bees and warren of rabbits from afar. He had also discovered that some of the men whom he had been brought up to honour and esteem, as the natural rulers of England, were emperors with very few clothes. George Chafin (1) had died in the same year as he was born. His father had talked about the Chafin family and the several members who held influential office. Their last years at Chettle had been a disgrace. Lord Uxbridge and Lord Shaftesbury seemed neither of them to be able to manage on their substantial incomes. He could not however allow that all men had equal rights. The French Revolution was extremely frightening and the Jacobins seemingly had little respect for anyone or anything. He now had property of his own that he was managing profitably, but he had no fine mansion, and it was the ownership of a beautiful house to which he now aspired. Chettle was a place he knew well. It was near enough to Wimborne to enable him to keep up his interests there and he had enough, with careful management, to renovate and repair the glorious house and get the other buildings into shape.

William Castleman typifies the bold entrepreneur who can see great potential benefits in changing circumstances and takes great risks to achieve them. His profound knowledge of the land, a self-confidence derived from the security of his early life in Hinton St Mary, and his legal experience, made him an enterprising and successful businessman. He was decisive, clear headed, bold, forward looking and energetic. He needed to keep himself well informed as he stood on constantly shifting ground. He was accused by some of working for himself and it was inevitable that the job itself made enemies. He also had many friends. He came from one social class and steered his way to a higher. His role as land agent reveals the ambiguities and discomforts of the situation; not entirely the master of the land, nor entirely the servant of the landowner who paid him. William, his wife Mary and their seven prematurely dead children are commemorated in a painted window in the north transept of Wimborne Minster with a brass plate under the window placed there by their three surviving sons, Edward, Charles and Henry.

William Castleman (2) had had his eye on Chettle for years. In fact he was never to live in the hundred-year-old mansion and spent all his working years at Allendale House in Wimborne. But he left the inspiration and the means for his son to fulfil his dream.

THIRTEEN

Lawless Chettle and the King of Smugglers

When William Castleman (2) died in 1844 his heirs were three well-educated and prosperous sons. All inherited extensive property but Chettle was not included. The title deeds of Chettle were still tantalizingly in the hands of John Swarbreck Gregory, Charles Augustus Symmons' solicitor. (see page 123).

Edward, William Castleman (2)'s eldest surviving son had married Anne Fryer in 1823. She was a daughter of the banking family of Fryer, Andrews and Co. of Wimborne. Her maternal grandmother Elizabeth Beale had been born, baptized and raised in Chettle. Elizabeth's father, William Beale had been a copyhold tenant of George Chafin (1) from 1751 and added further land to his tenancy in 1767 under George Chafin (2).[140]

In marrying Anne Fryer, Edward Castleman acquired a wife with a family history embedded in Chettle. Family recollections extended back to prosperous times before the Chafins lost their wealth. Anne also came with a considerable fortune. Her maternal grandmother Elizabeth Beale had married Isaac Gulliver the great smuggler.

William Castleman (2) was well pleased with the marriage of his eldest son. Anne symbolized the rich history of Chettle and the

---

[140] B F P Court Book Manor of Chettle transcribed Marie and Geoff Simcox 1996. William Beale had four children, Ann, Susan, William and Elizabeth born in 1739, 1744, 1747 and 1748 respectively. All four were baptized in Chettle Church by the Reverend Charles Dobson, rector in the parish for fifty-seven years despite complaints about his immoderate drinking.

achievements of the smuggling fraternity of the south coast.

The Reverend William Chafin had appointed her great grandfather, William Beale his churchwarden. It was the churchwarden's responsibility to administer the secular affairs of the church as an assistant to the parish rector. Beale was also the village farrier. In 1758 he took the lease of the inn at Thorney Down nearby[141] from the owner Mr William Cross of Blandford, and in September of that year he applied for a victualler's licence. The inn, which he called the Blacksmith's Arms, was for use as a warehouse for smuggled goods, and the victualler's licence, giving sanction to sell spirits to the public, provided a legitimate front for the transactions in case of a surprise visit from the excise men.

As a farrier William Beale was part of the horse transport network so essential for the distribution of smuggled goods. Box tombs also provided a hiding place for contraband. They were capacious and excise men were hesitant to desecrate a tomb. The box tomb of the Beale family, now in need of repair, still stands in Chettle churchyard. Tombs and monuments were, from the sixteenth century onward often designed and installed by their subjects in anticipation. Beale probably had his tomb made by a local stonemason and installed in the churchyard of St Mary's, Chettle with the kind permission of the Reverend William Chafin some years before he died. The stonemason, churchwarden, parson and all others in the village were beneficiaries of the illegal imports that were sometimes hidden in the Beale family box tomb.

On 5 October 1768 Elizabeth Beale, William's eldest daughter married Isaac Gulliver in the Parish Church of Sixpenny Handley. The marriage was by licence instead of banns, an unusual procedure, rather expensive, but quick. Normally banns were called on three successive Sundays in the parish churches of both betrothed. There were several possible explanations of this haste. Elizabeth was almost certainly not pregnant. Their fist child was born in 1770. Isaac, who

---

[141] Known at different times as The Blacksmith's Arms, The King's Arms, or The Arms.

first appears in the records of Dorset at the age of thirteen in 1758 when he was involved in a scuffle with excise men in Bitman's Chine,[142] was building up his very profitable contraband business that required a careful watch on winds, tides, and intelligence as to the whereabouts of excise men, employment of mariners, carriers and availability of concealed accommodation for the storage of smuggled goods. Protracted wedding arrangements would not have fitted well into these unpredictable circumstances of working life, but the real reason for the speed of arrangements was probably William Beale's impending death. Beale and Gulliver had been working hand in glove for possibly a decade. Gulliver imported contraband and Beale received and distributed it. The Blacksmith's Arms at Thorney Down was a vital nerve centre of Gulliver's enterprise and he could better maintain control of the tenancy as a family member.

The inn at Thorney Down had several advantages as a site for the promotion of such a business. It is in a part of Cranborne Chase interlaced with footpaths, spinneys and hides known to local inhabitants, who moved goods speedily from place to place, away from the prying eyes of the law. It was on the post chaise route from the west to London, by which silks, lace, spices, tea and alcohol could be dispatched to profitable markets in the city, and it is less than sixteen miles from the nearest inlet of the English Channel. The inn has good cellars, very suitable for accommodating contraband and Beale's victualler's licence provided a façade of legality. All these advantages Gulliver gathered to himself when he married Elizabeth Beale. He took over the tenancy of the inn, which he renamed the King's Arms. The victualler's licence was applied for annually by Ann Beale, Elizabeth's mother.

This marriage effected a seamless transition of all the practical requirements for the smuggling enterprise from one generation to the next, and gives us the first glimpse of that skill and foresight with which Gulliver conducted his profitable business.

Beale's son, Elizabeth's brother, another William, described as a

---

[142] Now known as Canford Cliffs Chine.

'*merchant, dealer and chapman*'[143] was also a copyhold tenant at Chettle. He held a dwelling house called Wheelers and thirty-six acres. In 1788 he was declared bankrupt. The Salisbury and Winchester Journal of 21 February 1788 announced that particulars of the letting of his '*sundry estates and sale of stock*' were to be handled by Mr Isaac Gulliver of Kingston near Wimborne. Here is another clue to Gulliver's success. He was living two separate lives. He promoted himself as a man of straightforward legitimate business and made full use of advertising facilitites in the Salisbury Journal and elsewhere to announce his activities. At the same time his fifty-strong work force of smugglers were plying their way across the Channel, into the inlets along the south coast to Wimborne, Chettle and Thorney Down. His legitimate business provided him with many a wide-eyed and innocent explanation to the excise men.

He had several relatives apparently also in legitimate trade.

The Gulliver family came from Malmesbury in Wiltshire, which is about eighty miles from the coast. His brother John was a butcher in Collingbourne, Wiltshire. He had another brother, Jacob, in Lymington and it may have been there that he became involved in the 'free trade'. Jacob had a family but how far these relatives were involved in smuggling must, like much else in the smuggling enterprise, remain hidden. Although illegal, all classes of society were in one way or another connected with smuggling. The direct perpetrators ran the most risk of publicity and punishment but receivers and beneficiaries were to be found amongst otherwise law-abiding commoners, gentry and nobility. This family kept on the move for many years. Isaac Gulliver and Elizabeth Beale were married in 1768 in Sixpenny Handley and they stayed at the inn at Thorney Down, or very close by at least until 1773 as both of their daughters were baptized in the parish church of Sixpenny Handley in 1770 and 1773. They were back at Thorney Down '*near Cashmore*' again in June 1778 as the following advertisement for staff appeared in the local paper:

---

[143] The term chapman was usually applied to itinerant pedlars and implies somewhat dubious trading standards.

'VOLUNTEERS Notice is hereby given to all young and Able Men who are willing to serve his Majesty either by SEA or LAND, that they are wanted to enter immediately: and each man approved of will receive a Bounty of TEN GUINEAS, and FIVE GUINEAS to drink his Majesty's health. Apply to Thorney Down, lying on the western road between Salisbury and Blandford. GOD save the KING.'[144]

In the following year the King's Arms, Thorney Down changed hands and George Moore became the proprietor. In March 1779 he assured the public at large that *'all gentlemen who shall please to honour him with their company may depend on his utmost endeavours to please.'* He was able to offer *'genteel post chaises, careful drivers, and exceeding good horses.'*[145]

A fortnight later the same newspaper reported on a *'desperate fray'* between an excise officer and six Dragoons on one side, and fifty or sixty smugglers on the other in a coppice near Hook's Wood.[146] Hook's Wood Coppice is just over a mile north of Chettle village and abuts Chettle Down. Several men were seriously injured and a smuggler died of his wounds. Possibly it was some of the young men who had been recruited through the advertisement of the previous summer, still a bit callow, who got involved in this bloodshed. The close proximity of the parish of Chettle put its residents under suspicion, but no names emerged.

At the time of this fracas Gulliver was living in Longham, near Wimborne. An advertisement in the same issue of the Salisbury and Winchester Journal as the report of the Hook's Wood encounter, announced that an auction would take place *'at the White Hart Inn Longham, near Winbourne, Dorset of twenty good HACK HORSES the property of Isaac Gulliver, of the same place.'* Having set up his fifty or sixty men in a major smuggling operation Gulliver advertised his legitimate presence several miles away.

The long outdated Tudor Sumptuary Laws motivated smuggling as the long outdated Chase laws motivated illegal deer poaching.

[144] *Salisbury and Winchester Journal* 1 June 1778.
[145] op.cit. 8 March 1779.
[146] op.cit. 29 March 1779.

Sumptuary Laws had been imposed as a restraint on the purchase of luxury goods, particularly of clothing and food. During the Tudor period when feudal society was giving place to capitalism, birth no longer necessarily determined social position. This gave rise to anxieties about deception and disguise, about the prospect of servants masquerading in the clothing of their masters, of the lower orders getting above themselves. Duties on luxury goods of clothing, particularly lace and silk, and of food, especially wine and spirits, were designed to keep them out of reach of all but the rich. Various Customs Acts passed between 1714 and 1760 added to the list of prohibited goods. One historian has described these Customs Acts as being *'for the promotion of the honourable profession of smuggler; and for the general advancement of frauds, abuses and riots among all ranks of his Majesty's subjects.'*[147] Deer poaching and smuggling converged and reinforced one another in the vicinity of Chettle. The gentry, sitting on the bench in their capacity as JP's, amongst their number the Reverend William Chafin, might tut-tut noisily but only took exemplary punitive action when violence erupted. They were as keen as any to get home to their contraband French brandy and venison.

Virtually everyone was involved in smuggling in one way or another. The staple industries of the area, agriculture and the wool trade were both under threat. Government prohibition on a variety of goods readily available eighty miles away across the Channel combined motivation and opportunity to an irresistible degree.

Two eighteenth-century rectors of Chettle, in addition to Chafin, were almost certainly involved in smuggling. The immoderate drinking of the Reverend Charles Dobson has already been mentioned. Legitimate alcohol was expensive. When Dobson died the Reverend William Feltham was appointed by George Chafin (1) in 1750. William Feltham combined the job of parish rector with that of *'Chaplain of His Majesty's Ship the Princess Mary.'* He died in Jamaica in June 1756. A profitable combination of Christian ministry with rum smuggling may reasonably be inferred. Edward Smith, a parishioner

---

[147] H D Traill (Ed) *Social England* 1896 p119–120.

of Chettle, was a colleague of William Feltham and helped finance this endeavour. He had lent his rector £130 in connection with his travels on H M S the Princess Mary.[148]

Isaac Gulliver had a reputation for maintaining a work force of about fifty men who were knowledgeable, quick witted and sure footed enough to avoid rough confrontations with the excise men. Outlaws contrive to minimize their traces and to leave no record, which gives rise to myth and legend. They have no bills of lading, keep no diaries or account books, payment for goods and wages must be in cash and all concerned have to abide by omerta. There is little evidence about Gulliver the outlaw – he never for example seems to have appeared in court – though there is enough evidence from contemporary newspapers and other public records about Gulliver the man.

The young Gulliver, strong, intelligent and calculating came into his own with his marriage to William Beale's daughter, and his acquisition of William's inn and business and then his son's house at Chettle and his business.

In October 1778 the Salisbury Journal reported on the seizure of smuggled goods near Thorney Down, the site of the King's Arms, by then under Gulliver's control. Sixteen hundredweight of tea and nine casks of liquor were taken to the supervisor's house in Blandford. The smugglers (unidentified) came in the evening and 'carried the whole off in great triumph'.[149] The goods were weighty and voluminous and could not have been removed without the connivance of local residents, and possibly of some of the excise men in Blandford. The network of miscreants of Cranborne Chase would have had little difficulty identifying the culprits.

Tea drinking, the preserve of the wealthy in the early eighteenth century, was by this time a national addiction. The poor took their tea with lots of sugar. It gave them immediate energy. 'As much superfluous money is expended on tea and sugar as would maintain four

[148] Will of William Feltham.
[149] Salisbury Journal 10 October 1778.

millions more subjects on bread,' Arthur Young, agriculturalist and author claimed in 1767.[150] In 1784 it was calculated that only 42% of the 5,803 tons of tea consumed in the year had been imported through the customs houses.

Overseas trade was expanding and imports were providing food and clothing for the middle classes instead of luxuries for the very rich. Respectable families were very willing recipients of smuggled goods. Mary Chafin's Recipe Book compiled between 1698 and 1709 makes liberal use of wine and spirits. In a different part of England Parson Woodforde of Norfolk makes his diary entry for 29th March 1777: *'Andrews the Smuggler brought me this night about 11 o'clock a bagg of Hyson Tea ...... he frightened us a little by whistling under the parlour window just as we were going to bed'.*[151] Where Parson Woodforde was open and frank, Parson William Chafin was more guarded. In his *Anecdotes* he refers to the establishment of a musical club which met at a *'little inn called the Hut, situate on Salisbury South Plain on a little eminence, which gave* [an] *extensive view even as far as the Isle of Wight rocks.'*[152] On making his way to the Hut, he tells us *'I perceived on the road from Salisbury a post chase...My friend* [used to] *walk to the Hut and arrange the music books and instruments for the next day; but this he never did till after he had attended divine service ...he was ...truly religious and a strict adherer to the Estab-lished Church.'* The *'friend'*, in all likelihood William Chafin himself, interleaved the musical papers he was carrying with nooses *'and set them with great dexterity at every pathway'* thus capturing some of the *'finest deer suspended by their necks'*. The conviviality and *'festivals at their hospitable boards'* that followed these musical evenings leaves little doubt that there was access to contraband liquor as well as stolen deer.

In 1788 William Chafin had resigned from his rangership of Bursted Walk proclaiming in a letter concerning his resignation *'I*

---

[150] Arthur Young *The Farmer's Letters to the People of England* 1767.
[151] James Woodforde *The Diary of a Country Parson* 1758 - 1802 entry for 29 March 1777.
[152] William Chafin op.cit.

shall always be ready to give my assistance to the best of my power in the support of Lord Rivers Rights in the Chase.' Lord Rivers, then Lord of the Chase had exclusive deer hunting rights. The freedom that his twelve thousand deer had to roam at will over everybody's property was at the bottom of all the troubles that were mounting up on Cranborne Chase. These rights were being vigorously challenged and one of the more telling arguments for disenfranchising the Lord of the Chase was that the law breaking it encouraged in respect of deer attracted other law breakers, especially smugglers who exploited the intimate knowledge that residents on the Chase had of pathways and hiding places. William Chafin was involved in both deer poaching and smuggling. He was also a Justice of the Peace with a public role of law enforcer. In this letter to Lord Rivers, and in his *Anecdotes* written half a century later, he gives us a glimpse of the intimacies between outlaw and establishment, both of which he embodied, and of his own duplicitous role in benefiting from those intimacies.

In 1768 Arthur Young commented approvingly on the enhancement of agriculture on Brownsea Island in Poole Harbour, by the Sturt family (William Chafin's mother's family). Manure, chalk and coal were being imported, though the disproportionate size of the sloops being used for the undertaking led to the suspicion that smuggling was included.

In 1780 William Pitt the Younger entered Parliament and quickly rose to the high office of Chancellor of the Exchequer and then Prime Minister. His reduction or abolition of many of the high duties was the death knell to smuggling. The *Gentleman's Magazine* of 3 May 1782 announced that *'A Proclamation was this day issued for granting a free pardon to all smugglers.'*[153]

A Poole customs official's report dated 10 December 1788 *'on the general character of Isaac Gulliver'* says that *'in the year 1782 he took the benefit of his Majesty's proclamation for pardoning such offences and as we are informed dropped that branch of smuggling and afterwards confined himself chiefly to the wine trade which he carried on to*

---

[153] *Gentleman's Magazine* Vol LIII 1782 p258.

a considerable extent having vaults at various places along the coast to the westwards of this port... he constantly sold wines considerably under the fair dealers price from which circumstances there is no doubt but that he illicitly imported that article... He is a person of great speculating genius and besides the smuggling he has carried on a variety of other business, but ... now lives retired at a farm in this neighbourhood having acquired ... a very considerable property.[154] This Poole customs officer had been able to make an assessment of Gulliver on the basis of over twenty years of contention. The authorities knew well enough what he was up to but never caught him red-handed. Legal and illegal enterprises were woven so smoothly into his colourful life that he may eventually not have entirely distinguished between them himself.

Three months after the free pardon was issued an advertisement announcing a house to let in Kinson, then in the occupation of Mr Isaac Gulliver, appeared in the Salisbury and Winchester Journal: '*Mr Gulliver is about to remove to Tingmouth, in Devonshire, where he proposes to carry on the wine and Brandy trade.*' Like Matthew Arnold's Scholar Gipsy, Gulliver was '*seen by rare glimpses*' in his customary haunts. This advertisement was designed more to put customs officers off his track than to inform of his whereabouts. There is no evidence that he ever went to Devon. It is certain, however, that Gulliver took advantage of the free pardon and took steps to establish himself in respectable society. He had plenty of friends already there, some of whom had benefited from his undoubted courage and talent. At a time when the beaches and inlets along the Dorset coast were often blood spattered, and sometimes corpse littered, Gulliver had the reputation of conducting his business without violence. It was a reputation helped by a habit of the judiciary (Colonel Hooper, chief excise officer in particular) of turning a blind eye whenever possible. Gulliver had amassed a fortune in less than twenty years since he had taken over the inn at Thorney Down. It taxes human credulity to suppose

[154] DRO Poole Letter Books HM Customs Excise London. The writer was JLRHW. Collector (or Comptroller). He may have been dismissed a year or two later for giving information to smugglers.

that this profitable enterprise was given up in 1782 and one Poole customs officer at any rate was not hoodwinked. Gulliver lived for another forty years, re-fashioning himself as an upright and law abiding townsman of Wimborne where he retired into a wine and spirit business.

In 1807–8 he was living in Long Crichel, in 1815 he was in Kinson and in 1822 in Wimborne. Kinson, a property of about a thousand acres, became Gulliver's own and was passed to his successors.

By 1789, after nearly three decades as the orchestrator and brains behind a successful posse of smugglers, Isaac Gulliver was styling himself 'Gentleman'. The term meant a good bit more than it does today. A gentleman did not work with his hands, but the term also implied a distinct position in land owning society, with the right to bear arms, and with a traceable pedigree. The College of Arms had to be persuaded that an aspiring gentleman could meet the essential criteria before a coat of arms could be claimed. Almost a hundred years later Anthony Trollope in his novel The Prime Minister (1876) had a character say '...a man doesn't often become a gentleman in the first generation'. The College of Arms was unable to trace either coat of arms or pedigree for Gulliver and they concluded that the 'smuggler...applied his illicit practices to Arms as well as contraband'. The Coat of Arms eluded him.

Nevertheless his will requires that his major beneficiaries should incorporate the surname Gulliver, and the Gulliver Coat of Arms into their own. There are other signs that he may in later life have become somewhat fanciful about his status. For example, he requested his executors to 'procure from the Official and churchwardens of the ...parish [i.e. Wimborne] a Grant or Facility for a vault for my family.' There is no Gulliver family vault in Wimborne Minster, only a roughly executed stone bearing the name 'Gulliver' on the wall of the Minster. They were also to 'apply for and endeavour to obtain an Act of Parliament or proper license from the Crown or take such other means as may be requisite or necessary or proper to enable or authorize him, or them, respectively to take, use and bear the surname and Arms of Gulliver.' This did not happen either. Thomas Gosse, an itinerant portrait painter on a visit to Wimborne in 1817 was commissioned to paint '*a likeness of Mr Gulliver who was formerly a smuggler of disreputable notoriety.*'[155]

The ever-ambitious Gulliver was not simply re-inventing himself in society as a legitimate businessman; he had set his mind on joining the gentry. Class boundaries were rigid and he was to find that he could not buy his way in as he had hoped. Dress, speech, gesture, deportment carried their subtle but unmistakable signals of membership. Lady Spencer of Althorp, a lady at the peak of the social pyramid, wrote in the 1790's to her daughter on the subject of the symbolism of dress: '*Let* [the dress] *be simple and noble, but pray do not let it be singular…the credit such conduct would be to your character would far outweigh the trivial and really false idea of your looking more shewy.*'[156]

Isaac Gulliver's excessively prolix will is about 20,000 words long. Lawyers charged by the length of a document and it is likely that in drawing up the will the solicitor, probably William Castleman, exploited Gulliver's increasing sense of his own grandeur. Reference to his copyhold and leasehold estates, '*all my freehold manors, farms, houses, hereditaments, freeholds and copyholds, tenements,*' lands, stocks, investments, funds and securities, profits, dividends and interests, timber and so on, is made repeatedly, but no place names or geographical descriptions are given.

But he was always Isaac Gulliver the smuggler and therefore not acceptable on equal terms in the upper ranks of Wimborne and Dorset society, and certainly was not to be entertained as an applicant to the College of Arms. What distinguished Gulliver from the many contemporary smugglers was his capacity to save and invest. He knew his fortune was as great as some of the esquires and dignitaries who had been pleased to purchase their bargain wines and spirits from him, and he was indignant at his exclusion from their inner circle. If he could not achieve his own goals in his lifetime he could at least lay down the foundations for future generations. Some

[155] Raymond Lister *Thomas Gosse* 1953.
[156] Amanda Foreman *Georgiana Duchess of Devonshire* 1998.

of them acquitted themselves with a distinction that vindicated his family aspirations.

His only granddaughter became the co-owner of Chettle, a grandson and a great grandson were knighted, one was appointed Lieutenant Governor of Bengal, a grandson was appointed Master Extraordinary in the High Court of Chancery and a great grandson was Lord of the Manor of West Moors.

Of the marriage of Isaac Gulliver and Elizabeth Beale there were three children. Elizabeth, known to the family as Betty, was born in 1770, Ann in 1773 and Isaac in 1774. Isaac, the only son, died unmarried at the age of twenty-four. Ann married twice but there were no children.

Elizabeth was Gulliver's favourite. She conformed more closely to aspiring family expectations. To her Isaac Gulliver left all his property. In 1793 she married William Rolls Fryer, scion of a family of successful bankers in Wimborne. William Rolls Fryer had commercial and mercantile interests as well as being partner in the bank, and owned a ship called *The Eagle of Poole,* which had been built in Barrington, Nova Scotia in 1801. It has been alleged that the *'Gulliver and Fryer families of Kinson were both much engaged in the trade'* (of smuggling).[157]

William and Elizabeth Fryer had six children – five boys and a girl. Anne was their second child, born in 1799. In 1823, at the age of twenty-four, she married Edward Castleman. When they were first married Edward and Anne lived at Dormers, a house which had been one of ten public houses owned by her grandfather, Isaac Gulliver. Shortly before 1830 they moved to Allendale House, the Castleman family home built by William (2) about forty years earlier. The Fryer family were not to be outdone by the Castlemans and Gullivers in their display of approval of this marriage. Anne's father William Fryer *'for the purpose of making a suitable provision for the said Anne his daughter'* invested £5,000 in a trust to be managed by her uncle, John Fryer and the Reverend Charles Bowle. The Reverend Charles

---

[157] M Dacombe (Ed) *Dorset Up Along and Down Along* 1935.

Bowle had been appointed by Isaac Gulliver in 1808 to be one of two executors of his will.[158]

The property that had been mortgaged to Samuel Bignold in order to repay the loan of £10,400 to William Castleman in 1827 (see page 135 above), was in 1834 remortgaged by Mary Clapcott to William Rolls Fryer for £13,500.[159] So the property for which William Castleman was mortgagee in 1818 came back into the family eventually.

The Castleman and Fryer families had long been part of the overtly respectable, quietly delinquent and financially successful subculture of Dorset. Some of Gulliver's fortune was acquired by legitimate business, but he was better known, and is better remembered, as an outlaw. They formed a tightly integrated ambitious and wealthy clan.

The old land dependent gentry were floundering and many were in serious debt. William Chafin had been one of them. The working population were losing their jobs, their rights to common land and were seriously distressed. The new men were quick to perceive, exploit and provide for the needs of a rapidly changing society. Chafin and Gulliver were linked through the Beale family. Chafin promoted Beale within the village and when Gulliver married Elizabeth Beale he was able to use the facilities that existed in Chettle and the Blacksmith's Arms. The parishioners of Chettle took their part in concealing contraband, moving it on quiet nights and keeping silent when the excise men arrived. They welcomed the much-needed income that they helped to generate and shared the stolen deer.

The two banking families of Castleman and Fryer, and the smuggling family of Gulliver, were intertwined well before the marriage of Anne Fryer and Edward Castleman took place. This marriage cemented financial and property interests that had been cultivated between their families for fifty years or so. Isaac Gulliver's granddaughter Anne had two sets of wealthy grandparents, the Gullivers and Fryers. With her marriage to Edward the considerable Castleman wealth was added. William Castleman's hope of acquiring Chettle for

---

[158] WRO 2667/1/14/94. There had been a banking house of Bowles, Collins and Tamlyn in Wiltshire in about 1800.
[159] George Bruce op.cit. p60.

himself and his family did not work out quite as he hoped, but before he died in 1844 he knew that everything was in place and that the Castleman ownership of Chettle would not be long delayed. His son was a lawyer, he had made a propitious marriage and the finances were secure.

The discriminatory laws that had done so much to promote smuggling and deer stealing had been repealed. Cranborne Chase and Chettle became peaceful once more. The heritage shaped by a generation of resourceful and courageous entrepreneurs was passed to the next generation. The prizes which had eluded Isaac Gulliver and William Castleman were now within the reach of their successors.

FOURTEEN

Chettle Waits

Chettle waited, semi-paralyzed, from 1824, when its title deeds disappeared into the vaults of the Bank of England, till 1847. Its legal status, its owner and its future were all in doubt for those twenty-three years. Numerous Acts of Parliament that affected the parish were passed while Chettle was marking time, so that the estate that finally emerged to the light of day in 1847 was very different from the manor that it had been in 1823.

Cranborne Chase was disenfranchised, fields were enclosed on the Chettle estate, the method of payment of tithes was altered, the new Poor Law came into effect, the first Copyhold Act affected feudal landholding and the Great Reform Act of 1832 and the Municipal Reform Act of 1835 redistributed political power. The Corn Laws were repealed. It was an extensive raft of legislation that radically altered the parish and the people.

With the exception of the Cranborne Chase disenfranchisement all this legislative activity was of national significance and all affected Chettle. Agricultural practice changed, the parish lost much of its authority, the tithe was commuted to a money payment, land tenure changed and the number of voters in Chettle increased. This all happened when leadership and authority in Chettle was distinctly ambiguous.

Chettle's geographical position as part of Cranborne Chase had drawn it into the illegalities and disorder that prevailed. The special status of Cranborne Chase as a royal hunting ground was brought to an end in 1828. The state of affairs on the Chase in the early nineteenth century was *'extremely injurious to owners of Lands... and ... tends greatly to demoralize the habits of the Labouring Classes'* as well as being *'a great hindrance to the cultivation of such Lands,'* wrote one of the local gentry.[160] Lord Rivers announced that he was *'willing to accept the clear yearly sum of £1800 ... in compensation'.* It was on this basis that the necessary Act of Parliament disenfranchising the Chase was passed. In 1828 *'Parliament approved the Bill disfranchising the Chase on the following conditions: that compensation should be payable to Lord Rivers from October 1829 and that his right to preserve deer throughout the Chase should be extinguished in October 1830.*[161] Nearly eight hundred years of aristocratic privilege was thus ended. The rate charge to Chettle was calculated at ten pence per acre. The total charge to the estate was £35 15s 6d[162] so the estate was then assessed as just over 858 acres. The deer disappeared almost overnight and with them the poaching, smuggling, hypocrisy and corruption to which they had given rise.

England was becoming a nation dominated by factories, towns, trade and commerce with an urban elite and an ever-growing population exerting its inexorable pressure on agriculture for more and cheaper food. King George III's speech at the opening of Parliament on 11 November 1800 had referred to the high price of food and to the petitions and riots that resulted. He went on to promote *'the permanent extension and improvement of agriculture.'*[163] The several Acts of Parliament that arose to carry forward this aspiration for agriculture had a direct effect on Chettle, transforming the appearance, the social relationships, the economy and the political and religious leaning of the estate.

In 1818 much of the farming on the Chettle estate was still based on the medieval strip, or ridge and furrow system. Each farmer had several strips of land scattered about the estate. It was a wasteful and

[160] B F P, CHA/9.
[161] Desmond Hawkins *Cranborne Chase* 1980 p57.
[162] B F P, CHA/9.
[163] D V Glass *Numbering the People* 1973 p57.

inefficient mode of tenure that had been, together with the 'rights of common' changing gradually throughout England for centuries. Between about 1750 and 1850 Parliamentary Enclosures accelerated the process. Re-arrangement of the strip holdings was often done by consensual agreement. Commissioners for Enclosure had the power to enforce when local agreement could not be reached. Hoskins estimates that 10–30% of land in this part of Dorset was enclosed in the eighteenth and nineteenth centuries.[164]

In Chettle John Tregonwell Napier (adopted son of William Chafin), rector of the parish from 1810–1820, Thomas Brewer, Gentleman, Sarah Brewer, widow, and Isaac Rabbits, yeoman, all communicated together to rearrange the strips of land they held *'in three arable fields, Drove Field, Middle Field and Longlands'*. The four of them agreed that *'it would be advantageous and beneficial … to have their several allotments or parcels of land … put into one piece,'* and the Reverend John Napier undertook all the essential correspondence. (Some of the parishioners were still unable to write and did their signing with a cross.) They appointed *'three respectable persons … to view and measure their several allotments… and to… mark a certain quantity of land equal to their several allotments in one piece … each person shall fence out his allotment in such manner … as the said three persons shall in writing direct … and will keep up such marks as shall always hereafter show where their allotments are. None shall permit their cattle (either sheep or black cattle) to feed or trespass on each others allotments'.*[165] The three respectable persons were summoned from other villages. They recorded how they carried out their job for the Glebe lands (that is the land belonging to the parsonage, John Tregonwell Napier's). There were seven separate pieces in Longlands totalling 7 acres 1 perch and 4 rods; in Middle Field three separate pieces totalling three acres and in Drove Field three separate pieces totalling just over nine acres. In all, the total was nineteen acres, one perch and six rods. Previous assessment of the Glebe lands had been twenty-three acres in 1634, twenty-one acres in 1768, now in the

[164] W G Hoskins *The Making of the English Landscape* 1955.
[165] B F P CHA/14.

early nineteenth century only just over nineteen acres! A constant difficulty with the strip system was the insecurity of the boundaries that were usually moveable. The parson's piece had been subject to slow but sure encroachment. Discordant assessments like this, as well as disagreements between neighbouring farmers had to be reconciled and entailed protracted correspondence. Happenings in Chettle were repeated throughout the nation. It was an enormous and time-consuming job, which had frequently to be resolved by local Commissioners.

Together with the reorganization of arable land went the enclosure of common land. Parishioners had customarily had grazing rights on common land and could take wood, furze and fruit from it. The parsonage of Chettle had *'common of pasture for three score sheep in the fields and downs and common of pasture for six beasts at the woods'.* Disputes about these rights of common were going on more than twenty years later. John West, then rector of Chettle wrote in 1841: *'It is remembered by the oldest inhabitant of the village that there was always a right of depasturing cattle on Chettle Common and at the woods adjoining belonging to the rectory.'* [166] In place of common land, available to all parishioners, were individually hedged fields allotted to an individual. The appearance of the fields of Chettle and the economic basis of the farming on the estate was quite changed.

The rector and the church had from time immemorial depended upon receiving one tenth, or tithe, of agricultural produce. By the nineteenth century tithes and their assessment had provided potent ground for acrimony between church and landowning interests. With the enclosure movement tithe payment was replaced by a money payment assessed as the *'tithe rent charge'* under the terms of the 1836 Tithe Commutation Act. This became a charge on the agricultural land as a standard tax and released both church and landowning representative in the village from an undignified annual haggle over the value of the livestock, the harvest and the calculation of one tenth of them. Payment henceforth was by a money transaction. The

[166] B F P CHA/14.

rector did not come to choose his pig, sack of wheat and chickens.

The mapping of Chettle as a prelude to the tithe commutation was done shortly after the passing of the Act. The tithe map, showing the newly enclosed fields and signed by two of the three famous Tithe Commissioners (William Blamire, Chairman and the Reverend Richard Jones) shows Chettle much as it is today. Chettle was assessed by the Tithe Commissioners in 1838 as 1113 acres, over half of which was arable land (57%) producing corn and root crops, 21% was downland, that is less fertile land supporting sheep, 14% woodland and 6% was meadow and pasture suitable for cattle.[167] (The rate charge payable to Lord Rivers by Chettle in 1830 was based on 858 acres. It is unlikely that the estate had grown by nearly 30%. The most likely explanation for this discrepancy is that Lord Rivers was content to settle for an approximation while the Tithe Commissioners were more precise.)

In 1834 the New Poor Law came into effect. In William Chafin's day the parish vestry, consisting of a few of the better off residents, had organized provision for the poor, disabled and sick of the parish. The vestry had been responsible for determining the rate to be raised from farmers and landowners and distributing it to the indigent. The parish was the administrative unit throughout England. By the 1830's the increasing urban population and the constant movement of people from village to town meant that the parish unit could no longer function efficiently in dealing with the needy. One of the last beneficiaries of the Chettle vestry in June 1834 was Fanny Jupp who received '*for maintenance of William Pettis's female bastard child for four weeks – 6s.*'[168]

The New Poor Law of 1834 abolished this system that had served since Tudor times. Parishes were grouped together to form a Union and a workhouse built to serve several parishes and provide accommodation for those in need. Boards of Guardians took the place of the parish vestries. The standard of living in the new workhouse was designedly kept below that of the waged labourer, to discourage the

---

[167] B F P CHA/14.
[168] B F P CAS/ 66A.

feckless from voluntary unemployment. In the southwest of England there were more labourers than work, no statutory minimum wage and agricultural labourers had no trade organization. (The Tolpuddle Martyrs met sixteen miles from Chettle in the same year as the New Poor Law came into effect to consider starting one, and were sentenced to seven years transportation.) It was therefore an employers' market and wages were driven down, often to below subsistence level. The workhouse conditions for working men and women were applied with equal stringency to children, invalids and the elderly. Many a workhouse death certificate gave the cause of death as *'Want of the common necessities of life,'* (that is, starvation). The grisly spectre of the workhouse threatened the incapacitated for more than a century.

Chettle was part of the Wimborne Union. *'At the Wimborne workhouse the new "Board of Guardians" in 1839 acted on their medical officer's advice "that one meat dinner, instead of three, during the week will be sufficient for able-bodied male inmates".*[169]

From 1834 the indigent could no longer apply to another of the parishioners, a member of the vestry, for help. Their recourse was to an anonymous functionary in Wimborne. No longer could they receive alms and stay at home. Relief was provided through residence at the workhouse. The parish ceased to be the administrative unit of the nation and there was little resistance to this erosion of local authority. The Poor Rate had been rising inexorably and many parish vestries were pleased to be free of the responsibility of dealing with this thorny problem.

Chettle lost some of its independence and became part of the wider world. The poor of Chettle were in no hurry to participate and survived without recourse to the dreaded workhouse until the Jupe family fell into wretchedness. (Fanny Jupp with her *'bastard child'* may well have been of the same family – spelling was flexible.)

Charlotte Jupe was born in 1775 when George Chafin (2) was Lord of the Manor. Her daughter Esther was born in 1812 and after

---

[169] Cecil N Cullingford *A History of Dorset* 1980.

all the family had gone mother and daughter lived together in the village. Esther died in 1839 at the age of twenty-seven. Village affairs were confused at the time but young Robert Rogers who lived in St Mary's Farmhouse near the church looked after things and continued to do so even after Edward Castleman bought the whole village in 1847. Robert and his family were kind to Charlotte and she was contented enough living on her own for the next ten years or so. In her mid seventies she became very frail. The 'poor-prison' of Wimborne, as the workhouse was known, took her in but she did not live long. Her body was returned to St Mary's Church for burial alongside her daughter, so she was saved the final indignity of a pauper's burial.

In the hundred and fourteen years of its existence no-one from Chettle went to the workhouse on account of unemployment, no child, no young widow, and no unmarried mother found their way there. An informal communal support system continued in the village. The practice of caring for neighbours was not readily brought to an end after nearly two and a half centuries of parish care. Nine very elderly folk were admitted. Their average age was seventy-three.

Under the Chafins the business of the estate had been conducted as from feudal times *'according to the custom of the Manor.'* Meetings of the Court of the Manor, or Court Baron took place about every two years. The Court meeting was the place for allocating responsibilities, for maintaining order and efficiency on the estate, and – of overriding importance – tenancies were arranged. They were copyhold tenancies and their rationale derived from feudal law under which the Lord of the Manor was deemed to hold the land of the monarch as an inalienable right. At his will the lord could grant land for use by others, subject to a customary return of service, money or goods in kind. But he could not sell it or let it on any other terms. A farming tenancy was made reasonably secure by being agreed for a number of lives. For example, at William Chafin's Court Baron in 1793 *'Thomas Brewer took of the Lord of the manor... One messuage, two yardlands ... [etc etc]... for and during the natural lives of William Brewer (aged seventeen or thereabouts) Ann Brewer (aged twelve years or thereabouts) and Thomas Brewer (aged fifteen or thereabouts) his sons and daughter and the life of the longest liver of them successively at the will of the Lord according to the custom of the said Manor.'* Thus if Ann Brewer, the twelve year old daughter, lived to be seventy-two and complied with all customary requirements, the Brewers could use the land for sixty years.

The Copyhold Act of 1841 reduced this legal embargo to the disposal of manorial property and meant that sales or tenancies could be arranged on other than feudal terms, thus jeopardizing the stability of Chettle as an integrated manor. The possibility of parcels of land, and cottages, being sold freehold to individuals was opened up.

The Great Reform Act of 1832 extended the national suffrage to £10 freeholders and abolished the Rotten Boroughs. Milborne Port was one. The Uxbridge family's ready access to a Parliamentary seat was thereby demolished and that part of the Uxbridge property was sold the following year.

The Municipal Reform Act of 1835 gave the franchise to all ratepayers. Municipal authority was no longer the prerogative of *'Tory lawyers, Churchmen and noblemen's agents.'*[170] The electoral register of Wimborne was enlarged so that the Castleman authority and influence in the town was diluted. The legislative councils of the nation were, by these two Acts of Parliament, considerably widened to include urban and industrial interests.

The Corn Laws were repealed in 1846. Bitterly contested as this legislation was, it had little immediate impact, but it was widely recognized as the turning point when England's agriculture gave place to its industry and the great landlords of England had to share political power with the merchants and ironmasters. The role of the next landlord of Chettle would be very different from the feudal Chafins.

Two years after William Chafin's death John Tregonwell Napier, rector of Chettle also died at the age of thirty-three. By then the advowson, giving the right to present a nominee for the post of rector, was held by Abraham Henry Chambers. An advowson had both political and financial value. It enabled its holder to influence the

---

[170] G M Trevelyan *Social History of England* 1942.

politico-religious tenor of the parsonage, and also gave access to the church tithe of the parish. By retaining control of the parsonage the landowner could effectively influence the ideas that emanated from the pulpit. The advowson also secured an income for someone of his choosing, often a member of his own family. In the long list of rectors of Chettle it is reasonably certain that from the seventeenth century their publicly stated views accorded with those of the Chafins. Of the eleven rectors appointed between 1690 and 1810 at least four were relatives. Rectory and manor were a powerful combination, especially at a time when most parishioners were poorly educated, some illiterate.

Abraham Henry Chambers had appointed John West as rector of Chettle. He was well connected and well bred, a man of independent means and an Oxford graduate who had been ordained in 1806. He held a number of chaplaincies and was *collated to the rectory of Chettle …in 1820 on the presentation of A H Chambers esq.*[171]

The appointment of John West to the parsonage of Chettle brought a man of a very different spleen from those who had preceded him. He was one of the growing number of Evangelicals who had gained a foothold within the Church of England. Their concern was with the saving of souls rather than preserving the organization of the Church. Christianity meant a fervent personal commitment to the Saviour, not an adherence to rituals and formalities laid down over the centuries. Missions to the new industrial areas, and to the colonies inspired them. They were closer to the Dissenters and Puritans in their thinking than to the Church of England, though more comfortable in their upper class social background within the established church.

John West and his wife Harriet had been married in 1807. They had had twelve children of whom four sons and two daughters survived. They lived at the Parsonage House (now Lower Farmhouse). He was the incumbent from 1820 till 1846, the years when the Bank of England held Chettle, and the agricultural population of the area was miserably, abjectly depressed.

[171] *Gentleman's Magazine*, Feb 1846.

Abraham Henry Chambers had high hopes that John West would bring a spiritual and behavioural renaissance to his estate. He had found the parishioners surly, untutored and delinquent, egged on in their rough rustic ways by their previous Lord of the Manor, William Chafin. John West would help him achieve the Arcadia that he planned.

West was an evangelical Christian, bent upon the saving of souls and humanitarian good works, much of which he believed could be achieved through appropriate Bible based education. But he was not whole-hearted in his commitment to the ideal plan that Chambers had for Chettle. He had also made an agreement with the Hudson's Bay Company that he would, if required, go as chaplain to their trading station at Red River Settlement in Canada. Within a few weeks of his appointment to Chettle Hudson's Bay Company held him to his contract. He had given *'a bond to Mr Chambers in penalty of £1,000 to resign the rectory'*[172] if he went to Canada. He did not resign and there is no record of his having paid the bond. Chambers *'set him down as a dirty ungrateful Parson'*[173] for this duplicity.

John West performed one burial at St Mary's Church, appointed a curate and departed to Canada. He did not return permanently until 1829, by which time Chettle was under the supervision of Commissioners in Bankruptcy.

The Hudson Bay area had been opened up in the seventeenth century for fur trading. Sub-zero temperatures prevail for seven or eight months of the year, but West evidently expected temperate agricultural conditions such as he had left behind. In October 1820 he recorded in his journal *'in vain did I look for a cluster of cottages where the hum of a small population at least might be heard as in a village. I saw but few marks of human industry in the cultivation of the soil. Almost every inhabitant we passed bore a gun upon his shoulder and all appeared in a wild, hunter-like state'*.[174] The snow bound fur trading

---

[172] B F P CAS/19.
[173] B F P CHA/15.
[174] B F P *John West Rector of Chettle 1820-1845. Calendar of John West's Stay at the Red River Settlement.*

community he considered a *'dark interior of a moral wilderness … a wild waste of heathenism'.*[175] He built a school, and was courageous in his attempts to Christianize the Eskimaux, though whether he made much attempt to understand their culture and traditions is doubtful. He typified the Christian missionary moving into the colonies to enlist the natives into the benefits of an everlasting Christian life. Many performed an important social service by founding schools and hospitals. They had none of the anxiety about undermining cultural patterns and relationships of more primitive people that have grown with the advance of anthropology and its attempts to understand the values and bonds that form the fabric of every society. He had hoped to return to Hudson Bay with his wife and family but the Hudson's Bay Company did not renew his appointment. Disappointed in that direction he returned to Chettle to improve the lot of the benighted of whom he found many.

He promoted a residential school for gipsies in Farnham. It was not a great success and the building was used for many years as the home of the Pitt Rivers Museum.

Like his contemporary, William Castleman (2), West was concerned with the alleviation of poverty and distress. Where Castleman looked to help through social change, West's educational ideas were informed by the New Testament and were ahead of their time. But his vision never went much beyond a narrow religiosity and he lacked the stamina to see through many of his ideas of ultimate heavenly justice that he sought to indoctrinate in his economically distressed parish.

His heart was undoubtedly in the right place, but he was not a great success. He had little appreciation of the tough realities of agricultural life, which so marked William Castleman (2)'s character. Both men were very much aware of the hydra-headed nature of the problem of agricultural poverty. No evidence of their having met or corresponded has come to light though it is inconceivable that they were not acquainted. Edward Castleman (1) is said to have had a very

---

[175] B F P *John West Rector of Chettle* op.cit. *The Church and School.*

high regard for West and installed the commemorative east window in Chettle church to John and Harriet West and their family.

Shortly after West's return from Canada the British Government was encouraging emigration to reduce the surplus population. A steady fall in the death rate, with no commensurate fall in the birth rate had caused a steady rise in the population throughout the eighteenth century. In 1798 the Reverend Thomas Malthus (1766–1834) had published his *Essay on the Principle of Population,* pointing out that the population had a natural tendency to increase faster than the means of subsistence. If the death rate did not rise, or the birth rate fall, or food production increase, or some combination, doom would not be long delayed. Food shortages had sparked the French Revolution and there had been periodic rioting in England for the same reason. A palliative, though not a cure, was to move the surplus population of this country to the empty spaces of the world.

The Government of New South Wales was, at the same time, seeking immigrants. John Macarthur (1767–1834), an Englishman from Plymouth, had built up a fine-wool industry in New South Wales, based on the merino sheep that he had originally imported from the Cape of Good Hope in 1796. West was instrumental in arranging for two hundred and thirty five people to emigrate from Cranborne Chase to the Macarthur property at Camden, New South Wales between 1836 and 1841.[176] How many arrived safely is not known. Many working people were willing to contemplate the rigours and risks of the long journey in the hope of better conditions in a new country. Those who settled commemorated families and friends that they had left behind by forming a Chase Society in New South Wales. It still exists, made up now of the descendants of the original émigrés.[177]

Removal of the unemployed and dispossessed of the parish provided some relief in a reduction of the Poor Rate. Landowners and farmers were themselves experiencing difficult times and were very

---

[176] Ian Stratton *John West 1778–1845* Dorset Worthies Series (Dorset Record Society) 1998.
[177] Personal discussion with Edward Bourke.

restive about the ever-increasing Poor Rate. Poor Law expenditure in the County of Dorset had increased 214% between 1792 and 1831. This fact inevitably casts some ambiguity on the motives of the organizers and promoters of emigration. John West was himself a landowner, and was no doubt aware of his divided loyalties. Around twelve thousand people were assisted, under the English Poor Law, to emigrate during the whole of the nineteenth century.

West and his wife Harriet were considered by many to be saints.

Harriet West died in 1839. They had been married for thirty-two years. Three years after her death John published *A Memoir of Harriet*. It is a collection of her letters from Chettle Parsonage to various friends and members of her family; they are more homilies than letters, strong on piety and weak on news and gossip. They now read as exaggeratedly sanctimonious and sentimental. Her husband's final accolade for her is modestly restrained in comparison. '*She has finished her course. She is gone to deck her Saviour's mediatorial Crown – a jewel formed and polished by His own Divine Hand for his Glorious purpose...*'

It is very plain that the standard of behaviour at the parsonage, and the attitudes and values advocated by the Wests were very different from those of the earthbound though popular Reverend William Chafin. Chafin was a Chettle man. He was born at the mansion, had grown up in the village and thoroughly understood the ways and manners of country life. West was a 'foreigner' brought in by Abraham Henry Chambers who had brought a lot of trouble to the village. The Reverend John West had chosen the Eskimaux in preference to Chettle for nine years. The several parishioners who could remember Chafin as well as West were divided on the question of who was the better parson, though they could all agree that West was the more likely to find his place in heaven.

West brought an authoritative and novel humanitarian zeal to Chettle. Nearby Sixpenny Handley had constant trouble with riotous gatherings, fire setting, and Captain Swing letters during these years. Perhaps it is to the patient piety of John and Harriet West that a calmer life at Chettle can be attributed. A biddable local population would have been a considerable attraction to a potential buyer in this riven countryside. John West, appointed by Abraham Henry Chambers, surely helped to reduce some of the many tensions in his parish. It might be argued that had there been no John West, Chettle might not have been sufficiently attractive to the Castlemans and its recovery never effected.

FIFTEEN

Edward and Anne Castleman Take Over

In 1847 when Chettle finally came into the ownership of Edward and Anne Castleman he was forty-seven, she forty-eight years old. They had four daughters between the ages of eleven and twenty-three and one son of six. The Corn Laws had been repealed the year before, thus exposing the English farmer to external competition. It was not for another quarter of a century, when the corn harvests of the American prairies began to pour into the English granaries, that the full impact of this legislation was felt by British agriculture. But there was widespread awareness that the repeal of the Corn Laws symbolized the passing of the old England dependent on land, in favour of the new industrial pioneering power.

At a time when the agricultural outlook was precarious and many landowners were disposing of their properties, the Castlemans finally managed to buy the Chettle estate.

By the 1840's the Castleman family had acquired a reputable status in Dorset and respectability as public figures and landowners. The acquisition of an estate would confirm their standing. Chettle was no ordinary estate for them as it had nurtured some deep family roots, continued no doubt to sustain legends of past renown and exerted a magnetic force, particularly upon Anne. Any dynastic ambitions they may have had for their growing family would have seemed entirely laudable.

Isaac Gulliver had died in 1823. He left money to his childless younger daughter Anne and all his freehold property to his elder

179

daughter Elizabeth, in trust for her six children, his Fryer grandchildren, *'to be equally divided.'*

Until 1867 a married woman had no legal rights of property ownership. *'Everything she owned, earned or inherited belonged to her husband. The husband's right was absolute and paramount.'*[178] Gulliver's will was worded to secure both his daughters from predatory husbands and gave to his one granddaughter an inheritance equal to that of her brothers. (Her paternal grandfather John Fryer in contrast left bequests to four of the Fryer sons but nothing to Anne.) When Elizabeth Fryer (née Gulliver) died in 1839 a sixth of Isaac Gulliver's freehold property therefore passed to his granddaughter, Mrs Anne Castleman. The numerous properties in Dorset that she independently owned brought her a total rental income of approximately £1,615.

Edward's father William (2) died in 1844 and his will, like all his written communications, is unambiguous, specific and short. His annual income from property, investments and private loans had been approximately £4,330. This was to be divided between his three sons. Henry, the middle son was executor.

This was a typical income for the landed gentry class. There were no state provided services and gentlemanly families had many obligations. Maiden aunts, unmarried sisters, retired servants were amongst the variety of dependents. Education, medical and nursing care, such as they were, were charges on the family purse. The management of property required a constant input of capital, and of professional services of lawyer, bailiff and groom. Contributions, voluntary or obligatory, to the church and poor rate, the local hunt, political party, hospital, school and charity were unavoidable. Income tax on the other hand was negligible. It had been introduced to pay for the war against Napoleon and then abandoned till 1842 when it became a permanent feature of English life. For many years it varied between 2d and 6d in the pound (0.83%–2.5%).

During the year following William Castleman (2)'s death some of

---

[178] Margaret Forster *Significant Sisters* 1984.

his property was sold to raise cash and some loans were called in. The £30,000 that was raised was more than enough to enable Edward to acquire Chettle, and the Copyhold Act of 1841 had loosened the restrictions on the sale of feudal property. During 1846 and 1847 he was in communication with John Swarbreck Gregory, the solicitor acting for Charles Symmons who held the deeds of Chettle.[179]

The family's trusted factotum, James Oakley Chislett, kept careful record of the purchase price of Chettle and how it was paid. In addition to £24,000 for the estate there was £3,746 for 'timber at valuation.' A total of £7,000 was borrowed at 4% from Mrs Small, Mr H Bartlett, Mrs Fleet, Leonard Martin, Mr Brewer and one other mortgagee. Payment was made over four years between September 1846 and August 1850. So of the total purchase price of £27,746, £20,746 was derived from family owned capital.

When the Castlemans acquired the Chettle Estate in 1847 they were intent on restoring it as a unified single property wholly under their control. To achieve this they had to eliminate the freeholding of any individual parcels of land or house, a task not easily done since William Chafin had supposedly sold it freehold to Chambers and there had been years of ambiguity about its status. The picture had become more complicated because by 1847 the Castlemans were not alone in their interest in Chettle.

There were a few local people who had negotiated a copyhold through the Court Baron before 1824. The Copyhold Act created the possibility of commuting this to freehold if both lord and tenant were in agreement. There were five men from further afield who had staked a claim as well. Chettle's voting list for 1841 has nine names on it. (To qualify for enfranchisement a man had to hold land worth £10 a year.) The four local men on the list included John Hibberd Brewer who had deep roots in Chettle and Samuel Scammell, husband of Sarah, the widow of Elias Lane to whom Abraham Henry Chambers had granted copyhold premises, which on Samuel's marriage to Sarah became his. Then there were James Blanchard and the

---

[179] DRO D/CRL/A1/1/9-11.

Reverend John West, who had acquired the freehold of the rectory. The five other men on the voting list were Richard Groom, John Richardson, James Denew, Edward Legh and Richard Artis, who were the assignees appointed by the Bankruptcy Commission. They had taken the opportunity of acquiring freehold property in Chettle and the integrity of the estate was in jeopardy.

Edward Castleman acted quickly and firmly to reverse this creeping break up. In January 1847 Edward Castleman wrote to Rutter Esq. solicitor acting for the Scammells: *'I consider the sum asked by Mr and Mrs Scammell for the leasehold at Chettle is more than it is worth… I would prefer to take a lease from her and her husband for the remainder of the contract at the same rent as she is now receiving. Will you inform me whether Mrs Scammell will accept this and when the present tenants can be got out, provided I should wish them to be removed.'*[180]

In March 1849 he wrote to James Blanchard, a substantial farmer in the parish: *'I have purchased of Mr Brewer all his interest in the property which you rent of him at Chettle.'*[181] This Mr Brewer was a descendant of Thomas who had been granted copyhold in 1793. These two letters show how land originally granted as copyhold had become purchasable. Edward bought their pieces back from Blanchard and Scammell, together with the five pieces owned by the assignees and incorporated them all into one estate. The Reverend John West who had the freehold of the rectory had died the year before the Castlemans took over. By 1847 the Reverend Edward Prothero was rector. The freehold of the rectory was not relinquished and was still a matter of legal correspondence in 1963.[182] Prothero was a constant thorn in the side of the Castlemans, especially Anne. He had started on the wrong foot over the rectory and there were constant arguments.

In the early days Edward and his family continued to live at Allendale House in Wimborne and Edward frequently took the ten-mile drive from Wimborne to Chettle through Stanbridge and the Crichels.

[180] DRO D/CRL/A1/1/11.
[181] DRO D/CRL/A1/1/13.
[182] B F P CAS/41.

The rolling chalk downs, the ancient barrows spoke to him of the long history that had always fascinated him.

Edward Castleman had much on his mind at the beginning of 1847. His two elder daughters were shortly to be married, and the Southampton and Dorchester Railway Company of which his brother Charles was chairman, had arranged the formal opening of the line on which he and Charles had worked closely together.[183]

There was much to be done before the Chettle House could become his family's home, but Chettle Lodge was in reasonable repair.[184] His second daughter Elizabeth and her fiancé Douglas Currie had agreed to take it as their first home. It would be good to have someone from the family living in the village as soon as possible.

Edward took stock as he approached the village. It was a very different place from what it had been in the Chafins' time. Edward had been eighteen when the last Chafin had died. It was no longer a feudal manor, nor was it troubled by Lord Rivers' deer and the poaching and smuggling that had been associated with them. The enclosure of the common and the amalgamation of the strips had quite altered the appearance of the place. The vestry no longer met to consider the welfare of the parishioners, but the village was peaceful enough and had welcomed the news that he had bought the estate.

The mansion was in no fit state to be lived in. Indeed it was *'practically a ruin, no floors or ceiling . All the window sashes were gone and the house was used for storing grain.'*[185] The church was much the same, in a tumbledown condition. Shrubs and weeds were growing from the roof and walls. A newspaper report had claimed *'the old church…had become ruinous precluding the possibility of useful repair or judicious restoration.'* The time had come for the renaissance of dilapidated Chettle. The buildings had had little attention for the past century. Fields had been enclosed so the necessary hedging and ditching had been carried out in about 1838 and Abraham Chambers had done some tree planting. But there was no place for piece-meal

[183] Brian Jackson *Castleman's Corkscrew* Vol 1 2008.
[184] Now the Castleman Hotel.
[185] B F P Chettle Parish Book.

repair here and there. Improvements had to be radical, grand and leave the imprint of Castleman upon them.

Throughout England churches were being built and refurbished to accommodate the religious revival of the nation.[186] John West had left his evangelical mark upon Chettle and the redefining of St Mary's Parish Church as the central inspiration of the village was a priority. '*Without God Castles are nothing*' was adopted as the Castleman insignia to be portrayed in the new windows of the south transept of the church. There were a hundred and forty people living in the village, most of them God-fearing and hoping for a fine place where they and their children could worship.

On 8 May 1847 Emily Castleman, the eldest of the family, was married to Thomas Hanham, scion of a well-known Dorset family, in St Martin's in the Fields, London. Thomas was an officer in the Royal Navy. It was a fine occasion and the Castlemans were pleased to have their name linked by marriage with a family of such long-standing repute. The Hanhams lived in Manston House in the village of the same name about ten miles away.

A month later on 10 June Elizabeth Castleman and Douglas Currie, also a naval officer, were married at Wimborne Minster. Memorials of her Castleman, Fryer, and Gulliver forbears were there in the Minster to remind Elizabeth of her heritage.

Douglas was a keen yachtsman and harboured his yacht at the Royal Victoria Yacht Club at Ryde on the Isle of Wight. The club had been founded by Lord Uxbridge in 1815 so the Castleman family had always taken an interest in it and took holidays there.

The Southampton and Dorchester railway line, given the nickname of Castleman's Corkscrew because of its meandering route, was opened on 1 June. May and June of 1847 were momentous. Two weddings, an estate and a railway line made the Castleman family the talk of Dorset. Edward thought wistfully of his father William (2). How pleased he would have been to see plans and aspirations that he had nurtured for years coming to fruition.

---

[186] Between five and six thousand new churches were built and many restored during the Victorian period.

Shortly after coming into possession of the property Edward engaged a firm of architects, Morrison and Hibson of Wimborne to rebuild the church. The work was carried out by local artisans, Mr J Barrett, stonemason of Farnham and Mr J Bugden, carpenter of Wimborne Minster. The superintendent of works was Mr Blake, surveyor of Wimborne Minster, who acted under the control of the architects. The nave, chancel and transepts were demolished and the new church built *'of similar materials as the old church viz. stone and flint and covered with tiles ...the roof will be open, of fir, stained. Floor will be laid with encaustic tiles and several of the windows filled with stained glass ...'* The entire cost of the church rebuilding was met by Edward Castleman.

Wall monuments commemorating the Chafin family were carefully and prominently rehung. The Jacobean oak pulpit, made in the early seventeenth century to promote the new translation of the Bible of King James I, was carved up to make two chairs and two coffin stools, some bookcases and three statues. The West family who had been a calming influence in the village were gratefully memorialized in the new east window. West's style of evangelical Christianity was popular during the Victorian period and Edward Castleman was churchgoing and probably quite devout. Lord Shaftesbury of Wimborne St Giles a few miles away, supposed a more secular motivation. *'The Middle Classes know that the safety of their lives and property depend on having round them a peaceful happy and moral population,'* he wrote.[187] It was a sentiment with which Edward Castleman concurred. He had enlisted as a special constable in Wimborne to quell the riots in 1830 and fervently hoped such times would never be seen again in Dorset.

All the rebuilding of the church was done without the necessary faculty – that is permission from the ecclesiastical authority, the bishop. It is difficult to believe, with the range of people involved – architects, the surveyor of Wimborne Minster, stonemason, carpenter, not to mention the acutely knowledgeable Castleman family – that this

---

[187] G M Young *Victorian England: Portrait of an Age* 1936.

was simply an oversight or due to ignorance. Antagonism towards the Reverend Edward Prothero that had started over the freehold of the rectory was probably the cause. Either he was not consulted or he declined to advise the bishop favourably. The position was regularized and a retrospective faculty granted in October 1850, at a cost of £500 to Edward Castleman.

The new church was completed. There was ready access from the mansion, across the garden to the west door. Most of the parishioners entered by the gate in the northeast corner of the churchyard, near the box tomb of Anne Castleman's great grandfather, William Beale.

The mansion was also restored. It had originally been built to display the status of a wealthy prosperous eighteenth-century family. Within three decades of its completion the extensive property that would have justified, and made possible, its upkeep had been lost. Extensive repairs and alterations were put in hand and the mansion became the family residence some time during the 1850's. Built as a showpiece, it was restored with similar aspirations. Country house life of the mid nineteenth century with its hunting and shooting required a full time gamekeeper, so Keeper's Lodge was built in the woods. The line of a road was altered and a hill lowered, no doubt to improve the view.[188]

The newly wedded Douglas and Elizabeth Currie moved into Chettle Lodge (now the hotel) where they lived for the next twenty-two years. They were the first of the family to arrive in the parish. They had six sons, all baptized in Chettle parish church. Douglas divided his time between Chettle and the Royal Victoria Yacht Club at Ryde on the Isle of Wight.

On 29 November 1847 Edward Castleman Esq. formally marked his entry as Lord of the Manor of Chettle by holding his first Court Baron. James Oakley Chislett was his steward. Thomas Dashwood, who had been steward through the many difficult years, and who had negotiated the troublesome sale to Chambers in 1807, returned to his attorney's practice in Sturminster Newton.

---

[188] B F P CAS/33.

James Oakely Chislett was son of George Chislett, who had been innkeeper of the King's Head in Milborne Port.[189] The constant disturbances following the Napoleonic wars had not been good for business and his inn keeping was not a success. George Chislett was one of the many tenants of Lord Uxbridge who had been unable to pay his rent. William Castleman (2) had absorbed him into his office staff in Wimborne. This was another mark of his considerate nature that he had been somewhat at pains to disguise. James Oakley Chislett was the eldest of his family of nine.

An early letter from the adolescent James Chislett seeking patronage of Lord Uxbridge is from a very well schooled pen. His loyalty and devotion to the Castlemans is palpable. He became Edward's agent and right hand, signing letters on behalf of Edward Castleman in the manner of the day with *'for whom I am gentleman.'*

Relatives usually held the central positions of trust and authority in the Castleman domain. But George Chislett had repaid William Castleman's kindness to him with devoted service and the Chisletts had grown up in the shadow of the Castleman family business and knew its credo and its lodestones, had absorbed its standards as their own. James Oakley Chislett was treated as an honorary Castleman.

His correspondence is voluminous. He lacks the focused incisiveness that marks the communications of William and Edward, but is painstaking and thorough. He became an indispensable member of the Castleman entourage keeping track of creditors, debtors, purchasers of underwood,[190] manure, and timber as well as keeping an eye on insurance policies and investments of various members of the family. He would later found the estate agent's firm of Chislett and Rawlence, still in operation today.

There were a number of irregularities in the first years of the new regime. A great deal of rebuilding was set in hand, and there was the estate to run. It was not clear who was to be responsible for paying wages and other bills. Building contractors did not get their accounts settled on time. Edward sometimes called upon Douglas Currie, his

---

[189] Kelly's *Directory* 1823.
[190] Sold by the acre – in 1850 £7 8s, in 1851 £9 5s.

son-in-law, the only family member resident in the village for the first three years, to sort things out.

The bailiff, Robert Rogers at Chettle famhouse was getting his farm into good heart and knew more than anyone else in the village about the agricultural side of things. The indefatigable James Chislett from the law office in Wimborne kept careful account of every sale, purchase, and tenancy, he knew the market price of oak, ash and beech timber, who could be trusted, and who could not. Very little escaped his notice. Occasionally there was a threat of court proceedings that braced everyone to action. Good order and discipline were eventually established when all had successfully worked out their roles and responsibilities. There had been over thirty years of misrule, or no rule at all, so it is little wonder that form and function took a while to take shape. The social changes at Chettle were huge. For the first time for more than forty years the parishioners knew who their landlord was – a Dorset man familiar with Dorset ways – in place of the variety of Commissioners in Bankruptcy from London who had had taken little interest in the villagers, and whose only interest in the village seemed to be to acquire land. Edward Castleman put an end to their schemes for gaining control and had brought with him men who understood the locality, were interested in farming, and in the village and its residents. The people of Chettle understood their speech and their ways, and willingly worked on the various schemes for improvement that were set in hand.

By 1851 Edward (1) with Anne his wife were living in Chettle Cottage.[191] With them were their youngest daughter Jane, then fifteen, their son Edward Arthur Hammond Castleman (2) aged ten, Margaret Priest a governess for the children, Elizabeth a servant/nurse, Susannah Carter a handmaid, Jane Pottle a cook and William Hampshire a footman. In Chettle Lodge Douglas and Elizabeth and their two sons had one manservant, Abraham Ferrett, and four women servants. There were five servants for each family.

The 'servant question' obsessed the Victorians. The living-in servant

---

[191] Now known as Chafins Cottage.

was often at close quarters with the family. Neither could survive without the other but resentment and exploitation easily crept in. Middle class families disliked the company of social inferiors and their inevitable intrusion, or inadvertent eavesdropping, into family confidences and discussions with all the threat that that implied. Servants rarely had any enforceable contract and were at risk of long hours and unreasonable demands. Devoted and considerate relationships between master and servant certainly existed, but it was an ambiguous area of subtle negotiation if successful, or deceitful scheming if not. The manservant at Chettle Lodge, Abraham Ferrett, received a wage of £3 a month. Edward Castleman made provision for a retirement pension for the family governess, Miss Millington. Chettle and the Castlemans had reached the Victorian age.

The year after they had moved to the village, Edward Castleman was *'seriously and dangerously ill.'* Edward's health was a matter of constant concern. In 1853 he went *'for a cruise for a week on his yacht, which was really necessary for his health.'* His eldest daughter Emily, wife of Thomas Hanham, had died in Bournemouth at the age of twenty-nine. Edward had worked himself to exhaustion at her bedside. Commemoration of a young wife would normally have fallen to her husband. Thomas Hanham, who was unconventional, had a reputation of being anti-Christian. By contrast Edward had all the marks of being entirely conformist to established Protestant church principles. It was a deeply religious period and a titanic struggle for the soul of Emily took place between her father and husband at the time of her final illness and death.

Like his father in many ways, Edward did not enjoy the robust resilience to life's assaults that had carried William through many difficulties, though he survived this and other health scares and fulfilled his public duties. In 1859 he was appointed Deputy Lieutenant of Dorset.[192]

Edward did not want for loyal support. Relatives and friends, as well as several men in formal relationships were unstinting with their

---

[192] B F P CAS/3.

help. Douglas Currie in the early years was his right hand man who later became a Magistrate of the County.

In 1858 Edward Castleman wrote to Robert Rogers, who was living at Chettle Farm[193] with his wife Margaret, several children and four servants: '*I shall be ready to let you Mr Blanchard's farm... from Michaelmas next at £290 you paying rates and taxes.*' Rogers was farming most of the land of the estate by then. He was overseer of the village. He and his son Robert after him were for years the backbone of the parish with a variety of administrative responsibilities. They were enumerators for the decennial census, dealt with the various rates that had to be raised, managed elections, and were Churchwardens.

The relationship between the Castlemans and the Rogers family mirrored on a smaller scale the eighteenth-century pattern of the great landholders and their tenant farmers who, with the rector, ran affairs of the parish, a symbiotically satisfactory arrangement. Rogers directly employed upwards of twenty agricultural labourers. His income was derived from the agricultural produce that he was able to sell. From it he paid rent for the land to Edward Castleman, wages to his labourers, and any rates and taxes chargeable on the land. Robert Rogers was to Edward Castleman as Edward's grandfather William (1) had been to Thomas Freke in Hinton St Mary.

Edward (1)'s health deteriorated further a year or two later and he died in 1861, at the age of sixty-one. In his fourteen years as the owner of Chettle the estate had been transformed. The mansion as a family home had been restored to its former splendour. There were outbuildings to accommodate horses and a variety of carriages for all members of the family. Cottages had been repaired and some new ones built to house the increasing population. The keeper in the new lodge properly managed the woods and the game that lived there. The restoration of the church had encouraged regularity of worship and a respectful orderliness that had not prevailed in the village for a century. The estate was valued for probate purposes at £20,722, with rents due at the death '*say £725*'.[194]

[193] Now St Mary's Farmhouse.
[194] B F P CAS/21. These rents almost certainly arise from the Chettle estate alone.

Valuation for probate cannot be equated with market value, but the probate valuation was approximately 25% less than the purchase price of what had been a derelict property. On 19 January 1848 Edward (1) had made his simple nine line will and never changed it. He bequeathed *'the whole of my property and estate both real and personal unto my dear wife Anne.'* With Edward (1)'s departure affairs at Chettle began to change. The bonds that held family and village together began slowly but surely to loosen.

Edward had always been the public face. He had continued his legal business, the stewardship of Kingston Lacey and the stewardship of the Uxbridge property till it was sold in 1854. His interests were wide and he knew many people. With his death these sources of income and outside contacts came to an end. Anne had always run the residential and domestic affairs of Chettle. Accounts, bills, receipts, the Game Book and lettings had always been under her control. Records were kept with meticulous precision. Her interests and field of vision were more limited than her husband's and her roots in Chettle were deeper. With Edward's death she became responsible for everything and had to take a more public position. Without Edward's level head and broad mind Anne became rather inflexible.

At his death Edward (1)'s only son Edward (2) was nineteen. At his coming of age two years later, he did not inherit and for the rest of his life was subordinate to his mother who maintained her position as sole owner till she died in 1883. She dominated Chettle and all who lived there for the next twenty-two years.

The Castleman family had some colourful members. Edith, the third daughter married Captain John Swinburne of the 18th Regiment of Foot, an Irish regiment. They lived in Chettle and had two children, John and Surtees. After Swinburne's death Edith made a second marriage in 1868 to Thomas Hanham her deceased sister Emily's widower and lived, as her sister had done, at Manston House. She was Thomas Hanham's third wife. Marriage to 'deceased wife's sister' was illegal so the marriage took place in France. It was another forty years before such marriages were permitted in England with the Marriage Act of 1907, but they were quite widely tolerated. Dorset's most famous son, Thomas Hardy was twenty-eight when this marriage took place. The Hanham family was well known in Dorset and Hardy made good use of newspaper cuttings and local gossip and wove them into his novels. He puts a comment into the mouth of Tess of the D'Urbervilles who says to Angel Clare, *'people marry their sister's in law continually around Marlott.'*[195] Marlott (Marnhull) is three miles from the Hanham house at Manston. W.S. Gilbert satirized the irksome nature of the law with *'And he shall prick that annual blister, Marriage to deceased wife's sister'* in Iolanthe, first performed in 1882.[196] Edith and Thomas had made their mark with their marriage.

Edith had proposed that her husband Thomas Hanham be appointed trustee on a family trust to take the place of Douglas Currie following his death. The lawyer, John Ruddall of Lincoln's Inn expostulated: *'The appointment of Captain Hanham would be exceedingly improper, as, in the event of Mr Smith's death* [a brother-in-law] *there would be no party to protect her interests and those of her children from the very individual against whom they would need to be protected. Moreover, the fact that Captain Hanham is not by the law of England the recognized husband of the lady would make the appointment even more objectionable.'*[197]

Edith and Thomas espoused another illegal cause – human cremation. Manston House burnt down in 1851; this could have been caused by early experimentation. Cremation had been the means of disposal in pre-Christian Britain but was considered inconsistent with the Christian belief in the bodily resurrection of the dead. Cremation was not sanctioned until an Act of Parliament of 1902 *'for the Regulation of Burning of Human Remains'.*

Edith died in 1876 and her corpse was interred in a mausoleum[198] at Manston House. The following year Lady Hanham, Edith's mother-in-law died in her ninetieth year. She had made a specific request that she should be cremated, not buried. Her body was similarly interred.

---

[195] Thomas Hardy *Tess of the D'Urbervilles* 1891.
[196] Sarah Brown ' Deceased Wife's Sister Act' *The Literary Encyclopedia* 26 June 2004.
[197] B F P, CAS/5.
[198] The mausoleum is still there.

By 1882 '*a simple and inexpensive furnace*' had been constructed at Manston and Edith's body was cremated on Sunday evening 8 October, and Lady Hanham's the following day. The *New York Times* and the *Pall Mall Gazette* both reported on 30 October 1882 that Mrs Edith Swinburne Hanham's remains were cremated at Manston on Sunday evening 8 October 1882. This was the first recorded cremation in England in modern times and was '*in opposition to the ruling of the Home Secretary*' Sir William Harcourt. Anne, Edith's mother, was still alive aged eighty-three at Chettle. She was bedridden, but in command of her faculties. (She was still signing cheques and conducting business at the estate.) Though unconventional in many ways herself, cremation was considered anti-Christian and would have been offensive to her. Thomas Hanham died five years later on 27 November 1887. His funeral was conducted a week later '*under Masonic rites (no clergy officiating), his body was interred in the Mausoleum, but removed, later that day … and cremated that evening.*'[199]

He had executed a deed three weeks before his death with '*John Comyns Leach of Sturminster Newton, Dr of Medicine to Ratify and Confirm the deed*' which served in place of a will. All his clothes were left to Sarah Jane Chapman of Manston House. Bequeathing expensive clothes, sometimes encrusted with jewels, was not unusual in the Tudor period. Towards the end of the nineteenth century clothing was more functional, washable and expendable and it was not generally bequeathed. This bequest seems like another eccentricity in a lifetime of idiosyncratic behaviour.

Hanham left Manston House to his stepson, John Castleman Swinburne-Hanham, who was the son of his third wife Edith and John Swinburne. He became managing director of the company that created Golders Green Crematorium. At its opening, credit was given to the '*zeal and foresight of… Mr J C Swinburne-Hanham its managing director… who …had already played a decisive part in the history*

---

[199] I am grateful to Brian Jackson, railway historian and author of *Castleman's Corkscrew*, for drawing my attention to this event in the Castleman story.

of the Cremation Movement by assisting at the cremation ceremony which took place at Blandford Dorset, in 1882.'

The great weight of respected opinion at the time would have found cremation repugnant to its Christian views. In the quiet corner of rural England that comprised Manston and Chettle it was a flagrant affront to sensibilities. Swinburne Hanham was known locally as 'The Stoker of Woking.'[200]

Jane, the youngest daughter, married Edwin Augustus Smith, a lawyer in 1854. Elizabeth, her elder sister who had married Douglas Currie, was widowed in 1869 and remarried two years later to the Reverend John Collis D.D. There was a great falling out between Jane and Elizabeth. Smith v. Collis became a high court case in 1884. The details of the case are obscure, but it is believed by a present member of the family that it arose from a dispute over the provision to be made for the care of their mother, Anne Castleman in her final decrepitude. The two sisters were then, at the age of forty-six and fifty-six respectively, the only surviving members of that generation. As a result of this dispute Allendale House was sold at auction on the instruction of High Court Judge Pearson in 1885. The house, designed for William Castleman (2) and his young family by Jeffry Wyatt in 1805, was an heirloom lost to the family. It is still there in Wimborne. It has been a girls' school, offices and has recently been restored.

Shortly after Edward (1)'s death Anne sought ways to supplement the income of the estate. She had let some of the stabling accommodation to Squire Osbaldeston. The man's amazing sporting record in hunting, shooting, and racing had earned him the sobriquet of *'The Squire of England.'* He had brought some horses to Chettle for the *'splendid training ground'* nearby at Tarrant Monkton. Osbaldeston records in his autobiography that the *'stay at Chettle was terminated by friction with the owner of the place, Mrs Castleman, over use of the stables.'* Osbaldeston complained that Edward (2) and his friend kept very late hours with their horses thus disturbing his, which *'could not*

---

[200] Woking was the location of the first public crematorium.

be tolerated' so the Osbaldestons sought new quarters.[201] Anne Castleman wrote to her son-in-law Edwin Smith requesting his help as a lawyer. *'I am very anxious about this affair with O-. I am sure they do not intend to pay anything and will make the affair of the stables an excuse... if they mean to cheat me their horses and all ought to be turned out ... I cannot stand swindling and I hope you will take the matter up in earnest.'* [202]

The women in Edward's family did not comply readily with the Victorian ideal of dutiful submissive womanhood. Anne Castleman, their mother was one of those exceptional early nineteenth-century women brought up on terms of reasonable equality with the men in the family. She was at heart a Gulliver, strong-minded, independent, and resourceful, and had always had control of her own income. She was a near contemporary of Florence Nightingale, who said of her father *'My father is not as other men are. He thinks that daughters should serve their country as well as sons. He brought me up to think so.'*[203] Anne Castleman, too, had been nurtured to think of herself as an equal with the sons of the family. They were both, in very different contexts, women brought up not to assent to any inferior role on account of their sex. They were well in advance of the age in which they lived and there was very little to support them. Women were treated legally, and often socially, as children. Anne Castleman, like other Victorian women with a strong sense of their own identity reacted to restraints with belligerent energy. She had four daughters who learned from her. The daughters had all married at a very early age, as if subconsciously, or otherwise, needing to get away. Elizabeth and Edith settled in the village when they were first married. Elizabeth had six sons and Edith two, all baptized in St Mary's Church. But when their husbands died they moved away within months. Anne Castleman had a good relationship with her son-in-law Edwin Augustus Smith, husband of her youngest daughter Jane, and he was one of the stalwarts of the family who worked in a professional

---

[201] Squire Osbaldeston *His Autobiography* 1926.
[202] B F P CAS/21.
[203] Hugh Small *Florence Nightingale: Avenging Angel* 1998.

capacity as Anne's solicitor. They never lived in Chettle however, and he maintained his legal business in Blandford. The discords of this family became noisier when Edward was no longer there and Anne became increasingly isolated.

William Castleman (2) and his sons had worked cooperatively together, and they had incorporated a variety of disparate people into their circle. Personal differences were subordinated to the bigger purpose of making a fortune. Edward Castleman (1) had continued his father's tradition of getting people to collaborate for achievement. But when Edward had gone Anne floundered. Edward (1)'s only son, Edward (2) was nineteen years old when his father died.

Five years later in 1866 when he was twenty-four he married Fanny Martha Fuidge who was eighteen. In the eight years of their marriage they had five children. Edward (2) died prematurely in 1874 at the age of thirty-two, leaving Fanny to bring up the five children. He never became the owner. Anne in accordance with Edward (1)'s will became the Lady of the Manor, officiated at the Court Baron meetings and retained the ownership until her death on 1 October 1883 at the age of eighty-four. Only two of her daughters survived her; Elizabeth for only eleven months. Jane lived till 1905.

They all bickered, quarrelled and went to law against each other and various of their neighbours with energy. Anne lived in Chettle House with a lady's maid, a cook, a housemaid and a footman, but none of her family,[204] till the end of her life, by which time she was disabled and bedridden. Her personal difficulties were made more complex by the deepening agricultural depression. From 1870 onward the true impact of free trade in agriculture was all too apparent. British farmers could not compete with the great prairies of America and the future was bleak.

Anne Castleman spent the last three years of her life in Chettle House. From May 1880 the Institution of Nursing Sisters of Bishopsgate supplied a private nurse, Sister Sully, to look after her. There was no nationally recognized nurse training, which was only beginning

[204] 1871 Census MC (R) 782.

to take shape. Most of the voluntary hospitals with medical schools had started their own programmes of training 'ladies' to be nurses, and there was a lively demand for their services. The Institution in Bishopsgate would have recruited nurses trained at St Bartholomew's or the London Hospital. To have acquired a private nursing sister from such a source in 1880 was quite avant garde.

Anne Castleman died on 1 October 1883 in her eighty-fifth year. She had been thirty-five years at Chettle. With her own son dead, the estate went directly to her grandson, Edward William Fuidge Castleman (3) who was then a schoolboy of thirteen at Harrow School.

Under the terms of Anne's will several servants received small bequests and *'Decent mourning to all servants.'* That meant new clothes so that they would turn up at the funeral looking smart. Her son-in-law Edwin Smith (Jane's husband) and the rector William Truell were her trustees. Her grandson Edward (3) was left *'messuages, farms, lands… in Great Canford, Hampreston and West Parley.'*[205] This property, originally Gulliver's, was still in family possession. But there was a Schedule of Real Estate directed by the will to be sold to pay debts – 13 dwellings, a freehold estate of 100 acres at West Stower and about 8 acres of land. This realized in total £10,935 upon which tax was payable at 1%, that is £109 7s 10d. Anne had been living beyond her means and the estate was depleted. *Rents due at Death* were assessed as £1360, £714 from Chettle and the rest from the properties inherited via her mother from Isaac Gulliver.

Mrs Fanny Martha Fuidge, Anne's daughter-in-law took over the running of the estate. She had no plan to move into Chettle House, which was to be let. Some of the contents therefore had to be sold and within about six weeks of Anne's death Waters and Rawlence arranged the auction on 13 November 1883. The sale included the library of one thousand three hundred books that reflected the interests of the family in history, religion and literature (there were several first editions of Dickens) and property law. There was furniture and kitchen paraphernalia and a range of horse drawn vehicles and

[205] B F P CAS/43.

197

various animals. There were two double-seated broughams, a one, and a two-horse landau, a four-wheel pony carriage and two-wheel pony cart with a folding hood and a light spring trap. Harness, horses, dogs, including a pointer and retriever, and pigs were sold.[206] This was the break up of a Victorian gentleman's family home.

During Anne's final years the tide of modernity flowed in. The railway and the steam ship enabled cheap food to be imported in ever increasing quantities and to be distributed to all parts of the country. The days of the brougham and the landau were over and British agriculture faced a profoundly depressing prospect. The Castleman family was not a united one. Almost all of the family had left Chettle and there was very little preparedness for the stringencies that lay ahead.

[206] B F P CAS/32.

SIXTEEN

After Anne

At this critical time in its history the nominal owner of Chettle was at boarding school. He was not well informed on the details of his legacy or what was entailed in being Lord of the Manor. He owned other properties at Great Canford, Hampreston and West Parley, relics of the Gulliver estate. He had never known his grandfather Edward (1) and was three years old when his father Edward (2) had died. Until he went away to school he had lived with his widowed grandmother, widowed mother and three sisters. His sisters were at Cheltenham Ladies' College under the educational eye of the formidable feminist Dorothea Beale. She had been headmistress there for twenty-five years and had transformed the reputation of the College. It had been an establishment where young ladies acquired the gentle accomplishments of music and drawing. Miss Beale made it one of the foremost academic schools for girls in the country. She was prominent and successful in the development of both secondary and university education for women. Anne Castleman left money in her will for the continuing education of her three granddaughters. The long influence of Isaac Gulliver for equality for the women of his family stretched down through four generations. The women in the family were the stonger characters, and there were more of them.

The management of Chettle fell to Edward (2)'s widow, Fanny Martha (née Fuidge), now aged thirty-five. Her family were co-owners of Fuidge and Fripp, one of the three great sugar refineries in the city of Bristol. Much of Bristol's prosperity had grown from the slave plantations of the Caribbean. The abolition of slavery and cheaper beet sugar from Europe was by the second half of the nineteenth century causing some decline in the city's wealth. Nevertheless Fuidge money did make its way to Chettle during the 1870's. Two tantalizing account books in the archive of the descendants of the Castlemans are to be found amongst the Bourke Family Papers. They are neat, leather bound, brass locked and beautifully written summary accounts of Fuidge and Fripp from 1845 till 1878. Sugar purchased in the year 1845-1846 cost £221,600 11s 9d. It rose steadily to £765,910 in 1875. Payments are consistent with a trading business, to steamship companies, Portishead Docks and railway companies. In 1874, the year that Edward (2) died, there is a payment of £500 to him and a further £200 to Mrs Castleman in 1874, 1875 and 1877. These relatively small sums would have been for personal expenditure rather than for the estate. Nevertheless Fuidge and Fripp were subsidizing their daughter from the profits of imported food as the agricultural depression began to bite. Anne Castleman who controlled the purse and the bank account at the time was finding it increasingly difficult to balance the books so both Edward (2) and Fanny turned to another source.

Fanny Martha had been a widow for eleven years and under her mother-in-law's thumb, when at thirty-five she became responsible for Chettle. Her children were all at boarding school, and she had had little opportunity of learning about the estate while her mother-in-law was alive. Her two surviving sisters-in-law, Elizabeth Collis and Jane Smith were much older than she was and were recovering from serious losses incurred by the court case in which they had been involved. Elizabeth died within the year and Fanny held out little hope of any cooperative succour from the immediate family. Her only moral support came from her mother Eleanor and unmarried sister Edith who came to live with her shortly after Anne Castleman's death. They were welcome companions, though probably little help for the task in hand, which was to make Chettle a profitable enterprise.

Assets had been sold off for the settlement of debts accumulated during Anne's lifetime and in connection with the Collis v. Smith legal case. Many of the contents of Chettle House had been dispersed at the auction in November 1883.

Robert Rogers' son was now living at St Mary's Farmhouse and farming many of the acres of the Chettle estate. The Rogers family thoroughly understood the parish but were themselves afflicted by the agricultural depression.

Fanny Martha moved out of Chettle and rented a house in Pimperne, a village four miles to the west. The plight of Chettle was by no means unique. Landowners no longer had a monopoly of power and were unable to control the freetrade circumstances that were damaging them. Recourse to income from other sources was essential for survival.

Fanny Martha diversified to the extent of letting Chettle House to two separate families, with their several servants, as tenants. Edward came of age in 1891 and should have taken control of Chettle but the Census data for that year shows the population of the parish to be one hundred and twenty-one, and once again there was no Lord of the Manor resident in the village.

Of the fifty-eight occupations specified for the residents of Chettle seventeen were agricultural labourers, eleven domestic servants, four carters, three grooms, three shepherds, two cooks, two gardeners, two trained nurses and one carpenter, baker, grocer, rector, surveyor, tobacconist, dressmaker, farmer, bailiff, butler and gamekeeper. The large majority of the village was dependent for its employment on the estate, and all their incomes were being generated ultimately from the soil of Chettle. More than three quarters of the population of the parish had been born within fifty miles of the parish and considered themselves as locals. Their roots and their forebears were close at hand. They were Dorset men and women, attuned to the seasons, cognizant of the soil and of the nature of growing things.

The life of the village centred round the shop and the post office, both run by Henry Sherring who was also the local baker. He held a key position in the communication network of the parish. He would have been the first to see the letters that *arrive at 8.45am and 2.30pm and are dispatched at 9.25am and 4.25pm. On Sunday at 10.25am.*

Henry would have known the origin and destination of the postal packets of the village, and was a valuable source of information and gossip.

The Parish School, built to accommodate forty children, had an average attendance of twenty-five, with Miss Sarah Ann Barrett as their schoolmistress. The Education Act of 1880 required Miss Barrett, though she may not have known it, to continue the educational endeavour, under State sponsorship, which John West had initiated voluntarily in the locality sixty years earlier. Her task was to inculcate the three R's and to give some religious teaching. The children of primary school age made up 20% of the population of the village. The school leaving age was ten (and rose to eleven in 1893). Any chance to continue their education beyond that age would, for most of her pupils, have been slender. They were then ready to join the work force. The commercial interests in the village were William Inkpen, farmer, Tom Ridout, carpenter, and Robert Rogers, farmer. (This Robert Rogers is the son of the Robert Rogers who had been a copyholder in 1834 and Edward (1)'s bailiff.)

At the turn of the century this was a village that was surviving with difficulty. As more and more food imports came in, the value of agricultural produce went down, as did the value of land.

A very small proportion of the parish had an education beyond the basic minimum of the three R's then required. Mrs Emily Campbell at Chettle House came from New Zealand and her cook from London. The other cook at Chettle House came from Kincardine in Scotland. These were anomalies segregated from the parish in part by their background, but also by their place of residence. There was, and had always been a marked social and economic distance between the mansion and the rest of the village, but they were dependent on each other.

Although the population of the country was increasing the numbers engaged in farming declined by 11% between 1881 and 1901,[207] and some two and a half million acres of arable land had been put

[207] W H Armstong *Farmworkers* 1987.

out of production. In the search for employment, people, especially young people, moved from rural to urban areas, or to the colonies. Many went from the southwest of England to the coalfields of South Wales. Agricultural economics from the 1880's exerted a strong centrifugal force on Chettle. The Castlemans had moved out and the population was declining.

Edward (3) had no personal or financial resources to help him counteract the troublesome forces that were ravaging his inheritance. His predominant interest was foxhunting. There were three accessible hunts that met regularly. The Cattistock and the Portman had both been started by Mr J J Farquharson – a near neighbour of Chettle – in the early nineteenth century. In 1858 the 2nd Viscount Portman had taken over one of them and Cattistock formed its own separate hunt in 1869. Then there was the Blackmore Vale Hunt that had started in 1831 when it belonged to Lord Uxbridge. (The last two Chafin brothers had had their own foxhounds until George (2) died in 1776 when they had been dispersed.) With judicious choice of meeting places a full time occupation could be made of foxhunting. There is nothing to suggest that Edward (3) was motivated to maintain either the economy or the community of Chettle. The Castleman bonds, which had held the estate and the parish together for half a century, were extremely fragile.

Kelly's Directory of 1895 describing the village itemizes Chettle House as '*the residence of Ed. Cay Adams … Edward William Fuidge Castleman is lord of the manor and sole landowner.*' Edward (3) was then twenty-four and living in Pimperne with his mother and her relatives.

Edward (3)'s Fuidge relatives all died in the early years of the twentieth century. Eleanor, his maternal grandmother died in 1901, his aunt Edith in 1904 and his mother Fanny Martha in 1907. All are buried in Chettle churchyard. Edward (3) continued to live at Pimperne and to devote much of his time and energy to foxhunting.

Inevitably the sale of Chettle was considered. Many country houses, with or without their estates, were being sold. Many were standing empty. By 1909 Edward had, however, saved the situation in the time-honoured way by marrying a rich woman, Jessie Anne Morris. She came with sufficient resources to enable a lot of building and maintenance work, including further work on the mansion, to be carried out. Edward (3) and Jessie moved into Chettle House that was once again inhabited by the Castleman family; the first time since Anne had died twenty-six years earlier. But the estate as an agricultural enterprise was not paying its way. Even had Edward (3) had an interest in its management it would have been an uphill task.

Then came the 1914 war. Siegfried Sassoon's *Memoirs of a Fox-hunting Man*, largely autobiographical, resonates wonderfully well with the life of Edward Castleman (3). George Sherston, the Fox-hunting Man was, like Edward, effete, ineffectual and lonely. Both had taken to foxhunting with a passion, and when war came they joined, with their horses, their County Yeomanry.

'I ruminated on my five weeks' service as a trooper in the Yeomanry ...I had also got yesterday's Times, which contained a piece of poetry by Thomas Hardy. "What of the faith and fire within us, men who march away ere the barn-cocks say night is growing grey ?"...I did not need Hardy's "Song of the Soldiers" to warn me that the Remounts was no place for me...My incompetence, compared with the relative efficiency of my associates, was causing me perturbed and flustered moments...I had the advantage of being a better rider than a good many of the men in my squadron, which to some extent balanced my ignorance and inefficiency in other respects.'...[208]

Thousands of young men who had lost their bearings in the landed gentry class to which they belonged, and had footled their way through the vacuities of the Edwardian social scene joined their County Yeomanry, not because of any *'faith and fire within'* but because it offered activity apparently to some purpose. Sassoon and Castleman, unlike many, survived, though as changed men.

Edward (3) joined the 2nd Dorset Yeomanry. He was involved in

[208] Siegfried Sassoon *Complete Memoirs of George Sherston* 1937.

the second phase of the Gallipoli expedition in August 1915. A letter from '*The Camp in Gallipoli Sunday 29 August 1915*' from E G T Bullock to Lieutenant Colonel Colfox O C 2nd Dorset (20) Yeomanry, Bowood Camp, 20 Chippenham, describes the encounter in two closely typed pages.

'We left our comfortable quarters in Egypt on Friday 13 August 1915 and entrained to Alexandria that night embarking next morning on a very crowded transport. We put to sea that evening (14th)… a second attack had started… Our casualties were very large. The Brigadier and all his staff wounded. We lost Castleman, wounded in the arm …out of eight officers I am the only one who escaped unhurt, the worst of it is that we can get no information about the wounded from the Ambulances as all reports go to the base and none come back here to us. … We lost 119 men out of the Regiment of whom five are, I believe dead, out of 301 who went into action… a terrible business, and I hope I may never see another day like it.'[209]

Edward had sustained a serious shoulder wound. As with Sassoon it was his riding and hunting accomplishments and devotion to his horse that had beckoned him to the Yeomanry. He was forty-five years old with no outstanding aptitude for military life.

While he was away Jessie ran the estate. For the four years of the war farming revived as once more the nation came to depend on homegrown food. Chettle came to life and the parish worked with a will to compensate for the several young men who were away. German prisoners of war from the camp at Fordington became part of the labour force later in the war. Homegrown food was at a premium and agriculture became profitable for a few years. Accounts for Chettle during the time that Jessie was in charge have not been found. Accounts for the year ending 29 September 1918 however show that there was a deficit of £898 19s 1d (this is 4.76% of the total expenditure). The wages bill for the year to English employees and

[209] DRO D/DOY/A/6/5.

prisoners of war was £1651 5s 5d. The prisoners of war kept the total bill down. An agricultural labourer's wages ranged between £1 and £2 a week. The labour bill fluctuated from year to year. In 1920, when the prisoners had returned to their own country, it was £3,342.18s. 0d. The annual deficit fluctuated too, but the account was always in the red. For the year 1924–5 there was a separate Pig Account, with a Panglossian comment: *'Loss of £52 on the year which about equals the manurial value.'*[210] Matters were obviously desperate when pigs, reared for food, had to be assessed by their *'manurial value'.* Matters only got worse after the onset of the Great Depression in October 1929.

Following the Parliamentary enclosures of the eighteenth and nineteenth centuries the tithe in kind had been commuted to a money payment – a rent charge on land. In time this became saleable as an investment, known as a Fee Farm Rent. In April 1918, before the war had ended, several Fee Farm Rents were auctioned at the Auction Mart, Tokenhouse Yard, London E C. Lot 3 was the Fee Farm Rent amounting to £35 15s 6d per annum on 850 acres 2 rods 26 perches, property of Edward Castleman.[211] Every enclosed field and building, its name, acreage, and use (arable, pasture etc) were listed in the sale brochure, which claimed that these commodities constituted *'Investment of the safest character.'*

With this anticipated income Lot 3 would have sold, if we assume a 5% return, for around £715. There was evidently a lively sale in Fee Farm Rents, which were bonds with a fixed interest. The landowner, instead of paying the tithe to the parson, paid the fixed rate to the bondholder. It perhaps gives us some idea of the plight of landowners and the lengths to which they went to realize some of their assets.

Between 1918 and 1939 Edward (3) returned to the life of a country squire. The farms of the estate were let and Edward spent much of his time hunting. Each year the estate was in deficit. Bankruptcy was staved off by sale of other assets. Jessie died in 1937. There were no children and Edward was then sixty-seven. If there was any solace,

---

[210] B F P Account book 1919–1956.
[211] DRO D/CRL/B3/5/2.

it was that many of his neighbours and colleagues were facing the same difficulties.

Edward (3)'s sisters had never returned permanently to Chettle after their schooling at Cheltenham Ladies College in the 1880's. Alice, the eldest had married Bernhard Oswald Roe in 1900. He had followed his father, Sir Charles Roe into the Indian Civil Service. The Indian Civil Service was formed after the Indian Mutiny of 1857 and for the ninety years of its existence (till Indian independence in 1947) was '*the most powerful body of officials in the English speaking world.*'[212] One thousand civil servants ran the subcontinent with a population of about three hundred million.

When the newly married Alice Roe, great great granddaughter of Isaac Gulliver, first went to India a great grandson of his, Sir Frederick William Fryer was Lieutenant Governor of Burma. They were part of a select and influential stratum of British colonial society. Alice and Bernhard Roe had four children, Betty, Esther, Corrie and Dora. When World War I started in 1914 Alice and the children returned to England and lived in Marnhull. Marnhull is within walking distance of Manston where Alice's aunt Edith Swinburne Hanham had lived. The mausoleum was still there and her cousin, John Castleman Swinburne-Hanham now lived in Manston House and was managing director of Golders Green Crematorium. Edward (3) and Jessie were in Chettle House, so the Castleman-Gulliver clan was reassembling. Esther, the second daughter of Alice and Bernhard, was an impressionable young girl teetering into adolescence when her Uncle Edward was wounded in Gallipoli. It is likely that she helped her Aunt Jessie look after him when he returned. A firm bond between Esther and Edward (3) was established during the four years that she lived at Marnhull during the war. She visited from time to time after she returned to India. She became a fine sportswoman and notable tennis player. In the early 1930's while on a visit to Marnhull she met at a tennis party in Manston, Leslie Ernest Bourke, a military man and another tennis enthusiast. In 1933 they married and went

[212] Clive Dewey *Anglo-Indian Attitudes: Mind of the Indian Civil Service* 1993.

to India with the British Army. Their first child, Susan was born in 1935. Their second child, Patrick was born in Bushey, Hertfordshire, two years later. With the outbreak of war in 1939, families, particularly those with young children, scurried to what they hoped would be safe havens.

Esther with her two small children arrived in Chettle. They were a leaven and delight to her Uncle Edward (3), by then a bereft, rather dispirited, aimless man of sixty-nine.

The Bourkes had been for five or six years part of the colonial elite of the British Empire, where the women were not expected to roll up their sleeves. Esther, establishing herself in Chettle at the beginning of the war found herself, as Uncle Edward's niece, the de facto Lady of a Manor heading fast into bankruptcy. Her husband was working in the War Office and in 1941 their third child was born. Edward Timothy Castleman Bourke was christened in St Mary's Church on 3 January 1942, almost certainly the first child of Chettle House to have been christened there since William Chafin in 1731. Three weeks before Edward Bourke's christening the Japanese had attacked the United States Pacific Fleet at Pearl Harbor. Shortly afterwards, with the war at its gloomiest, Leslie Ernest Bourke returned to India where he became part of Field Marshal Sir William Slim's 14th Army (the so called Forgotten Army) which finally defeated the Japanese in Burma. Few men came away unscathed from that bitter encounter. He was never reunited with his family.

Esther Bourke, physically strong and athletic, had always been well servanted. In 1942 she found herself with three small children, an absent husband, an elderly uncle in decline, a large house, very little domestic help or advisory support (most had been called-up) and responsible under the eye of her Uncle Edward (3) for a thousand acres of Dorset. Just eighty miles due south of Chettle across the English Channel was Nazi occupied France. Winston Churchill in the first of his wartime speeches had told Parliament and the British people that there was nothing for it but *'blood, toil, tears and sweat.'* This straightened the backs and stiffened the sinews of millions on a beleaguered island: for the spouse of an army officer it was inspiration. She faced responsibilities for which her life had provided no preparation. A combination of fear for the future of her children, the challenge of Chettle and a rekindling of Castleman pride released a dauntless energy.

Her solutions were often innovatory and did not always meet with approbation. She is said to have driven about in a Bren gun carrier, there being no car. She felled timber, renovated houses, ran a poultry business and was instrumental, under the eye of her Uncle Edward, for keeping Chettle together. No one had tried very hard to do this since Esther's great grandmother Anne Castleman had died nearly sixty years before.

Uncle Edward William Fuidge Castleman died on 19 March 1946. He appointed Esther, her unmarried sister Elizabeth Alice and her unmarried brother Corrie as executors. There were small bequests to various nephews, nieces and servants. A third of the property was left to Esther, a third to Corrie and a sixth to each of the other sisters, Elizabeth Alice and Dora Diana.

There is little doubt that Edward (3), with his appreciation of the difficulties of making this agricultural estate economically viable, assumed that the beneficiaries would realize their assets and that Chettle would, after nearly nine hundred years, be broken up and sold as a collection of freeholds.

In her six years at wartime Chettle Esther had worked tirelessly to maintain the village and the estate. Despite her initial ignorance of country matters and some consequent mistakes, she had achieved what many had considered impossible. In the process she had fallen in love with the fields, woods, church, houses, the estate of Chettle that was so very different from the India where she had grown up. Chettle had provided safe haven from the horrors of the great struggle for herself and her children. She was determined to secure its future. During the six years that she had striven so hard to maintain the estate she had come to the view that it could and should be kept together. Her children, then aged eleven, nine and five, should enjoy the benefit of her endeavours and carry on the family concern for Chettle which she could trace back to her great great grandfather

William Castleman (2) and her great great great grandfather Isaac Gulliver. In order to achieve this she not only had to try to buy out the other beneficiaries, but there were considerable debts to deal with.

Probate was granted on Edward (3)'s will on 2 July 1946. The probate valuation was £70,000; debts and death duty amounted to around £35,000.[213] Just over three weeks later a Sale by Auction was held on 25 and 26 July *'By the direction of the Executors of Major E W F Castleman, deceased.'*[214] (The war was not finally over until a fortnight later and a note on the sale catalogue insists that Identity Cards must be produced by purchasers.) The six hundred lots would bring interested bidders, with their wallets bulging, from the far corners today, but travel was still restricted. The only new furniture available during the war had been *Utility*, so the items of furniture would have been particularly attractive. Lot 162 was a *'Fine marqueterie on figured walnut china cabinet...Attention is drawn to the rich figure of the walnut, the exquisite inlays and ormolu mounts of this fine cabinet.'* This was sold for £52. Lot 167, a *'Late 17th century burr-walnut chest'* for £78 15s 0d and Lot 168, a *'Set of six Sheraton mahogany frame chairs'* for £75. There were forty-two oil paintings including one by Carlo Dolci, the seventeenth-century Florentine painter, that went for four guineas. Another by Guido Reni (1575–1642 Bologna) failed to sell. Some of the items had a rarity/interest value that would probably make them priceless today. The 1946 sale gives a final glimpse of the opulence that was once Chettle, its finest hour sometime in the early eighteenth century.

There were further sales of Sheep on 2 August, 93 Pedigree Guernsey Dairy Cows and Heifers on 2 September and Agricultural Machinery and Horses on 4 October. Chettle House was advertised *'To Be Let'* in the catalogue for these auctions. The furniture, live and dead stock sales and a further sale of timber raised £15,000 in all. [215]

With loans from various members of her family Esther Bourke

---

[213] Information from Edward Bourke.
[214] B F P Catalogue at Chettle House 25 and 26 July 1946.
[215] Information from Edward Bourke.

was able to assemble £35,000 with which she paid off the debts and by the early 1950's she was able to buy out her two sisters Elizabeth and Dora. Her brother Corrie's life interest in his portion of the estate reverted to the family on his death.

By such Draconian measures was the Chettle estate kept together.

The accumulated symbols and values of over two centuries were dismembered. It was a terrible price to pay but many fine country houses, contents and all, were lost at the end of the war. When Esther Bourke died in 1967 she was able to leave the Chettle estate, with its fine mansion, to her three children, who live there today.

Acknowledgements

I would never have embarked on the story of Chettle without the kick-start of his inspiration from my son, Dominic.

From the outset the Bourke family, Susan, Patrick and Edward, the present owners of the estate, have been wonderfully supportive. Edward in particular has discussed successive drafts, and made available books and documents from his unique reference library. He and Susan have been ever willing to make room in the estate office for me to make notes from the extensive Bourke Family Archive. Father William Johnstone resident priest of Chettle allowed me access to church records in the hospitable surroundings of Church Cottage (the rectory). Several residents of Chettle, especially June and Ron Head, John Sansom and Alistair Arnold have shared their memories and views with me.

Archivists at the Dorset, Hampshire, Northamptonshire, Oxfordshire and Wiltshire County Record Offices and at the Bank of England have been helpful quite beyond their remit. *The Stalbridge Inheritance* by Irene Jones opened new doors to the Castleman element in the story of Chettle. The librarians of the County Library in Dorchester pursued my enquiries with an impressive tenacity. In meandering about the countryside seeking for keys to churches, the whereabouts of houses, Roman roads, gravestones and smuggling entrepôts I have met people generous with their time, interest and good humour.

For the transposing of research notes into an ordered narrative I

213

am indebted beyond words to Robin Harvie. He, Naomi Bowen and Julian Humphries have applied their special skills unstintingly and Janice Cliffe made the three family trees.

Loving thanks to those of my family and friends who have boosted, commented, criticized and encouraged in appropriate degree. Dominic and Rose Prince have a special interest in Chettle and their two children, Jack and Lara have helped in checking various features of the village. I am pleased to acknowledge the help of John and Sarah Carrier, Simon and Anne Cawkwell, Anne and Virginia Crossman, Alf and Heather Davey, Jane and David Davies, Sheila Dillon and Peter Koenig, Ranjita Lohan, David Perry, A K Rajan and Manjula and the transatlantic Rupert Prince whose patient guidance through technological wizardry, as well as wry coments on the text, has been invaluable.

Joyce Prince 12 May 2008

Bibliography

Books

Ackroyd, Peter *Shakespeare: the Biography* 2005.

Armstrong, W H *Farmworkers* 1987.

Bayley, A R *The Civil War in Dorset* 1910.

Brown, Deni *Encyclopaedia of Herbs* R H S 1993.

Bruce, George *A Family and a Fortune* 1987.

Buchan, John *Oliver Cromwell* 1941.

Chaucer, Geoffrey *The Canterbury Tales* Translated into modern English by Neville Coghill 1951.

Dacombe, M (Ed) *Dorset Up Along, Down Along* 1935.

Chafin, Mary *Original Country Recipes* (Reprint Macmillan) 1979.

Chafin, William *Anecdotes of Cranbourne Chase* 1818.

Cullingford, Cecil *History of Dorset* 1980.

Dewey, Clive *Anglo-Indian Attitudes: Mind of the Indian Civil Service* 1993.

Fraser, Antonia *Cromwell: Our Chief of Men* 1973.

Foreman, Amanda *Georgiana Duchess of Devonshire* 1998.

Forster, Margaret *Significant Sisters* 1984.

Glass, D V *Numbering the People* 1973.

Hardy, Thomas *The Mayor of Casterbridge* 1886.

Hardy, Thomas *Tess of the D'Urbervilles* 1891.

Hawkins, Desmond *Cranborne Chase* 1980.

Hawkins, Desmond *The Grove Diaries* 1995.

Hemming, Basil *History of Parliament* 1983.

Hoskins, W G *The Making of the English Landscape* 1955.

Hutchins, John *The History and Antiques of the County of Dorset* 1773.

Jackson, Brian *Castleman's Corkscrew* Vol 1 2008.

Jones, Irene *The Stalbridge Inheritance* 1993.

Kaines, H *Diary of a Dorset Farmer* Dorset Year Book 1928.

Lister, Raymond *Thomas Gosse* 1953.

Lloyd, Rachel *Dorset Elizabethans at Home and Abroad* 1967.

Nicholson, Adam *Power and Glory* 2003.

Ogg, David *England in the reign of Charles II* 1934.

Pitt Rivers, A *King John's House, Tollard Royal* 1890.

Randall, Gerald *The English Parish Church* 1982.

Riden, Philip (Ed) *Victorian History of the Counties of England: Northamptonshire* 2002.

Sebba, Anne *The Exiled Collector* 2004.

Sedgwick, Romney *The House of Commons 1715–1754* HMSO 1970.

Seymour, Richard *The Compleat Gamester* 1754.

Snell, K D M *Annals of the Labouring Poor: Social Change in Agrarian England 1660–1900* 1985.

Stratton, Ian *John West 1778–1845* 1998.

Thirsk, J (Ed) *The Agrarian History of England and Wales* 1967.

Traill, H D (Ed) *Social England* 1896.

Trevelyan, G M *Social History of England* 1942.

Williams, Ann & Martin, G H (Eds) *Domesday Book* A Complete Translation 1992.

Woodforde, James *Diary of a Country Parson 1788–1802* 1935.

Young, Arthur *The Farmer's Letters to the People of England* 1767.

Young, G M *Victorian England: Portrait of an Age* 1936.

Journals

Country Life: Geoffrey Webb *Chettle House in Dorsetshire* 6 October 1928.

The Gentleman's Magazine Vol. LIII 1782 & Feb. 1846.

Kelly's Directory for Milborne Port 1823.

Midland History Vol XXXI C S L Davies *Conspiracy Kinship and Preferment* 2006.
Salisbury Journal & Weekly Advertiser various dates.
Somerset & Dorset Notes & Queries Vol 10 1907.

Primary Sources
B of E Archive Bank of England Archive.
BFP Bourke Family Papers. Contains some Chafin records (1572–1818), Castleman family records and photographs (1847–present).
DRO Dorset Record Office for relevant parish records, CRL file (Chislett Rawlence) ANG file (Anglesey) and SEN file (Pitt).
HRO Hampshire Record Office.
NRO Northamptonshire Record Office.
ORO Oxfordshire Record Office.
PRO Public Record Office
WRO Wiltshire Record Office.
(County Record Offices are now known as County History Centres.)

Index